Essential law for accountancy students

A R Leal MA (Cantab), LLB, Grad Cert Ed

Head of Business Studies, Plymouth College of Further
Education
Chief Examiner in Law for the RSA
Moderator in Law for the AEB

52

Edward Arnold

© A R Leal 1982

First published 1982
by Edward Arnold (Publishers) Ltd
41 Bedford Square London WC1B 3DQ

British Library Cataloguing in Publication Data

Leal, A. R.
  Essential law for accountancy students.
  1. Accounting — Law — England
  I. Title
  344.206′63   KD2042

  ISBN 0-7131-0605-0 ✓

To Helen

Printed in Great Britain by
Richard Clay (The Chaucer Press) Ltd,
Bungay, Suffolk

Contents

Preface

The justification for this book is twofold. Firstly, at present there is not a textbook on the market designed for accountancy students taking law examinations. The books available are written for law students and not for accountancy students. This book is not written for prospective lawyers; it avoids copious footnotes and references to cases and articles. It concentrates on explaining simply, with suitable illustrations, the *basic* law required by the accountancy student. The author has restricted the content so it is suitable for part-time students faced with the completion of professional examinations in their spare time. Unlike most law books, this one can be read in the limited time available to the professional student and, because it restricts itself to basic law, the memory load is manageable. The second justification is the new syllabus of the Association of Certified Accountants which is completely covered.

The Nationality Bill being considered in Parliament in 1981 has not been incorporated into the text as at the time of publication it was impossible to forecast the final shape of the Act.

A list of cassette tapes complementing this book can be obtained by sending a sae to
Barl Enterprises,
Lake House,
78 Radford Park Road,
Plymstock,
Plymouth,
Devon.
PL9 9DX.

Acknowledgements

The author would like to thank the Association of Certified Accountants and the Institute of Chartered Accountants for permission to quote questions from past examination papers. I am also grateful to my wife for her secretarial assistance and to my many colleagues for their useful suggestions. All errors and omissions remain, of course, my responsibility.

The Publishers wish to thank the following for permission to reproduce copyright material:

Halifax Building Society, page 23;
Securicor Limited, pages 90 – 91;
The Boots Company Ltd, pages 219 – 24.
Oyez Publishing Ltd, page 265

Section 1

Law of contract

1

Agreement

Agreement is one of the necessary ingredients in the formation of a valid contract; the others are consideration (unless the contract is under seal) and an intention to enter into a legally binding relationship. (Consideration is dealt with in Chapter 3, intention in Chapter 2.)

Agreement arises when the offeror expressly or impliedly makes an offer (which is capable of acceptance) which the offeree accepts. Many of the rules surrounding offer and acceptance stem from the courts' reluctance to interfere with contractual promises because they believe the parties should be free to make their own bargains.

Offer

Main rules

1 An offer capable of acceptance must be distinguished from an indication by one party that she is prepared to enter into negotiations or from an invitation to the other party to make the offer. In some contracts one party expressly states he or she is open to offers.

> *Gibson* v. *Manchester City Council* (1979)
> In September 1970 the Conservative-controlled council decided to sell council houses. They sent a letter to the plaintiff stating 'the council may be prepared to sell the house to you at a purchase price of £2725 less 20%.' It continued '*if you would like to make formal application* to buy your council house please complete the application form.' This was headed 'Application to buy a council house'. The plaintiff completed and returned the form to the proper authorities. He later wrote to the council requesting the transfer of his property as per his application. Before contracts were exchanged local elections caused a change in the council's composition. The new council discontinued the policy of selling council houses to tenants. The plaintiff sought a decree of specific performance. Was there a contract that could be enforced? Was the council's letter an offer capable of acceptance or was it inviting the tenant to make an offer? If it were the latter, because

the council had never accepted the offer there would be no agreement and no contract. The court decided the council's letter was only an invitation to treat, hence the plaintiff's action failed.

Where the party's intention is not expressly stated it must be ascertained from the circumstances. The court will examine the consequences of holding the statement to be an offer and, if these are undesirable, it will assume the party was inviting offers, making in legal terminology an invitation to treat. Consider the table below which explains further.

Situation/statement	If this was an offer then
a) Goods on a supermarket shelf	when the customer selected goods this would constitute acceptance. The customer could not return them if he or she found a more suitable item without being in breach of contract. Therefore invitation to treat.
b) Goods 'offered' for sale by an auctioneer	the first bid would be acceptance thereby terminating the auction. Therefore invitation to treat.
c) Display of goods in a shop window	when the customer requested the item this would be acceptance. The retailer would have to sell the item although he or she felt the sale was undesirable, eg alcohol to a drunk. Therefore invitation to treat.
d) An advertisement offering a car for £1600	everyone who responded to the advert would be entitled to the car. The vendor could have numerous contracts but only one car. Therefore invitation to treat.
e) Offer to sell shares	everyone accepting would be entitled to shares. The offer could be oversubscribed. Therefore invitation to treat.
f) Offer of £15 to anyone returning a lost dog	Only one person can accept this offer by returning the dog. This is reasonable. Therefore offer.

2   The offer can be to an individual, a class of persons or the whole world. It may be rash to make an offer to the whole world but the idea of 'freedom of contract' means that the courts will not usually

intervene because the parties' actions appear foolish to a reasonable man. They presume that the party must be happy otherwise he or she would not have made such an offer. Although the offer can be made to anyone, only that person or persons can accept. If X offers to marry Y then Z cannot accept!

3   The offer must be certain and definite. If the parties were to start legal proceedings to enforce a contract the court would need to ascertain the terms of the contract; hence the rule. Where the court can render a vague offer certain, perhaps by implying terms or ignoring meaningless terms, it does so.

4   When making the offer the offeror may stipulate the method of acceptance. (see below.)

Whilst an offer to sell an item such as a painting is still capable of acceptance, the offeror cannot sell it elsewhere because should the first offer be accepted there will be two contracts and with only one item the offeror would be forced to break one of them. It is therefore obvious that an offer must eventually end. The main ways of **terminating an offer** are time, revocation, death, rejection and acceptance.

a) Time   An offer open only for a stipulated time ceases at the end of that period and in other situations the offer lapses after a 'reasonable' time. What is reasonable varies from case to case.

☐   George Reedy, an accountant who is working late every night in an attempt to build up his practice, decides to buy his wife some red roses. It is winter and only one florist has red roses. Reedy asks their price and is offered six for £12. He does nothing. Reedy returns two weeks later and says that he accepts the offer. Because of the perishable nature of flowers, the offer would have lapsed within the fortnight.

b) Revocation   An offer can be withdrawn at any time before acceptance. As the offer only becomes effective after communication to the offeree, however, fairness dictates that the same rule apply to revocations. The communication of the revocation can, however, be from the offeror or a reliable third party.

☐   A businessman who collects antiques sees an advert in his local newspaper from a householder who is emigrating and wishes to sell the contents of his house. He visits the house and notices an antique desk. The householder offers it to him for £200. Although its real value is £2000 the businessman is greedy and says he will need to think about it. He tells the householder it is an imitation. He hopes to return later and negotiate a lower price. Two hours later a friend in the antique trade telephones him to inform him of the antique desk he has just obtained for £200! The offer is effectively withdrawn and cannot be accepted.

c) *Death* An offer lapses on the death of either party where the offer is of a *personal* nature but otherwise contracts may arise despite the death of one of the parties.

d) *Rejection* This may be an express rejection or disguised as a counter offer. The latter destroys the offer, the offeree making a new offer (ie subject to the amended terms) which the original offeror can accept or reject. The original offer is destroyed and incapable of acceptance.

> *Butler Machine Tool Co Ltd* v. *Ex-Cell-O Corporation (England) Ltd* (1979)
> The plaintiffs offered to sell a machine tool for £75 535, the price being subject to a price variation clause to cover inflation. The defendant buyers replied by sending their form agreeing to pay the price but subject to their conditions, one being that there would be no price variation clause. At the bottom of this form was an acknowledgement that the other party agreed to these terms. The plaintiffs duly signed and returned it to the defendants. Delivery was delayed and the plaintiffs claimed another £2892 because of the price variation clause. The defendants refused to pay, claiming this clause was not incorporated into the final contract.
> Lord Denning analyzed the documents. 'The quotation of 23 May 1969 was an offer by the sellers to the buyers containing terms and conditions on the back. The order placed on 27 May by the buyers purported to be an acceptance but it contained differences and therefore was, in law, a rejection of the offer and constituted a counter offer. The letter on 5 June from the sellers was an acceptance of that counter offer as shown by the acknowledgement which the sellers signed and returned to the buyers.'
> The final contract did not therefore include the price variation clause and the plaintiffs were unable to claim the £2892.

A counter offer must be distinguished from a request for further information which leaves the original offer in existence and capable of acceptance. If in the above case the defendants had written asking whether the plaintiffs would remove the price variation clause this would have been a request for information and not a counter offer. If the plaintiffs had replied in the negative the defendants could still have accepted the original offer.

e) *Acceptance* See below.

Acceptance

Main rules

1 The offeree must be aware of the offer at the moment of acceptance. People cannot accept offers which they have forgotten or were never aware of.

☐ To boost sales during a recession a garage offers free petrol for one month to anyone buying one of their cars. Reedy returns home from a foreign business trip and buys a new car, unaware of this offer. After purchasing the car he discovers the free petrol offer. Reedy has no legal right to the petrol because he could not accept the offer of which he was unaware.

2 Only the person or persons to whom the offer is addressed can accept it.

3 The acceptance must be unqualified. An acceptance subject to con-tract' is not a qualified acceptance but merely means that the agree-ment is not legally binding until a formal contract is signed.

4 The acceptance must be in the manner stated (either expressly or impliedly) by the offeror. Where the offeror stipulates that only *one* mode of acceptance is acceptable then the offeree must accept in that and no other manner.

☐ Gerald Rope, a businessman with a liking for attractive secre-taries, offers an applicant a job but says if she wants to accept she must indicate this by meeting him at 7.30 pm in a local night club. If she wants the position she can only indicate her acceptance in the manner stipulated.

Where the method specified is not exclusive then any method more advantageous to the offeror is acceptable.

☐ Dolittle, Plunder and Grabbit want to commission a portrait of the senior partner for the board room. They approach a well known artist who offers her services for £5000 but says because of other work she requires an answer 'by return of post.' The method stipulated is not exclusive but relates to time (ie within 48 hours). A telephone call the same day as the offer would therefore be a valid acceptance.

5 An acceptance is only valid when communicated to the offeror. If the offeror fails to receive it then it has not been communicated and no agreement has been reached.

☐ When the artist is telephoned the line goes dead just as Dolittle is about to agree to the terms. Because the acceptance is not com-municated to the offeror it is not valid. Dolittle must phone again.

The general rule that acceptance is valid only upon communication to the offeror, has exceptions. To understand these the student must appreciate that the general rule is for the benefit of the offeror. Until acceptance is communicated to the offeror there can be no binding contract. If acceptance did not have to be communicated, a contractual relationship could arise without the offeror's knowledge. Such a situation would not be for the offeror's benefit.

As the rule exists for the offeror's advantage, he or she can dispense with the need to communicate acceptance. If I offer to sell you my car for £500 stating that you need not inform me if you accept, then a binding contract is made when you decide you want the car even though I am totally unaware of your acceptance.

This is different from a situation where the offeror attempts to impose on the offeree an obligation to reply by saying, 'If I don't hear from you in 48 hours I will assume you have accepted'. No offeror can stipulate that silence constitutes acceptance but he or she can waive the need for the offeree to communicate acceptance.

The offeror can waive communication of acceptance either expressly or impliedly. The above situation would be an example of the former.

Examples of implied waiver include:

1 Reward cases

> *Carlill* v. *Carbolic Smoke Ball Co.* (1893)
> As was stated in this case: 'If I advertise to the world that my dog is lost, and that anybody who brings the dog to a particular place will be paid some money, are all the police or other persons whose business it is to find lost dogs to be expected to sit down and write me a note saying that they have accepted my proposal? ... The essence of the transaction is that the dog should be found and it is not necessary in such circumstances that in order to make the contract binding there should be any notification of acceptance ... A person who makes an offer in an advertisement of that kind makes an offer which must be read in the light of the common-sense reflection. He does, therefore, in his offer impliedly indicate that he does not require notification of the acceptance of the offer.'

Communication of acceptance is, therefore, impliedly waived where the offeror specifies performance as the method of acceptance. It is sufficient to perform the required act.

2 Postal rule

This states that when the postal rule operates an acceptance is valid the moment it is posted and not when it is received by the offeror.

If I post an acceptance on 14th October and it arrives on 16th October, the agreement was reached and hence the contract made on the 14th, (the date of posting). This can be crucial if the offeror attempts to revoke the offer, because after the 14th this becomes impossible. An attempted revocation on the 15th is ineffectual. A letter posted on the 13th (the day before the letter of acceptance was posted) will also be ineffective if it arrives after the 14th, because revocation is only valid when communicated to the offeror. The postal rule only applies to acceptance and a revocation never becomes effective on posting.

The effect of the postal rule is clear, but when does the rule operate? It operates when the offeror impliedly waives the need to communicate acceptance *and* the post (or telegram) is an acceptable method of replying. If an offer is made by telephone requesting a reply within the hour, the post (or telegram) is obviously an unacceptable method of acceptance and so the postal rule is inapplicable.

Even where the offeror specifies (expressly or impliedly) that the post is acceptable the rule does not automatically apply. The offeror may stipulate that the reply can be sent by post but that acceptance is not to be valid until it is received. Such a proviso clearly indicates the rule is not to operate — the court cannot say that the offeror impliedly waived communication of acceptance because the offeror has expressly stated the opposite. Even if no such proviso is used the rule is inapplicable if its application would lead to absurdity. In such a situation the court will hold that the offeror did not waive communication because such a waiver would be completely unrealistic. If a man proposed marriage by post it is inconceivable he would be prepared to waive communication of acceptance (ie to accept the postal rule).

Most of the 'postal' cases were decided in the nineteenth century when the post was often unreliable. Without the rule it was said 'no mercantile man who has received a letter making him an offer and has accepted the offer, could safely act on that acceptance after he has put it into the post, until he knew that it had been received.'

This, of course, was convenient for the offeree but it penalized the offeror. A reply to the offer might not be received but he or she would not be free to sell elsewhere until the offeree was contacted to see if acceptance had been made by post in case the letter had been lost or delayed.

Any loss as a result of lost mail was to fall on the offeror, the reason being that the offeror had chosen the post knowing it was unreliable and so the acceptance might be lost. As it was the offeror's decision he or she must bear the risk should the letter of acceptance go astray. If he was unhappy about his situation he was free to select another medium through which to conduct his negotiations. The law thus favoured the offeree. The last important postal case was decided in 1892 until.

Holwell Securities Ltd v. *Hughes* (1974)
In October 1971 the defendant granted the plaintiffs a six month option to purchase property. The option was to be exercised 'by notice in writing to' the defendant. Within the six months' period the plaintiffs exercised the option by post. The letter failed to reach the defendant. Neither side disputed the facts, both agreeing that the post was an acceptable method of communicating the acceptance. The dispute was over whether the postal rule operated. The plaintiffs claimed it did and so the contract was valid when the acceptance was posted. The defendant stated that the rule was inapplicable and so the general rules on acceptance applied. As the acceptance had not been communicated to the defendant there was no acceptance and hence no contract. The case was decided on the words 'notice in writing to', as it was held that this clearly indicated the offeror required notification of the acceptance. It was impossible to imply that he had waived communication.

In this case Lord Justice Lawton stated that even though the post was used the postal rule did not automatically apply. He said, 'Does the rule apply in *all* cases where one party makes an offer which both he and the person with whom he was dealing must have expected the post to be used as a means of accepting it? In my judgment, it does not.' He stressed that it only applies where the offeror waives communication of acceptance. He stated, 'The rule does not apply if, having regard to all the circumstances, including the nature of the subject matter under consideration, the negotiating parties cannot have intended that there should be a binding agreement until the party accepting an offer or exercising an option had in fact communicated the acceptance or exercise to the other.'

Clearly the court is not going to impose the postal rule on *any* postal offer but is now going to consider the realities of the situation. As the post is now more reliable than it was one hundred years ago there seems no point in penalizing only one party (the offeror) if a letter goes astray.

To summarize, the postal rule will only operate when the following conditions are satisfied:

1   the post is an acceptable means of communication;
2   the offeror does not stipulate the acceptance is only to be valid upon receipt;
3   the 'other circumstances' do not suggest the rule is inapplicable.

Past examination questions

1 Consider and discuss whether a contract has been made in the following situations.

a) Alice sees in a shop window a fur coat marked 'Sale price £200'. She tries on the coat and agrees to buy it, but is then told by the shop assistant that there has been a mistake, and the coat is priced at £2000.

b) Bert offers to sell his car to Cecil for £500. Cecil replies 'I'll give you £350, no more'. Bert says he will not take less than £500 and they part. Later in the day Cecil telephones Bert and says he will accept Bert's offer to sell the car for £500.

c) George offers a reward of £500 for the return of his stolen silver. Harry, who has not heard of the reward, accidentally finds the silver in a wood and claims the reward.   C A 1980

2a) To what extent is it true to say that a contract does not arise until acceptance is communicated to the offeror?

b) Robert wrote a letter to Anthony offering to sell Anthony his car for £1500. Anthony replied 'I accept your offer but I can only pay £1200.' Robert rejected the offer of £1200. Anthony then replied 'Very well, I will pay £1500.' In the meanwhile, Robert has sold the car to Kalubya. Anthony now claims that he is entitled to the car. Advise him.

       A C A December 1977

3a) In what circumstances may an offer
lapse;
be revoked?

b) Brian enters a supermarket, picks up one of the wire baskets provided and fills it with groceries from the shelves. He then remembers that he has left his money at home and begins to replace the goods on the shelves. The manager of the supermarket stops him and says that Brian has bought the goods and must pay for them. Advise Brian.

       A C A June 1978

4a) What are the rules which govern the acceptance of an offer in a contract?

b) Mike writes to Peter 'I will sell you my car for £2000. If I hear nothing from you before next Saturday, I will take it that you have accepted.' Peter does not reply by Saturday. Mike is now threatening to sue Peter for breach of contract to buy the car. Advice Peter.

       A C A June 1979

5a) 'Silence can never amount to acceptance of an offer.' Discuss.

b) Biggles finds a gold watch in the street. He recognizes it as one belonging to his neighbour, Tom, and so he returns it to Tom, who thanks him profusely. On returning home Biggles opens his newspaper and sees an advertisement describing the watch and giving Tom's name and address, and offering a reward of £20 for the return of the watch.

Can Biggles claim the reward?   I A S June 1979

6a) Describe briefly how contractual offers are terminated.

b) Alice advertises her car for sale for £1000 in the local newspaper. Brian replies by telephoning Alice, and offers £900 for the car. Alice says she will not take less than £1000. Brian agrees to pay £1000 if on inspection he finds the car suitable. Inspection is arranged by them at noon on the following day. Before Brian arrives to inspect the car, Charles calls on Alice and she agrees to sell the car to him for £950. Advise the parties.   C A 1980

2

Intention to create legal relations

An agreement is only legally enforceable if the parties intended, when making the contract, to instigate legal proceedings in the event of any dispute. This is expressed in legal terminology by saying they intended to enter into a legal relationship. To help determine if this intention is present the court divides agreements into two major areas: Family, social and domestic, and business.

1 Family, social and domestic

In these agreements there is usually no intention to enter into a legal relationship, the parties relying on each other's honesty to honour the agreement. The court therefore *presumes* that family, social or domestic agreements *lack intention. The party seeking to enforce them must rebut this presumption* by showing that the parties intended their agreement to possess legal consequences.

☐ A R Leal promised to divide his royalties 50:50 with his wife if she types his manuscript. She does this and the book is published. It is enormously successful and he refuses to honour his promise. His wife is not entitled to the royalties unless she can prove they intended their agreement to be legally binding. If she produces no evidence to rebut the presumption, she must lose.

The parties' intention is to be inferred from the language they use and from the circumstances in which they use it. The presumption rests with any supporting evidence on the one side and evidence against the presumption on the other side. Only if it outweighs the presumption (plus supporting evidence) will a binding contract exist.

☐ Dolittle orally promises to 'look after' his son whilst he is qualifying as an accountant and, once he qualifies, make him a partner in the family practice. The son eventually qualifies but because he votes Labour the father refuses to give him a partnership.[1]

---

[1] The alert student might question the offer. Is it too vague?

13

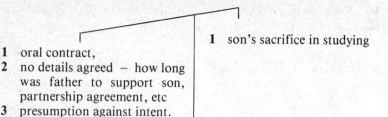

1 son's sacrifice in studying

1 oral contract,
2 no details agreed – how long was father to support son, partnership agreement, etc
3 presumption against intent.

As these facts do not rebut the presumption the son cannot sue the father.

☐   Sidney Harp, an accountant, wishes to retire but his son cannot qualify and take over the business. He therefore promises his nephew, who is qualified, that if he and his family move from Brighton to Plymouth (where the business is) and the nephew works in the practice he will leave it to him in his will. The nephew must however guarantee that he will employ the son at £8000 pa (to be inflation indexed). Their agreement is written. After working for his uncle for five years the nephew quarrels with him and his uncle changes his will.

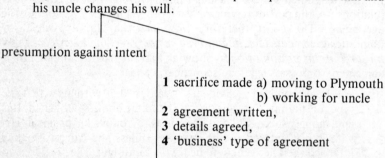

presumption against intent

1 sacrifice made a) moving to Plymouth
                   b) working for uncle
2 agreement written,
3 details agreed,
4 'business' type of agreement

The presumption, on these facts, has been rebutted and the nephew can sue his uncle.

Parker v. Clarke (1960)

The defendants, an elderly couple living in Torquay, found difficulty in maintaining their residence and suggested that their niece and her husband should sell their cottage and move in with them and in return agreed to make certain bequests in their will. The plaintiffs sold their cottage and moved to Torquay but the situation became difficult and the plaintiffs left. The agreed provisions in the will were not made and the plaintiffs sued for breach of contract. The parties had discussed and agreed details concerning their living together (such as who paid for the petrol on shopping trips) and the plaintiffs had made a considerable sacrifice in selling their cottage and moving to Torquay. The presumption was rebutted and they were successful.

Note: It must be emphasized that the existence of consideration does not automatically mean intention is present. Somebody who agrees to travel 200 miles to visit friends has provided consideration but their agreement still lacks intent.

2 Business

In these agreements if one party breaks the agreement the other anticipates the use of legal sanctions. The court therefore *presumes* that the parties *intended to be legally bound and the party seeking to prove that no intention exists must rebut this presumption*. The burden of proof is heavier than with domestic or social agreements but the parties may, by using clear words (such as 'binding in honour only', 'gentleman's agreement'), show their intention to make their agreement binding in honour only and not in law.

☐   George Reedy orally promises an employee at the interview that once she is 'suitably experienced' he will offer her a partnership. Six years later after a heated argument Reedy informs her he has no intention of making her a partner. As this is a business agreement (its oral nature is irrelevant) the courts presume that intention is present and on the facts it would appear unlikely the accountant could rebut the presumption.[2]

Jones v. *Vernons Pools Ltd* (1938)
The plaintiff sued the defendant for losing his 'winning' football coupon. It was held the agreement was not legally binding because the presumption was rebutted by the clause which stated 'It is the basic condition of the sending in and acceptance of this coupon that it − 'shall not be attended by, or give rise to any legal relationship, rights, duties or consequences whatsoever − The pools arrangements, agreements and transactions are binding in honour only.'

Past examination questions

1   'There can be an agreement which is not a contract.' Explain this assertion.   C A October 1979

---

[2] Is this offer too vague? Has the employee provided consideration? (see page 16.)

3

Consideration

English law is concerned with bargains and not promises, hence if X agrees to give Y £100 this is a promise and unenforceable. If however Y gives, or promises to give X something in return for the promise, it becomes a bargain and is enforceable. Any simple contract (ie one not under seal) therefore requires consideration to be enforceable. This can be executed or executory. The former is an act performed in return for the other party's promise or act. Executory consideration arises when the party promises to perform an act in the future.

☐ A R Leal agrees to write a book called *Essential law for accountancy students*. The publishers pay him £5000 when he signs the contract in which he agrees to deliver the final manuscript within one year. The publishers' consideration is executed, the author's is executory.

A working definition of consideration could be 'a sacrifice (act or promise) made in return for the other party's promise or act'.[1] By reference to this definition the reader can obtain the main rules relating to consideration.

The promise or act must be made IN RETURN for the other's promise or act.

☐ A R Leal's wife types the manuscript for *Essential law for accountancy students*. When she has finished it her husband promises her 50% of the royalties. He later refuses to pay. Can the wife successfully sue? Assuming she rebuts the presumption against intent she succeeds if she provided consideration. Is her act in typing the manuscript consideration for his promise? Is it made in return for the promise? As her action occurred *before* the promise it cannot be consideration.

Re McArdle (1951)
Mrs McArdle's home went to her five children equally on her

---

[1] In *Currie* v. *Misa* (1875) consideration was defined as 'Some right, interest, profit, or benefit accruing to the one party, or some forebearance, detriment, loss or responsibility given, suffered or undertaken by the other'.

death. Improvements were made to the house by one daughter-in-law. At a later date the five children promised to recompense the daughter-in-law. When they failed to pay she sued but lost as her consideration for their promise was in the past.

Therefore:

1 **Rule one** Past consideration is no consideration.[2]

There is an apparent exception to this rule. Suppose X drove his car to a garage and asked them to repair it. Having done so they present him with a bill for £70 which he accepts. Can he later refuse to pay because their consideration, repairing the car, occurred before he promised to pay (ie it was past)? As this would be commercially unacceptable an exception to the rule exists. When a request implies payment the subsequent promise to pay x pounds relates back to the original request (thus the act theoretically follows the offer of payment).

☐ An accountant's employers ask him to work on Saturday and Sunday to prepare some accounts for audit. He does this and on the Monday is offered £100 for his trouble. As their original request implied payment, his weekend's work is valuable consideration and their offer is enforceable.

Lampleigh v. *Braithwaite* (1615)
B asked L to obtain a pardon for him. B received a pardon and then offered L £100. The court held 'the request and subsequent promise were ... to be treated as part of the same transaction. The request included an implied promise to pay a reasonable sum and the later offer merely fixed the sum.'

The promise must involve a SACRIFICE.[3]

☐ Harp, the elderly accountant with the unqualified son, discovers he is not, as he claims, studying at night but drinking and night clubbing with his friends. In a fit of anger he sells his practice to a competitor for £5. £5 is a sacrifice hence the contract is enforceable.

Mountford v. *Scott* (1971)
The defendant granted the plaintiffs a six months' option to purchase his house for £10 000 on payment of £1. In an action for specific performance the defendant claimed that £1 was not valuable consideration. Lord Justice Rusell said 'The ground of attack on the validity of the option agreement was that the

---

[2] A statutory exception exists to this rule regarding negotiable instruments.
[3] This could involve compromising a legal right but must be more than 'natural love and affection'. The latter is said to be good but not valuable consideration.

consideration ... £1 was a sum which the law would not regard as valuable consideration. Therefore there was no consideration in the eye of the law to support the application of the defendant not to withdraw his offer for six months. This I found a startling proposition. Anything of value, however small the value, is sufficient consideration to support a contract at law.'

Consideration requires a sacrifice and in giving up £1 the plaintiff is making a sacrifice, albeit a small one. This is consideration. The courts enforce contracts regardless of the wisdom of the bargain; they ignore the adequacy of the consideration providing some value is given.
Therefore:
2 **Rule two** Consideration must be valuable but need not be adequate.

The promise must involve a SACRIFICE.

☐   An accountant's employer promises her a bonus of £20 if, during an audit for an important client, she is punctual. If she is punctual can she enforce the offer? Is performing her job consideration? Under her contract of employment she should arrive on time. Performing her duty cannot amount to a sacrifice for her employer's promise. She has to perform the act anyway.

Stilk v. *Myrick* (1809)
Two seamen deserted during a voyage. The Captain promised to divide their wages among the remainder of the crew if they sailed the vessel home. He later refused to pay, claiming the agreement lacked consideration because the remaining crew were contractually bound to sail the ship home. Their contract of employment included a clause that the crew would continue under the usual emergencies of the voyage and in 1809 the desertion of two crewmen was an ordinary emergency. The crew were contractually bound to sail the vessel home and therefore the Captain's promise was unenforceable.

Therefore:
3 **Rule three** Performance of an existing contractual duty is not consideration.[4]

[4] A modification to Rule Three is that performance of an existing contractual duty may be good consideration for a promise of a third party. In *Shadwell* v. *Shadwell* (1860) the plaintiff, who was engaged to marry EN, was promised an annual income by his uncle on marrying. He later sued his uncle's estate for sums due and they claimed the agreement was unenforceable because the plaintiff was already bound to marry EN before the uncle's promise. The court held that the nephew had provided consideration – his action was successful.

The promise must involve a SACRIFICE.

☐ Dolittle is under subpoena to attend court (ie attendance is compulsory) to give evidence about a fraud committed by one of his clients. Because of a possible civil action one of the parties involved, who is anxious that the accountant gives evidence, offers to pay his expenses. This offer is unenforceable. It lacks consideration because the accountant is under a duty to attend the court.

Therefore:

4 Rule four Performance of a public duty is not consideration.

Consideration may however exist if one party performs more than his or her legal or contractual duty.

☐ The accountant who agreed to work one weekend can use this as consideration because he or she was acting in excess of his or her contractual duty.

Glasbrook Bros v. *Glamorgan CC* (1925)

The defendant colliery owners, concerned about possible violence during a strike, requested that police be billeted at their mine. The authorities refused, believing their mobile force would adequately cope with disturbances. The defendants therefore promised to pay the cost of billeting the police. They later refused to pay claiming that no consideration existed for their promise as the billeting was merely performance of the plaintiff's legal obligation, protecting public property. The House of Lords held the provision of a mobile force discharged their obligation and the billeting, being in excess of their legal duty, amounted to consideration. The colliery owners had to pay.

Therefore:

5 Rule five Performance of more than your public or contractual duty is consideration.[5]

Rules three and five are illustrated by the situation where a creditor promises to accept less than the full amount from the debtor in complete satisfaction.

☐ Harp decides to retire and sells his practice for £170 000, payable on March 1st. The purchaser is having trouble raising the price. Harp is purchasing a bungalow for £150 000 near Plymouth and

[5] In *Hartley* v. *Ponsonby* (1857) one third of the crew deserted. The captain promised to share their wages among the remainder if they sailed the boat home. His promise was enforced because the desertion rendered the voyage dangerous and the crew were not obliged to continue. They were performing in excess of their contractual duty.

is told he must complete by March 1st. He therefore tells the purchaser if she pays £150 000 he will forget the other £20 000. Harp can later claim the other £20 000.

Harp's promise not to claim the other £20 000 requires consideration to be enforceable. The payment of £150 000 cannot be consideration because of rule three. The purchaser owes £170 000 and payment of £150 000 cannot be a sacrifice.

Therefore: a debt cannot be discharged by payment of a lesser sum on the date due.

Foakes v. *Beer* (1884)

Mrs B obtained a judgment against Dr F for £2090, interest being payable from the date of judgment. She promised that if Dr F paid £500 immediately, and the balance by instalments, she would forgo interest. Having received £2090 she claimed the interest. As no consideration existed for her promise to forgo the interest she was entitled to succeed.

A promise not to enforce payment of the full debt if a lesser sum is paid will be enforceable if

a) the discharge is contained in a deed (ie under seal)

or

b) if the debtor has provided consideration. This could be payment before the debt becomes due, if at the creditor's request. Earlier payment entails sacrificing interest on the sum paid. If repayment is in London and the creditor requests payment in Paris this is also consideration. If the creditor requests £800 plus a gold ring (worth £50) this constitutes consideration as the debtor owes cash and therefore the ring is a different method of payment.

or

c) if the debtor can plead equitable estoppel as a defence. This doctrine states that if C promises not to enforce her legal rights and D acts on this promise to his detriment, C cannot enforce her rights until sufficient notice is given to allow D to resume his original position. The creditor's promise not to claim the remaining debt satisfies the first requirement and if the debtor spends £20 000 on a yacht the second condition is fulfilled. Leaving £20 000 in his bank is not acting to his detriment and the creditor can claim the sum. The doctrine is suspensory providing the debtor can revert to his original position but if this is impossible the creditor's rights are extinguished. Being an equitable doctrine it is discretionary.

☐   Harp, who has sold his practice for £170 000, has gambling debts of £10 000. His bookmaker is applying 'pressure' on him to settle. The purchaser knowing he needs cash very urgently tells him,

'Accept £150 000 in full settlement or suffer the consequences!' He agrees to do this. Having paid off his debts he claims the remaining £20 000. Even if the other ingredients are present a defence of 'promissory estoppel' would fail because the purchaser's conduct is inequitable.

D & C Builders Ltd v. *Rees* (1966)

Mrs Rees owed the plaintiffs £482. Knowing they possessed liquidity problems she refused payment, offering £300 in full settlement. Needing cash urgently they accepted, agreeing in writing to waive the remaining £182. Having cashed a cheque for £300 they sued for £182. Mrs Rees claimed that payment by cheque instead of cash constituted a different method of payment and so was consideration (see b) above). This was rejected by the court. She then sought relief under equitable estoppel. Although the necessary ingredients were present the court refused relief as her conduct was unfair and her claim totally lacked merit.

or

d) if the debtor makes a composition arrangement with the creditors whereby the debtor pays each so much in the £1. No creditor is permitted to sue for the outstanding debt.

Past examination questions

1a) Under what circumstances, if any, does payment of a smaller sum by a debtor discharge a debt owed to a creditor?

b) Soon after Peter married Pauline in January 1976, Maurice and John, the respective fathers of the couple, agreed to pay a monthly allowance into Peter's bank account to help the couple financially during the early years of their marriage. It was a term of the contract that Peter could sue either Maurice or John in the event of default. Two months after the agreement was made Maurice and Peter had a violent argument and Maurice announced that he would no longer give Peter and Pauline any financial help. Advise Peter as to his legal position.

A C A June 1977

4

Classification

Contracts fall into two main categories: those under seal and those not under seal called simple contracts.

1 Those under **seal** (often called **deeds** or **specialty** contracts). For a contract to be in a deed it must be in:

(i) writing,
(ii) signed by the party to be bound,
(iii) sealed,
(iv) delivered.

The two most important characteristics of a contract under seal are that it is enforceable without **consideration** (see page 16), and that, for the purposes of the Limitation Act, actions can be commenced within twelve years and not six as with a 'simple' contract.

Any contract can be made under seal to take advantage of the above characteristics. In the example on page 20 if the agreement had been in a deed it would have been enforceable. Certain contracts must however be under seal. These include:

a) the sale of a British ship,
b) the conveyance of a legal estate in land,
c) the creation of a legal mortgage,
d) leases exceeding three years.

If the agreement is not in the **form** of a deed no contract is formed.

☐ Trevor Wit agrees to lease an office for five years. The contract is written but not sealed. The agreement is ineffectual; there is no contract.

2 **Simple contracts** are contracts not under seal.

Most simple contracts can take any form — oral, written, implied from conduct — but some must satisfy statutory formalities. These state that either

a) The contract must be *in writing*. Examples include:
(i) contracts transferring shares in a limited company,
(ii) certain consumer credit agreements,
(iii) bills of exchange, cheques and promissory notes.

22

County and district ....

Title number ....

THE HALIFAX BUILDING SOCIETY - MORTGAGE DEED

Dated the   day of   19

The Borrower:

The Society: **THE HALIFAX BUILDING SOCIETY** of Halifax, West Yorkshire HX1 2RG

The Advance: £	The Initial Repayment Period years
Monthly Payment: £ (variable)	Interest Rate: % per annum (variable)

The Property:

A. The Borrower acknowledges receipt of the Advance

B. The Borrower as Beneficial Owner **Charges** the Property **by way of Legal Mortgage** with the payment of all moneys payable by the Borrower to the Society

C. This Mortgage is governed by the Mortgage Conditions 1975 - 1978 which have been prescribed by the Board of Directors of the Society and of which a copy has been supplied to the Borrower

D. This Mortgage is made for securing further advances

SIGNED SEALED and DELIVERED
by the Borrower in the presence of :-

Figure 1   The Halifax Building Society — mortgage deed

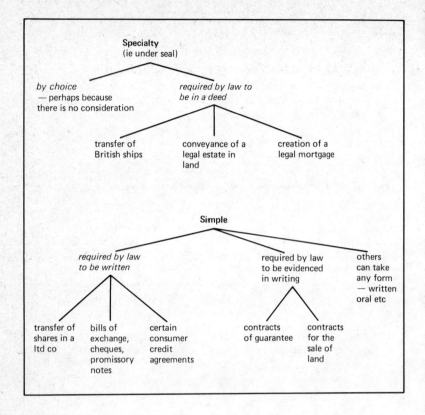

Figure 2   Contracts

If the contract is not in writing it cannot come into existence.
or
b) The contract must be *evidenced in writing*.

In a) the contract must be written but in b) the contract may be oral providing there is adequate written evidence of the contract's existence. Only two contracts need evidencing in writing and these are:

1   Contracts of Guarantee   Under s. 4 of the Statute of Frauds Act 1677

> 'no action shall be brought whereby to charge ... the defendant upon any special promise to answer for the debt, default or miscarriage of another person; ... unless the agreement upon which such action shall be brought, or some memorandum or note thereof, shall be in writing and signed by the party to be charged therewith or some other person thereunto by him lawfully authorised.'

A contract of guarantee arises when a third party (the guarantor) agrees to pay the creditor if the debtor defaults with repayments. The main contract is between the debtor and the creditor.

☐ A businessman's nineteen year old daughter is buying a sports car on credit. The garage wants her father to guarantee the repayments. Unless their agreement with the father is evidenced in writing the garage cannot enforce it if the daughter defaults.

2 *Contracts relating to land* Under s. 40 of the Law of Property Act 1925

'no action may be brought upon any contract for the sale or other disposition of land or any other interest in land, unless the agreement upon which such action is brought, or some memorandum or note thereof, is in writing, and signed by the party to be charged or by some other person thereunto by him lawfully authorised.'

A contract for the purchase of land must therefore be evidenced by written material containing all the relevant information.

A failure to comply with either of the above statutes means the contract, although valid (unlike contracts required to be under seal or in writing), is unenforceable in the courts.

☐ Trevor Wit, an aspiring businessman, agrees orally to purchase office premises and pays a £2000 deposit to Celia Rafty. He cannot force Rafty to convey the property – the court will not enforce the contract – but Rafty can retain the £2000 because the contract is valid and she is not seeking the court's assistance to enforce it.

The above is clearly inequitable and, as equity will not allow a statute to be used as a vehicle for fraud, it developed the doctrine of part-performance. This has been recognized in s. 40 (2) of the 1925 Act.

Doctrine of part-performance

If one party has partially performed his or her part of the contract the court may grant a decree of specific performance compelling the other to perform contractual obligations despite an absence of written evidence. Before the court will act the plaintiff must prove:

1 He or she has performed an act which implies the existence of the alleged contract.

☐ In the above example following Rafty's promise to convey the property Wit arranges for structural alterations to be done and has his brass name plate affixed to the front of the building. This would be a sufficient act of part performance.

Rawlinson v. *Ames* (1925)
Ames agreed to lease Rawlinson's flat but requested certain structural alterations. These were carried out under Ames' supervision. When the latter refused to take the lease Rawlinson obtained
a decree of specific performance because, although s. 40 (1) was
not complied with, the court held the alterations constituted a
sufficient act of part-performance.

2 It must also be unfair to allow the promisor to renege on his or her
promise *and*
3 there must be adequate oral evidence of the contract. Where the
doctrine applies it does not mean the contract is automatically
enforceable, merely permits one party to adduce oral evidence to
prove its existence.

Past examination questions

1a) Explain the equitable doctrine of part performance.
b) John wishes to purchase an old barn from Jim for £5000. Jim
agrees orally to sell at this price and he allows John to start converting
the barn into a weekend cottage. Jim subsequently changes his mind
and refuses to complete the sale of the property. Advise John.

ACA June 1979

5

Contents

When analysing a contract's contents it is necessary to distinguish between representations made prior to the contract which become contractual terms and those which do not. The latter are 'mere representations'. Prior to the Misrepresentation Act 1967, the distinction was important but now the innocent party possesses a remedy for a false representation whether incorporated into the contract or not. Although the remedies for breach of contract and misrepresentation differ in some respects, a detailed analysis of the tests evolved to distinguish between mere representations and contractual terms is unnecessary. It is sufficient to say that the answer depends on the parties' intention as inferred from all the facts.

Terms of the contract

Terms stated in the contract are **express** terms. Not all terms are expressly stated by the parties and additional terms may be **implied** by the court under:

a) *Custom*   Providing no contrary express terms exist the courts imply into a commercial contract any relevant trade customs.
b) *Statute*   The most well known implied statutory terms are those implied by the Sale of Goods Act (1979).
c) *'The Moorcock' principle*   This enables terms to be implied to give *business efficiency* to the contract; terms are not implied merely because they would be reasonable, they must be essential if the contract is to make sense. The test is 'at the time of contracting if the parties had been asked is it a term of the contract? They would have answered, of course.' The term is so obvious neither party bothered to state it.

☐   Cyril Sharp, a successful music publisher, employs a tax consultant. After examining Sharp's affairs the consultant presents a report. Neither party mentioned a fee. To give 'business efficiency' to the contract the court would imply a term that Sharp pay a 'reasonable price' for the consultant's work.

27

The Moorcock (1889)
The Plaintiff moored his boat at the defendant's jetty. Both parties knew at low tide the vessel would rest on the river bottom. This was rocky and the boat was damaged. A term that the river bed was flat was implied to give business efficiency to the contract.

Sharp purchases a second-hand Rolls Royce for £20 000. The garage selling the vehicle provide a warranty that they will repair, free of charge, any defects arising within one year. It breaks down within the specified period and is returned. The garage undertake, in writing, to repair the car within forty eight hours.

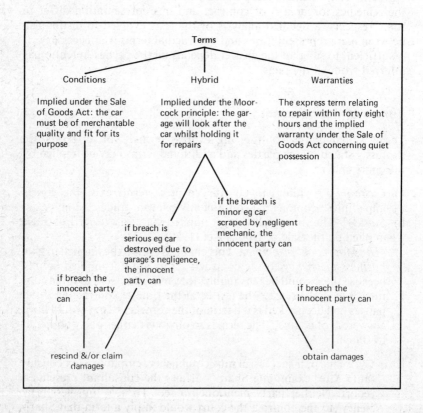

Figure 3 Terms of a business contract

Drizzle Tours

1.   If the holiday is arranged directly with the Company all correspondence will be sent to the customer at the address specified on the booking form If the arrangements are made through a travel agent all communications from the Company will be sent to the agent who, as regards communication from the Company to the customer, is the agent of the customer. All monies paid to the travel agent are held by the travel agent as the agent of the customer until the booking is accepted and thereafter as the agent of the Company.

2.   The customer must pay the specified deposit on completion of the booking form, or the full amount if the booking is made within 8 weeks of departure. The booking is not accepted until the date shown on the confirmation account issued by the Company. If the booking is not accepted the deposit will be refunded. Alteration or cancellation by a customer of an accepted booking will be subject to the provisions of paragraphs 8 – 9 of these conditions.

3.   Every effort will be made to operate all holidays as advertised but the Company reserves the right at its discretion or in the clear interest of the client, to modify or cancel any holiday, flight, schedule, accommodation or arrangement at any time up to 8 weeks before departure. In particular, holidays based on charter flights can only be provided at the advertised price if a satisfactory number of bookings are made, and the Company reserves the right to change the date of flights. In the case of any material modification or of cancellation, the Company will, if possible, offer alternative arrangements, or, if these are not acceptable, a full refund of the monies paid. When offering alternative arrangements, the Company will, if accommodation is affected, use its best endeavours to provide an alternative in the same area. If the Company is only able to offer a lower classification of hotel it will refund the difference in the brochure price, plus 5% of the original holiday price.

4.   The Company will not materially modify or cancel the holiday within 8 weeks of the date of departure unless compelled to do so because of circumstances beyond its reasonable control.

5.   If war or terrorist activities threatened or actual, civil unrest, closure of airports, industrial action, threatened or actual or any other event outside the control of the Company either delays or extends the holiday or compels a change in the holiday arrangements, the Company cannot accept liability for any resulting loss, damage or expense and any refund will be subject to the deduction of reasonable expenses. Your attention is drawn to the insurance provisions arranged by the Company to cover you and your party against risks of flight delays.

6.   If such events occur before the scheduled departure date of your holiday and consequently the holiday has to be materially modified or cancelled the Company will, if possible, offer alternative arrangements, or, if these are not acceptable, a prompt and full refund of all monies paid less any reasonable expenses.

7.   The Company does not control the day to day management of the hotels and it is possible that shortly before departure or on arrival at the overseas airport or resort the Company may be advised that the accommodation reserved is not available. In those circumstances the Company will use its best endeavours to provide alternative accommodation in the same area. The policy in such cases is to provide an hotel of similar or higher classification at no extra cost or, if this is unavailable, a lower classification of hotel and the Company will refund the difference in the brochure price plus 5% of the original holiday price.

8.   If the customer does not pay the balance of the holiday price at the prescribed time, the Company reserves the right, after due notice to the customer or the agent as appropriate, to cancel the booking. In this event, or if the customer cancels the arrangements after the booking is accepted, the insurance premium and the deposit will be forfeited. Additionally, if cancellation occurs for either reason within 42 days of departure, the insurance premium and the following cancellation charges will be payable by the customer.

Periods before departure within which written cancellation notice is received.	more than 42 days	29 – 42 days	15 – 28 days	1 – 14 days	departure day or after
Cancellation charge (including deposit paid) as % of total price.	deposit only	30%	45%	60%	100%

(Your attention is drawn to the insurance cover available for involuntary cancellation).

9.   After acceptance of the booking, if the customer alters the confirmed arrangements an amendment fee of £5.00 per person, plus any telex charges, will be charged. Additionally, if the alteration is within 42 days of the original departure date the cancellation charges in paragraph 8 will be applied unless the new holiday departs on or before the original departure date. These charges will always be applied where the new holiday date is outside the period covered by this brochure.

10.   The prices shown in this brochure are based on known costs and exchange rates as at 24 July 1982. Approximately 8/10 weeks before your holiday is due to commence the Company will send you a final invoice which will include any surcharge due on your holiday. The Company guarantees that no surcharge will exceed 10% of the advertised holiday price.

Any cost increase over 10% will be absorbed by the Company and moreover once the final invoice as detailed above has been sent to you no further price changes will be made.

In making this pledge the Company does accept a financial risk and in view of this no refunds resulting from cost changes will be made.

Only governmental action can alter this guarantee.

11.   Any flights forming part of the holiday arrangements will be subject to the conditions on the ticket issued by or on behalf of the carrying airline, which in most cases limit the airline's liability to the customer in accordance with International Law.

12.   The Company is only liable for loss of or damage or delay to baggage caused directly by its negligence. Valuable items as specified in the second sentence of Section 4 of the holiday insurance details are at all times at the customer's risk and should be covered by insurance. Your attention is also drawn to the provision in Section 4 of the insurance policy for the purchase of emergency clothing and personal requirements.

13.   In the event of any dissatisfaction with the accommodation or any other service provided by the Company in the resort the matter must be reported immediately to the local representative, agent, or hotelier so that action can be taken to remedy the problem. Unless the Company is given such notice it can accept no responsibility.

Any complaint made to the Company after the holiday should be made in writing to our Customer Relations Department within one month of return.

If you have cause for complaint and we are unable to agree on a suitable settlement the dispute may (if you so wish) be referred to arbitration under a special Scheme devised for the Travel Industry by the Institute of Arbitrators by arrangement with the Association of British Travel Agents. If you elect to seek redress under this Scheme, written notice requesting arbitration under the Scheme must be made within one year after the scheduled date of return from the holiday.

The Scheme provides for a simple and inexpensive method of arbitration on documents alone with restricted liability on the customer in respect of costs. Provision for a normal attended Hearing is also included in the Scheme but in this case the restricted cost liability on the customer would not apply. Details of the Scheme will be supplied on request.

14.   These Booking Conditions comply with the Tour Operators Code of Conduct drawn up by the Association of British Travel Agents and approved by the Office of Fair Trading.

Figure 4   Terms

Terms (express or implied) can be conditions, warranties or a hybrid term containing elements of both. A **condition** is a vital term so important that its breach destroys the substance of the contract. The innocent party may rescind the contract, which discharges him or her from future performance, and may claim damages. The party may however choose to continue with the contract and only sue for damages and if he or she affirms the contract after knowledge of the breach this is his or her only remedy.

☐   Rondel's restaurant specializes in catering for outside functions. FML Ltd arrange a farewell buffet for their Managing Director for January 24th and Rondel's are engaged. It is expressly stated that the buffet is on the 24th. If Rondel's fail to arrive there is a breach of condition because this goes to the root of the contract. FML Ltd can rescind the contract.

A **warranty** is not a vital contractual term but is subsidiary and collateral to the contract's main purpose. Its breach, no matter how serious, cannot destroy the substance of the contract therefore the innocent party's only remedy is damages.

☐ If Rondel's agree to provide the buffet and one bottle of vintage champagne, the wine being provided by FML Ltd, a failure to supply the champagne would be a breach of warranty. FML Ltd could only sue for damages.

The consequences of a breach of the above clauses can be easily ascertained. With many clauses the consequences cannot be ascertained in advance as a breach may result in minor or serious consequences. These hybrid terms are called **complex, intermediate** or **innominate**. If their breach is serious, effectively destroying the contract, they are treated as conditions but where the breach is minor the only remedy is damages.

☐ Rondel's agree to provide a buffet. If they fail to deliver any food it will be regarded as a breach of condition thereby allowing FML Ltd to rescind the contract. If they break the clause by delivering seventeen instead of eighteen gateaux the breach would be less serious and therefore only a breach of warranty.

Whether there is a breach of condition or warranty can be commercially important as illustrated in *Decro-Wall International SA* v. *Practitioners in Marketing Ltd* (1971). The plaintiffs were a French company who had entered into a sole agency agreement with the defendants whereby the latter sold their ceramic tiles. Their agreement stipulated that all goods should be paid for within ninety days of the date on the invoice. The defendants always paid but there was a delay which varied from two to twenty days. The tiles were commercially successful and the French company wanted to increase their UK agents. This however was impossible because of the sole agency agreement. The plaintiffs therefore claimed the delay in payment was a breach of condition. They could therefore rescind the contract and open new agencies. The defendants argued the breach was one of warranty and therefore although damages were payable the sole agency continued. The court held that the delay in payment did not go to the root of the contract. It was only a breach of warranty.

In theory parties negotiate over terms but today the growth of large organizations has resulted in the adoption of standard form contracts. These are either:

1 *Model contracts* These consist of standard clauses previously agreed by representatives of the main parties. Their object is to save time. It would be commercially impossible if businesses renegotiated each individual contract. Such contracts are typical in the commodity trade and their existence is morally acceptable.
2 *Contract of adhesion* These evolved to enable large organizations to exploit their economic power, often arising from a monopoly position. They take advantage of the inequality of bargaining power. Such contracts are issued on a 'take it or leave it' basis and

are not open to re-negotiation. If at the entrance to a motor racing meeting I am sold a ticket containing an exclusion clause nobody expects me to negotiate to modify the conditions. In many instances, at a car park entrance for example, the clause is contained in a notice. I would have great difficulty negotiating with that!

Where only one supplier exists, or all suppliers use similar clauses, the consumer has little option but to 'accept' any onerous terms. The most common standard clause of this type is the exclusion clause.

Exclusion clause

This excludes one party's (usually the stronger) liability for a breach of contract or the commission of a tort. Before a clause can be relied on by a defaulting party it must surmount a series of hurdles erected by Parliament and the courts. The main barriers are:

1 Statute
The Unfair Contract Terms Act (1977) affected the following areas of law:

  (i) Contracts for the Sale of Goods and Hire Purchase agreements (see pages 97 and 153).
 (ii) Other contracts   As with tort the sections relating to breach of contract have a limited application. Clauses excluding or restricting liability for breach of contract not arising from negligence are unenforceable unless reasonable where a) one party 'deals as consumer' or, b) where one party contracts on the other's 'written standard terms of business.' Contracts falling outside a) or b) are not covered by the Act (for example, where business people contract other than on standard terms or where two private individuals contract.)
(iii) Torts   With reference to torts the Act only relates to 'business liability.' This is defined as 'liability arising from things done or to be done in the course of a business or from the occupation of business premises.' *Any exclusion clause which excludes or restricts liability for negligence in a non-business situation is valid* as activities of a private nature are not covered by the Act. In business situations the Act attacks clauses excluding or restricting liability for negligence. This covers 'breach of a) any express or implied contractual obligation to take reasonable care or exercise reasonable skill, b) any such common law duty, and c) the common duty of care imposed by the Occupiers' Liability Act 1957.' The 1977 Act distinguishes two types of clauses:

  a) those excluding or restricting liability from death or personal injury arising from negligence. These are **void**. It is immaterial

whether the clause is contained in a contractual notice or a notice at, for example, the entrance to a motor racing circuit.
b) those excluding or restricting liability for other loss or damage arising from negligence. These clauses are effective if 'reasonable.' With contractual exclusion clauses the court must have 'regard to all the circumstances known or contemplated, or which ought reasonably to have been known or contemplated, by the parties when the contract was made.'

Note: The Act's provisions are specifically excluded from some contracts.

2 Is the clause part of the contract?

The clause must be incorporated into the contract. It must be brought to the other party's attention before the agreement is reached. Terms cannot be added to the contract after it is finalized.

If the contracting party signs the contract they are aware of its contents and bound by any exclusion clause. The only methods of avoiding liability are to plead non est factum (see page 122), when the contract becomes void, or to utilize the successful argument used in *Curtis* v. *Chemical Cleaning Co Ltd* (1951). In that case the plaintiff took her wedding dress to the cleaners; when asked to sign a document she enquired about its contents and was informed it only excluded the cleaner's liability for damage to the sequins. The clause excluded liability for all damage. The dress was badly stained. When the cleaners attempted to rely on the exclusion clause their claim was rejected as their assistant had misrepresented the nature of the clause. Apart from the two exceptions listed above if you sign a contract containing an exclusion clause it is binding.

In oral contracts the same rules apply; clauses brought to your attention before the contract is made are binding. A clause notified after the contract is made is ineffective.

☐   If after Rondel's and FML Ltd have signed their contract the former, realizing they will be using new and untrained staff, send a letter to FML Ltd. excluding their liability for their staff the clause is not incorporated into the contract.

Olley v. Marlborough Court Ltd (1949)

The plaintiff registered at a hotel, making the contract at the reception desk. When he reached his room there was a notice excluding liability for articles stolen from guests' rooms. The plaintiff's wife had property stolen and the hotel was successfully sued as the clause was notified after the contract had been formed. Although Olley won the court commented that had he stayed at the hotel on previous occasions he may have lost. A previous course of dealings between the parties may allow the terms to be incorporated into the later contract.

In *Thornton* v. *Shoe Lane Parking Ltd* (1971) the plaintiff approached the barrier of an automatic car park where a notice stated 'cars are parked at the owner's risk.' He placed his money in the machine to enter the car park. He received a ticket from the machine referring to additional conditions, one of which excluded liability for injury to customers. As a result of the defendant's negligence Thornton was injured and sued. Was he defeated by the exclusion clause?[1] The court said no, holding that the contract was formed when the money was put into the ticket machine. As Lord Denning eloquently expressed it: 'A ticket is issued by an automatic machine. The customer pays his money and gets a ticket. He cannot refuse it. He cannot get his money back. He may protest to the machine, he can even swear at it. But it will remain unmoved. He is committed beyond recall. He was committed at the very moment he put his money into the machine. The contract was concluded at that time. It can be translated into offer and acceptance in this way: the offer is made when the proprietor of the machine holds it out as being ready to receive the money. The acceptance takes place when the customer puts his money into the slot ... he is not bound by the terms printed on the ticket ... because the ticket comes too late.'

Most clauses are introduced before the contract is formed and so the crucial issue is whether the defendant has brought it to the plaintiff's notice. If the clause is contained or referred to in a contractual document or on the front of a ticket (on which one expects to find clauses) the party is bound even though he or she failed to read it. The other party is not usually obliged to expressly bring them to his or her notice. The plaintiff, acting as a reasonable man, would be unaware of clauses on the back of a document and unless one's attention is specifically drawn to them they are invalid. The same result arises if clauses are contained in a document of a non-contractual nature. We do not anticipate discovering exclusion clauses in such documents; the reasonable man would be unware of them.

☐   When terms have been agreed between Rondel's and FML Ltd the latter signs a formal contract which states date of event, price, time of payment etc. They also receive a detailed list of the contents of the buffet; on the back of this document is an exclusion clause. This is not incorporated into the contract.

[1] This case was decided before the 1977 Act.

Chapelton v. *Barry* UDC (1940)
The plaintiff hired a deck chair and was injured when it collapsed. The hiring conditions were on view at the hiring place and the customer was advised to retain the ticket as proof of payment. Chapelton placed it in his pocket without looking at it. On the front was an exclusion clause. It was unenforceable against the plaintiff as the reasonable man would not expect to find terms on such a document.

3 Interpretation

The clause's function is to avoid liability for a wrongful civil act. If you negligently damage a car a clause exempting liability for damage to owners is irrelevant! Exclusion clauses are however interpreted by the courts against the party relying on them (contra preferentem). In *Hollier* v. *Rambler Motors AMC Ltd* (1972) the defendants owned a garage. The plaintiff's car was undergoing repairs and, due to the garage's negligence, it was damaged by fire. One of the questions for the court was whether the following clause 'The company is not responsible for damage caused by fire to customer's cars on their premises,' excluded their liability. Lord Justice Salmon claimed the average individual would assume the clause meant that 'if there is a fire due to any cause other than their own negligence they are not responsible for it.' As interpreted it did not cover the breach in question. The clause as interpreted meant the company were not liable for not committing a wrongful act (but then they would not be liable anyway!) As interpreted the clause was meaningless.

4 Fundamental breach

The view that a fundamental (ie very serious) breach of contract destroyed any exclusion clause was refuted by the House of Lords in the following case.

> *Photo Production Ltd* v. *Securicor Transport Ltd* (1980)
> The defendants were hired to protect the plaintiff's factory, especially against fire. An exclusion clause in the contract stated 'under no circumstances shall the company be responsible for any injurious act or default by any employee of the company unless such act or default could have been forseen and avoided by the exercise of due diligence on the part of the company.'
>
> An employee, M, of the defendants, admitted deliberately starting a 'small fire' which eventually burnt down the factory. The plaintiffs claimed damages of £648 000 for breach of contract and/or negligence. The defendants' servant, whilst on patrol had deliberately started the fire and his employers were vicariously liable for their servant's criminal act committed in the course of his employment. (*Morris* v. *CW Martin and Sons*

(1966)). Both parties agreed that M's previous character had not indicated any fire raising tendencies and the defendants therefore relied on the exclusion clause. The court held that whether an exclusion clause covered the breach in question (whether it be of warranty, condition or fundamental term) was one of construction. If it covered the breach, as it did here, then liability could be avoided.

Past examination questions

1a) Explain the meaning and importance of the 'officious bystander' test in relation to ascertaining the existence of contractual terms.
b) Mrs Cobbing takes her expensive evening gown to the shop of Williment Dry Cleaning Ltd to be cleaned. Inside the shop is a notice which states: 'Customers are advised that compensation for loss or damage to garments is limited to a maximum of £10 per item.' Mrs Cobbing queries this notice with the manager who assures her that she will get adequate compensation for any loss or damage incurred. Mrs Cobbing leaves her gown with Williment Dry Cleaners Ltd who lose the gown. Mrs Cobbing receives a cheque for £5 but the dry cleaners refuse to consider any further claim. Advise Mrs Cobbing.
A C A December 1977
2a) What is the difference between a condition and a warranty? What is the practical importance of the distinction?
b) Jack told Derek that Christopher had a 1974 Range Rover for sale. It was true Christopher had a Range Rover for sale but it was a 1973 model. Derek telephoned Christopher and agreed to buy 'the Range Rover' without any mention of its date of manufacture. When Christopher delivered the Range Rover Derek discovered the mistake and refused to accept it. Advise Christopher.   A C A June 1976
3) Explain the main provisions of the Unfair Contract Terms Act 1977.   A C A December 1978
4) Write brief notes on
a) warranties and conditions,
b) collateral contracts,
c) implied terms in a contract.   C A October 1979
5) Albert, visiting Gloucham for the first time, parks his car in Motorpark Ltd's automatic car park. At the entrance is a sign which reads 'All cars parked at owners' risk'. Albert did not see this notice. At an automatic barrier a ticket is dispensed to drivers entering the car park. On the back of the ticket is written 'Parking subject to the company's terms and conditions'. Albert put his ticket into his pocket without reading it. Inside the car park is a notice board which, among other things, excludes the company's liability for personal injury to users of the car park. Albert, getting out of his car, slips on a patch of oil and is injured. What is the liability of Motorpark Ltd?   C A October 1979

6

Capacity: minors

A contract may possess the necessary ingredients but still be unenforceable. This chapter deals with the validity of contracts with minors and chapters 7 to 10 deal with various vitiating factors.

Because of their possible exploitation the court protects certain groups of people. One such group is minors (persons under the age of eighteen). Protection is afforded by only allowing them to enter into binding contracts which are for their benefit. Their contracts can be classified under three headings.

1 Valid contracts

These bind both contractual parties. They consist of:

a) *Contracts for necessary goods and services*   As one judge said, 'If a man satisfies the needs of an infant by supplying the infant with necessaries the law will imply an obligation to repay him.'[1] The minor must pay a *reasonable* price for necessaries, which are defined as goods or services suitable to the condition in life of that minor and to his actual requirements at the time of sale and delivery.

The plaintiff must therefore prove, firstly that they were suitable for *that* minor. Suitability depends on the minor's income, social status, occupation and other relevant circumstances. A sports car might be a 'necessary' for a wealthy student – being essential for the student's station in life – whereas it would be an extravagance for a penniless student. Secondly the minor must not already be adequately supplied with the item, and thirdly the item must be necessary when delivered; until delivery the minor can reject the goods or services and the other party possesses no legal recompense.

Even a contract for necessaries will be unenforceable if it contains an onerous term.

---

[1] The minor's liability to pay is probably quasi-contractual. *Quasi contracts* arise in situations where one party has benefited at another's expense in such circumstances that the law requires the latter to be recompensed. Although there is no contract between the parties they are put in the same position 'as if a contract' had existed.

☐   Andrew Fair's two seventeen year old children, Bertram and
Janis, both pass their 'A' levels and Janis, following her father's
wishes, goes to University to read Economics. Andrew covenants
to give Janis a yearly sum of £5000. Bertram rejects university and
joins a firm of accountants at £1400 pa. His disappointed father
insists he live on his salary. Both children incur certain
expenditure.

Consider the table below.

Article bought	Necessary	Explanation	Payment
(Assume the minor is not adequately supplied unless otherwise indicated)			
Janis			
(i) New economic textbooks costing £25	√	suitable for an economics student	£25
(ii) An economics book written and sold to by the lecturer for £10 which duplicates the textbook[2]	X	already adequately supplied with textbooks	nil
(iii) A second hand car costing £1200 worth only £800	√	suitable but only pays a reasonable price	£800
Bertram			
(i) An £85 bicycle for travel to work but rejected before delivery	√	suitable	nil
(ii) A guitar costing £500	X	not necessary given his income	nil
(iii) A brief case costing £15	√	suitable	£15

Nash v. *Inman* (1908)
The plaintiff supplied a minor with eleven fancy waistcoats.
Being a wealthy architect's son he required an extensive wardrobe
hence they were suitable to his station in life. However at the time
of delivery the minor already possessed sufficient waistcoats. The
plaintiff's action to recover the purchase price failed.

b) *Beneficial contracts of service*   Because these provide the individual with an opportunity to earn his or her living, those which are
substantially for his or her benefit are binding. A contract can be
substantially for a person's benefit although containing an onerous
clause.

☐   Janis signs the university regulations which stipulate that students
deposit £50 which is to be forfeited if they break university

[2] Is there undue influence present?

discipline. Although this is an onerous term the contract is binding, being overall for her benefit because it enables her to pursue a degree course. Bertram, although taking accountancy examinations, has aspirations of becoming a pop musician. Xavier Ploit Ltd agree to teach him musical composition but the contract gives them sole publishing rights over his material for a minimal consideration. This contract is not overall for his benefit, it is void.

Doyle v. *White City Stadium Ltd* (1935)
A minor contracted to fight for £3000 subject to British Boxing Board of Control rules (the contract was similar to a contract of service). One clause stipulated the purse would be withheld in the event of disqualification. He was disqualified and the purse was withheld. The contract was enforced because, despite the onerous term, it was generally for his benefit.

2 Voidable contracts

These involve a permanent or continuing interest in property such as a partnership or interest in land. They bind the minor unless they are avoided during infancy or within a *reasonable* time of reaching eighteen, (what is reasonable depends on the facts). Ratification of such contracts is unnecessary, they become binding unless avoided. A minor who avoids a contract cannot recover money paid before avoidance unless there has been a total failure of consideration.

☐   Janis signs a three year lease on a flat for £620 pa. During her second year, when she is nineteen, she is offered a place in the college residential block. She cannot now avoid the lease. It became valid when she failed to avoid it within a reasonable time of reaching eighteen. Bertram also signs a three year lease for £400 pa. On his eighteenth birthday he avoids it. The £400 already paid cannot be recovered but he avoids liability for any further sums. To further his musical career he and four friends decide to form a group and establish a partnership. They each contribute £600 to form the partnership and purchase electrical equipment. Before the partnership is formed Bertram withdraws. Because there has been a total failure of consideration he can recover the £600.

3 Void

Contracts for the repayment of loans or for the sale of non-necessaries are 'absolutely void.' The term void, when applied to minors' contracts, means they possess no legal effect and cannot be enforced by either party but a minor who has paid for and received a non necessary cannot recover payment although the contract is void. If Bertram has paid for the guitar then, provided he received it, he cannot recover the £500.

These common law principles sometimes caused hardship, especially where the trader was deceived regarding the minor's age. Equity therefore assisted the plaintiff in limited circumstances.

a) Where money is lent to purchase necessaries the creditor can recover that part spent on necessaries. Under the doctrine of subrogation the creditor stands in the shoes of the tradesperson supplying the necessaries.

☐   Janis's father is late in paying the covenanted sum. Janis informs her personal tutor she cannot afford to purchase textbooks. The tutor lends her £100 to buy them. Janis spends £20 on books but the remainder on other items. Although the whole sum was lent for necessaries only the £20 spent on textbooks is recoverable.

b) The equitable doctrine of restitution is applicable where the minor obtains goods or money by deception. Providing the minor is in possession of the goods or money she must return these to the plaintiff.

☐   Bertram is offered a job with a pop group but needs a new guitar and amplifier. By pretending he is nineteen he borrows £200 from Sidney Hark, (he spends the money on an amplifier) and obtains a £500 guitar from Music Centre on credit. The latter can recover the guitar but Hark is remediless.

The strictness of the common law means the plaintiff cannot frame an action in tort as an indirect method of enforcing a void contract. Bertram is guilty of the tort of deceit but Hark cannot sue him for this because it would be another means of enforcing the loan.

Past examination questions

1 Explain the rules relating to the contractual liability of minors.

A C A June 1977

2 David, aged 17, asks your advice as to whether or not he is bound by the following contracts:
a) John, a tailor, provides him with a new suit on credit.
b) He borrows £50 from Harry to buy books for his studies. He spends £30 on books and £20 on a party for his friends.
c) He takes a three-year lease on a flat at £1000 per annum.
d) He orders a sports car, valued at £3000. By giving his age as 21 he persuades the seller to deliver it before any payment is made.

A C A December 1978

3 a) What contracts made by minors are void?
b) Discuss the validity of the following agreements made by minors and the remedies available to the other party:
   (i) Jill, aged 16, takes a seven year lease on a flat.
   (ii) Mandy, aged 16, hires a horse which she injures by foolhardy riding.
   (iii) Harold, aged 17, subscribes for partly paid-up shares in a company. He now wishes to set aside the transaction when the final call is made.

C A 1980

7

Misrepresentation

Representations are statements made at the negotiation stage ie prior to the agreement, which induce one party to enter into the contract but do not form part of the contract.

A misrepresentation is an untrue statement of a fact which induces one party to enter into the contract. If it becomes a contractual term the innocent party can sue for breach of condition or warranty but even where it is not incorporated there is still a remedy. He or she can sue for misrepresentation under the Misrepresentation Act 1967.

A misrepresentation, as defined above, consists of two main ingredients.

1 An untrue statement of fact

☐ Trevor Wit, whilst negotiating to purchase a car, is told it is a 1977 model with one previous owner. The salesman emphasizes the car is 'excellent value' because of good petrol consumption, hence it is a 'much sought after car.' It is guaranteed for two years and Wit is told this means it will not require an MOT test during this period.

All the above statements are in fact untrue but not all are actionable as misrepresentations. The statements misled Wit and induced him to buy the car but he cannot sue where the statement was:

  (i) a statement on the general law,
 (ii) merely the salesman's opinion [see below],
(iii) advertising patter.

The statements are classified below.

Law	Opinion	Advertising	Fact
Statement re MOT	Good consumption of petrol; Excellent value.	Much sought after car;	Only one owner; 1977 model.
not actionable	not actionable	not actionable	actionable

Normally an opinion cannot be a misrepresentation but where one person is an 'expert', or possesses special knowledge, the court may hold that an opinion is actionable.

☐ George Reedy, an estate agent, is anxious to sell a property and informs a prospective purchaser that it could be let for £60 per week[1]. If this is incorrect he is probably liable because he possesses expert knowledge.

Where an individual's statement concerns a future state of affairs this is not a statement of fact, hence it cannot be a misrepresentation.

☐ Geoffrey is purchasing a partnership in C's practice and is told that C's daughter will join the practice once she qualifies. This is a statement of intention.

To avoid abuse the courts have held that when a person states an intention (or an opinion) he or she makes a representation about the state of his or her mind. If it can be proved otherwise then the person has misrepresented the state of his or her mind and this is actionable. The misled party must however prove the state of the other's mind, a burden difficult to satisfy.

☐ If Clive knew his daughter would not join the practice when making his statement he can be successfully sued in misrepresentation.

The statement constituting the misrepresentation is normally oral or written but it can take other forms.

☐ The car salesman is wearing a Cambridge tie and Wit, being an ex-Cambridge man, therefore automatically trusts him. The salesman deliberately conceals certain defects on the car. Wearing the tie is a misrepresentation (he misrepresents himself as a Cambridge graduate) and concealing a defect in an item may also be a misrepresentation.

Horsfall v. *Thomas* (1862)
T purchased a gun from H without examining it. The defect which had been concealed could therefore not have affected his decision and was not a misrepresentation. (See below.)

2   *Which induces the other party to make the contract*

☐ Before buying the car Wit is told it has been recently serviced and has only done 60 000 miles. The odometer reads 85 000 but Wit fails to check it although he does obtain an AA inspection before purchase. After terms are agreed he is informed the car is guaranteed for two years.

All the above statements are again untrue but not all are actionable as

[1] is this a statement of fact or opinion?

misrepresentations. The statement concerning the servicing did not induce the contract because Wit obtained a second opinion which indicates he was not relying on this statement. He can however sue for the misrepresentation over the mileage and his failure to check its veracity is immaterial.

> *Redgrave* v. *Hurd* (1881)
> S misrepresented his business takings when selling a partnership to P. Although P was invited to examine the accounts he declined. Rescision of the contract for misrepresentation was still awarded.

The untrue statement regarding the guarantee cannot have induced the contract, being made after it had been formed. It is not an actionable misrepresentation.

Silence

The general rule is that *silence cannot amount to a misrepresentation*.

☐   The car salesman knows the car is unroadworthy. He need not inform Wit of this fact although he knows Wit believes the car is roadworthy.

The silence rule possesses three main exceptions:

a) *Half-truths*   If a statement 'implies' something then the court considers the statement (the half-truth) *plus* the implication. If the latter is untrue the representee can sue although the spoken words were true and it was the silence that constituted the misrepresentation.

☐   If the car salesman states 'the clock shows 20 000 miles', this implies that the car has only covered 20 000 miles. If it has covered 120 000 miles then although the statement is accurate it is a half truth and he is liable.

> *Dimmock* v. *Hallet* (1866)
> The vendor stated his farms were let to desirable tenants. This was true but implied that they would be staying. As they had already given their notice to quit the implication was untrue. The vendor was liable in misrepresentation.

b) *Where the representation*, although true when made, becomes untrue before the contract is formed the representor must disclose this fact. If the representor remains silent she or he is liable for misrepresentation.

> *With* v. *O'Flanagan* (1936)
> In negotiating to sell his practice S told P its income was £2000 per

annum. This was true but before the sale S fell ill and the practice's income fell to £250. Because S failed to inform P of this fact the latter was entitled to rescind the contract.

c) In contracts of *utmost good faith* (umberrimae fidei) such as insurance policies the party must disclose all material facts of which he or she is aware. Remaining silent permits the contract to be rescinded (see *Woolcott* v. *Sun Alliance Insurance* (page 142).

Remedies for misrepresentation

The innocent party's remedies depend on whether the misrepresentation is fraudulent, negligent or innocent.

Fraudulent
This occurs when a false representation is made:

a) knowing it is untrue, or
b) without believing it is true, or
c) recklessly. This would arise where the representor made the statement without caring whether it was true or false.

It is therefore not a fraudulent misrepresentation if the representor can prove he or she believed the statement was true. The test is subjective (what did the maker believe?) and not objective (what would the reasonable man have believed?) hence there need not be reasonable grounds for the representor's beliefs.

☐ When selling his practice S told P that income would double next year. In fact it fell by fifty per cent. In the prevailing economic climate a prudent, reasonable man would have realised this. S however is an optimist and did believe, despite the warning signs, business would improve. S's statement cannot be fraudulent because of this belief.

Once fraudulent misrepresentation has been proved the innocent party can claim damages in the tort of deceit and also rescind the contract (or refuse to perform it if this is more appropriate).

Negligent
Any misrepresentation which is not fraudulent is **presumed** to be negligent unless the representor can prove he or she possessed 'reasonable grounds to believe, and did believe up to the time the contract was made that the facts represented were true' (s. 2(1) Misrepresentation Act 1967). The burden of proof is on the maker of the statement and the test is **objective** (would a reasonable man have believed the statement) and

not subjective as with fraudulent misrepresentation. A negligent mis-statement allows the innocent party to claim damages under either the tort of negligent mis-statement or s. 2(1) of the Misrepresentation Act. The innocent party can also apply for rescission but under s. 2(2) the judge can award damages instead.

Innocent
Where the representor successfully discharges the burden of proof outlined above the misrepresentation will be innocent. The misled party can *only* apply for rescission but under s. 2(2) the court can award damages instead if 'of the opinion that it would be equitable to do so having regard to the nature of the misrepresentation and the loss that would be caused by it if the contract were upheld, as well as to the loss that rescission would cause to the other party'. The innocent party cannot insist on damages, only ask the court to exercise its discretion in his or her favour. The table below gives a synopsis.

Types of Misrepresentation	Remedies	Authority
Fraudulent	1 Rescission, *and*	Equity
	2 Damages	Tort of Deceit
Negligent	1 Rescission although the court may award damages in lieu, *and*	Misrepresentation Act s. 2(2)
	2 Damages	Misrepresentation Act s. 2(1) or the Tort of Negligent Mis-statement.
Innocent	1 Rescission but court may award damages in lieu.	s. 2(2)

Rescission allows the innocent party to avoid the contract. Being an equitable remedy it is at the court's discretion which will not be exercised if in all the circumstances the grant would be unfair.

If the innocent party, after discovering the misrepresentation, *affirms* the contract (either expressly or by his or her conduct) it would be unfair if he or she could renege. Rescission will therefore not be granted after affirmation. Delay after discovering the misrepresentation in requesting rescission is evidence of affirmation and lapse of time defeats a claim for rescission in innocent and negligent misrepresentation but not fraudulent.

Where rescission would jeopardise an innocent third party this would be unfair, hence rescission is unavailable where an *innocent third party has acquired for value rights* under the contract.

☐ P pretends to be R when purchasing S's car. Before S can rescind the contract the car is resold to a third party. S's only remedy is damages.

Because rescission restores the parties to their pre-contractual position, where this is impossible, ie *restitution is impossible*, the remedy is also withheld.

☐ Reedy purchases a partnership in Dolittle, Plunder & Grabbit. The firm expands and to obtain additional capital a private company is formed. Reedy then discovers a misrepresentation induced him to enter into the partnership. Because the firm is now a company the parties cannot be restored to their original position. Damages is the only remedy.

Exemption clauses
A clause exempting liability for fraudulent misrepresentation is ineffective and in other forms of misrepresentation any contractual term which would exclude or restrict liability or the remedies of the representee is ineffectual unless the party seeking to rely on the term can prove it is fair and reasonable.

Past examination questions

1 Define the term misrepresentation.
2 Discuss the following situations:
  (i) David, a car salesman, describes a used car to Edward as being in 'tip-top mechanical condition'. Edward gets Fred, a mechanic, to check over the car for him, and then agrees to buy it. Later Edward discovers numerous mechanical defects in the car.
  (ii) Workings Ltd, in order to sell its Cornish tin mine, claims 'its future prospects are excellent'. Speculators Ltd buys the mine only to find it virtually worked out.   C A 1980

8
Mistake

At common law

The general rule is that mistake does not vitiate (destroy) a contract. This is an extension of the caveat emptor rule (let the buyer beware). It is the responsibility of the parties to undertake all necessary enquiries, only entering into the contract when they are completely satisfied.

☐ Simon Nobb, an aspiring young executive, buys a Rover from a private vendor in the mistaken belief that it is roadworthy. He has made a mistake but this does not affect the contract's validity. It is an inoperative mistake.

A mistake is *operative* and a vitiating factor when it destroys the agreement between the parties. Agreement is an essential ingredient for any valid contract and where it is destroyed by mistake the contract is rendered void. Operative mistakes can be divided into three areas:[1]

1 Mistake as to identity

To understand this the student must recall one of the basic rules of offer and acceptance which is that only the offeree (the person to whom the offer was made) can accept the offer. If Albert offers to marry Barbara then Christine cannot accept!

In most mistaken identity cases the seller is contacted by a rogue who negotiates a sale pretending to be a well-known person and offers to pay by cheque. Because the seller is impressed by the supposed identity of the purchaser he or she accepts the cheque. This is dishonoured but, before the contract is rescinded, the goods are resold to an innocent third party.

The crucial question is whether the contract with the rogue is void for mistake or voidable due to misrepresentation. The latter applies because the rogue misrepresents himself as a well-known person. Misrepresentation renders the contract voidable but the seller can only rescind the contract before third party rights intervene. Once the item is resold to an innocent third party the seller loses the right of rescission and the goods remain with the new purchaser. The seller can sue the rogue who has by now probably vanished. If the seller, however,

[1] Non est factum (a type of mistake) is discussed on pages 122 – 3.

48

successfully pleads mistake the contract is void. The rogue cannot pass a good title to the new purchaser and the goods thus remain the legal property of the seller.

☐ Simon Nobb, whose wife has left him because he was working such long hours, decides to sell her jewellery and inserts an advertisement in the local paper. R visits him in response to the advert and agrees to pay £2500 for the jewellery. Simon is reluctant to accept a cheque but R tells him he is John Owens. The accountant knows Owens is the grandmaster of the local freemasons and because he has aspirations of becoming a mason he accepts the cheque. The cheque is returned but by then R has sold the jewellery to an innocent third party. Can Simon recover it?

To succeed Simon must prove he made the offer to the person the rogue impersonated and would not have contracted with the rogue had he known his true identity. Thus because the offer was not made to the rogue he cannot accept it, hence his purported acceptance is invalid. There is no agreement and hence no contract – it is void. This situation was illustrated in the following case.

Lewis v. *Averay* (1972)
Lewis advertised his car for sale at £450. A rogue inspected the car and expressed interest. During the negotiations he represented himself to be 'R A G', a well-known television actor. Having agreed terms he wished to pay by cheque. Lewis requested proof of identity. The rogue produced a pass to a well-known film studio bearing his name and photograph with an official looking stamp. Lewis allowed him to take the car. The cheque was dishonoured. Averay purchased the car from the rogue before Lewis rescinded the contract and so action was joined between him and Lewis. The court had to determine whether the offer was made to the person physically present (the rogue) or to 'R A G'. If the former was true the contract was voidable, because of misrepresentation, but if the offer was made to 'R A G' there could be no agreement as 'R A G' would be the only party capable of accepting it. Lord Denning decided the contract was only voidable for misrepresentation and not void. He said: 'When a dealing is had between a seller like Mr Lewis and a person who is actually there present before him then the presumption in law is that there is a contract, even though there is a fraudulent impersonation by the buyer representing himself as a different man than he is.'

Judging from that case it appears the presumption is virtually irrebuttable, hence whenever mistaken identity arises in a face-to-face situation the contract will only be voidable.

The presumption does not arise when parties negotiate by post or telephone. Each case is dealt with on its special facts. Was the offer made to the rogue or only the person whom he impersonated?

☐   George Reedy decides to sell his business and emigrate because of the high rates of taxation introduced by the new left-wing government. He sells the 'goodwill' to a competitor and then receives a call from a person pretending to be a friend saying he wants to purchase the fixtures and fittings. They agree a price of £5000 and Reedy allows the other party to collect the goods that afternoon before payment is made. The goods are collected before Reedy discovers the deception. Because the offer was clearly made to his friend the rogue's acceptance is invalid. The goods remain the property of Reedy.

Cundy v. *Lindsay* (1878)
A rogue, (Blenkarn), ordered goods from Lindsay signing his name so that it induced Lindsay to believe the goods were ordered by Blenkiron & Co, a reputable customer. Having received the goods Blenkarn resold them to Cundy. The House of Lords held that Lindsay made the offer to Blenkiron and so Blenkarn's attempted acceptance was invalid. No agreement meant no contract and the goods were returned to Lindsay.

Kings Norton Metal Co Ltd v. *Edridge, Merrett & Co Ltd* (1897)
The plaintiff sold goods on credit to 'Hallam & Co' which was an alias used by a rogue called Wallis. He resold the goods to the defendant before the plaintiffs avoided the contract. The plaintiffs claimed their contract with Hallam & Co was void, hence the property remained theirs. The court held that the plaintiffs intended to deal with Wallis (unlike Blenkarn) and the mistaken belief that he was creditworthy was inoperative. The contract was voidable, hence the defendants obtained a good title.

2   Mistake as to subject matter
Where the parties are contracting over different items then real agreement cannot exist.

☐   When selling his wife's jewellery Nobb refers to 'the valuable ring'. He negotiates a sale but when he hands over the wedding ring the buyer states that he agreed to purchase the engagement ring. Viewed objectively there is no apparent agreement, hence no contract exists.

Raffles v. *Wichelhaus* (1864)
The parties contracted over a cargo of cotton 'ex Peerless from Bombay'. Unknown to either there were two ships carrying cotton from Bombay named Peerless. Applying the objective test it was unclear which Peerless the parties were referring to and so the contract was void through lack of agreement.

In ascertaining whether there is true agreement the court examines the parties apparent intention as indicated by their words and actions and not the state of their minds. In the above example if Nobb referred to 'the first ring I gave my wife' a reasonable man would assume the parties were discussing the engagement ring. Agreement exists and the court would reject a purchaser's contention that he thought they were negotiating over the wedding ring. Actions speak louder than thoughts.

3 Mistaken expression of terms
This is only operative where one party makes a mistake when expressing the offer *and* the other party is aware of this. In *Webster* v. *Cecil* (1861) P offered £2000 for M's property. M rejected this offer but said P could buy if for £1250. P accepted this offer but could not obtain specific performance because M made a mistake when making the offer. There was no real agreement. P knew M meant to offer his property for £2250, hence his purported acceptance of £1250 was a counter-offer. The parties never agreed on a sale price. If however viewed objectively there appears a 'meeting of the minds' (ie agreement) one party cannot avoid the contract by claiming he made a mistake when expressing his offer.

☐ If M's first offer to P was £1250 and P had no reason to doubt its genuineness then he may accept it. There exists a valid contract. M cannot plead mistake by saying he meant to ask for £2250.

In equity

Mistakes not falling into the above categories are inoperative at common law hence the contract remains valid. The party who was mistaken can however seek the assistance of equity:

(i) Where the other party seeks to enforce a valid contract (ie one where the mistake was inoperative at common law) the court may refuse specific performance in *limited circumstances* or make its award conditional on perhaps the payment of money to the mistaken party.

(ii) Where there is an operative mistake at common law the court must set the contract aside but equity can give ancillary relief and make rescission on terms as occurred in *Cooper* v. *Phibbs* (1867). A leased a fishery from B. Both parties believed B owned it whereas it belonged to A. B had however spent money improving it, hence the court agreed to set the contract aside providing A reimbursed B for his expenditure.[2]

(iii) Where there is an agreement but, because of a mistake, a later written document fails to record the prior oral agreement the court may rectify it so it reflects the earlier contract. The party seeking rectification must prove:

a) There was complete agreement on the terms of the contract, and
b) the agreement continued unchanged until it was reduced into writing, and
c) the writing fails to express the earlier agreement.

A businessman agrees to pay £2000 a year rent for offices. If the figure on the lease is £20 000 the court will rectify the agreement, reducing the amount to £2000.

(iv) If a mistake is inoperative at common law the contract remains valid but equity possesses a discretion to set the contract aside on terms 'if the parties were under a common misapprehension either as to facts or as to their relative and respective rights, provided that the misapprehension was fundamental and that the party seeking to set it aside was not himself at fault.' (*Solle* v. *Butcher* (1950).)

Note: The contract becomes *voidable* and not void.

☐ An accountant agreed to a restraint of trade clause in his contract. He wanted to work for another firm but both he and his ex-employer believed this was impossible because of the restraint. The accountant therefore agreed to pay his ex-employer £1000 to free him from the restraint. Unknown to either party a recent House of Lords decision had declared such restraints void. The court may set aside the agreement to pay £1000 for the release because of this mistake.

Magee v. *Pennine Insurance Co Ltd* (1969)
The plaintiff possessed a car insurance policy with the defendants. His son, who was covered by the policy, crashed the car and the company agreed to pay the plaintiff £385. At the time of this agreement both parties believed the policy was valid. Unknown to both parties the policy was invalid. Could the court set the contract aside once this became known? Applying the above test they decided yes and the plaintiff was unable to claim the £385.

---

[2] Where money has been paid under a mistake of fact it is recoverable. This is an example of quasi-contract ie the party benefitting must repay the sum 'as if a contract' existed between the parties.

Past examination questions

1a) In what circumstances, if any, will proof of mistake render a contract invalid?

b) A had notepaper printed showing the addresses of some large, but non-existent, factory premises and a whole string of offices abroad. Using this notepaper, he ordered and obtained from B a quantity of goods, which he promptly resold to C, who acted in good faith. A has now disappeared with the proceeds of the sale. Advise B.

A C A December 1976

2a) To what extent does a mistake by one party as to the identity of the other party affect the validity of the contract? Illustrate your answer by reference to decided cases.

b) Nicholas the manager of a domestic appliance store, receives a letter from Jon, a rogue, in which Jon orders on credit a refrigerator to be delivered to his address. He falsely signs the letter 'Lord Hopper' who is a local businessman, and whose address is very similar to that of Jon. Nicholas who has had dealings with Lord Hopper in the past and who does not suspect the deception, sends the refrigrator to Jon, who immediately sells it to Liz, an innocent purchaser. Nicholas seeks your advice as to his legal rights, if any, against Liz. A C A June 1978

3a) Explain the equitable remedies for a mistake which is not recognized at common law as affecting the validity of a contract.

b) Dominique, a Swiss national, was induced to endorse a bill of exchange by a representation fraudulently made by Erica, that the document was an airline ticket. Dominique is now being sued on the bill of exchange. Advise Dominique. I A S December 1980

4 Consider the following contractual situations:

a) Alice agrees to buy Brian's motor car for £1500. Unknown to both of them, when that contract is made the car has already been destroyed by fire.

b) Charles goes into Woolwoods' store and buys goods which he pays for with a cheque. Charles had stolen the cheque from Stanley, and in writing the cheque, forges Stanley's signature.

c) Giles buys a picture from Hugh which both wrongly believe to be by a famous artist. C A October 1980

9

Duress and undue influence

Where one party is forced to enter into a contract because of duress or undue influence they can avoid the contract (ie it is *voidable*).

Duress

This is present where there is actual or threatened violence (or the threat of imprisonment) to the contracting party or his or her family. The common law concept of duress has limited application but was relevant in *Barton* v. *Armstrong* (1976). The parties were both shareholders in a large Australian company; after certain events the plaintiff sold his considerable shareholding to the defendant. Later he asked the court to rescind (set aside) the contract because of duress. The list of events prior to the signing of the contract were as follows:

1　At a board meeting the defendant told the plaintiff: 'This city is not as safe as you may think between office and home. You will see what I can do against you and you will regret the day when you decided not to work with me.'
2　The plaintiff frequently received telephone calls between 4.00 am and 5.00 am. Usually no one spoke and only heavy breathing was heard. On one occasion however a voice identified as the defendant's said 'You will be killed.'
3　The plaintiff's house was watched by one of the defendant's 'strong-arm' men.
4　The defendant told the plaintiff: 'I am of German origin and Germans fight to the death. I will show you what I can do against you and you had better watch out. You can get killed.'
5　The defendant once burst into a board meeting shouting 'You stink, you stink. I will fix you.'

The court held that the threats put the plaintiff in fear of his life and so amounted to duress. The contract was set aside.

It is however possible to 'pressurize' a party by more subtle means.

☐　Tate and Spencer are partners. Tate is purchasing land from Spencer and insists it is sold at £500 below market value otherwise Tate will dissolve the partnership. This 'pressurizes'

Spencer but is not duress.

To cover such situations equity evolved the concept of undue influence.

Undue influence

Where one party's free will has been *excessively* influenced the contract is voidable. The borderline between permissable persuasion and excessive influence is blurred as illustrated by the cases[1] of *North Ocean Shipping Co* v. *Hyundai Construction* (1978) and *Pao On* v. *Lau Yiu Long* (1979). In the former the plaintiffs ordered a tanker, The Atlantic Baron, from the defendants' shipyard. It was a fixed price contract, expressed in dollars, payable in five instalments. The defendant company agreed, as part of the contract, to open a letter of credit for the contract price as security for the repayment of instalments should they default in their performance. After the first instalment had been paid the dollar was devalued by 10% thereby effectively reducing the amount payable to the defendant company by 10%. They therefore asked for a 10% increase on the remaining four instalments. The plaintiffs, being advised that they were under no legal obligation to increase the payments, refused. The shipbuilders, knowing that the plaintiffs were negotiating a lucrative charter contract, decided to pressurize them by refusing to finish the vessel unless they agreed to the 10% increase. This would have involved a breach of their contract. Because of the lucrative contract under negotiation the plaintiffs stated that, although not legally obliged to do so, they would pay the additional 10% 'without prejudice to their rights.' They stipulated that the defendant must make corresponding increases in the letter of credit and this was done. The re-negotiated instalments were paid without further protest.

The vessel was delivered in November 1974. In July 1975 the plaintiffs claimed the additional 10% they had paid on the last four instalments (with interest) because they were rescinding the contract which was voidable. Did the defendants' threat to break the contract unless the plaintiffs agreed to pay the increased price allow the contract to be avoided? A threat to break a contract may permit such a remedy if the other party has no choice but to accede. On these facts the judge held the contract voidable. The plaintiffs could, therefore, ratify (or affirm) the contract or avoid it once the pressure had ceased. If, after this has ceased, the plaintiffs continued with the contract this amounted to affirmation. Their silence when paying the increased instalments coupled with the delay in commencing an action for eight months after delivery of the vessel meant the plaintiffs had affirmed the contract.

[1] The court considered both cases involved economic duress but students will find them easier to understand under the concept of undue influence.

Their action was unsuccessful.[2]

In *Pao On* v. *Lau Yiu Long* the plaintiffs, a private company, owned buildings the defendant public company urgently required. After negotiations the defendant's offer for the property was accepted in February 1973. The payment consisted of shares in the public company. If, however, these had all been sold immediately it would have depressed the share price. The plaintiffs, therefore, agreed (at the defendant's request) not to sell 60% of the shares until May 1974. As share prices fluctuate both parties accepted that the plaintiffs would require protection against a fall in the share price.

A separate contract was, therefore, drawn up whereby the defendants were to repurchase 60% of the shares on 30th April 1974 at $2.50 per share (ie the market price prevailing in February 1973). After agreeing, the plaintiffs realized that in the attempt to safeguard their position they had forfeited any increase in the share price between February 1973 and May 1974. They requested a new agreement. The defendants refused. The plaintiffs knew that any delay in the acquisition of the building could result in a loss of public confidence in the defendant company. They therefore refused to complete the first agreement until the defendants agreed to their request. Although aware of the illegality of the plaintiff's actions the defendants agreed, being unwilling to risk the delays involved if legal proceedings were commenced. They signed a written guarantee of indemnity that in consideration of the plaintiffs agreeing not to sell 60% of their shares for thirteen months they would indemnify them against any fall in the share price during this period. The share price fell and the plaintiffs sought to enforce the guarantee. The defendants refused to pay claiming the contract, which was voidable, had been avoided. The court drew a distinction between acceptable commercial pressure and pressure which involved a 'coercion of the will of the other party' and rendered the contract voidable. Each case depends on its special facts; on these there was no 'coercion of the will vitiating consent' whereas in the first case the coercion had been such that the agreement was not a voluntary action on the plaintiffs' part.[3]

[2] Where was the consideration for the promise to increase the contractual payments? The defendants claimed that because they were under no legal obligation to increase the amount of the letter of credit this action constituted consideration. This argument was upheld by the judge.
[3] Was the defendants consideration past? The defendants argued that the consideration, agreeing not to sell the shares, was provided months BEFORE the second contract of indemnity was signed. Whilst accepting the time sequence the court applied the exception to the rule, past consideration is no consideration, expounded in *Re Casey's Patents* (1892). In that case the plaintiffs wrote to Casey stating that 'in consideration of (his) services as practical manager' he would receive a share in certain patents. It was held that although Casey's consideration, working for the firm, was past (ie was given before the promise) it was nevertheless valid because his services raised an expectation of payment.

The courts divide cases of undue influence into those where:

a) They *presume* (because of the parties' relationship) that undue influence was present. This places the burden of proof on those seeking to enforce the agreement. They must prove to the court's satisfaction that no undue influence was exercised and that the other party's consent was freely obtained. Relationships raising the presumption include parent and child, guardian and ward, solicitor and client, doctor and patient, priest and parishioner and trustee and beneficiary.
b) No presumption is raised. The party seeking to have the agreement set aside has the burden of proving the existence of undue influence which vitiated (destroyed) their consent.

The remedy sought is rescission but, being equitable, it will be refused if there is unreasonable delay in applying for it (see above).

The request (working for the firm) and the subsequent promise (the share in certain patents) was regarded as part of the same transaction. In the case under consideration the court held that when the plaintiffs agreed not to sell the shares for thirteen months it was understood that they would receive some benefit for their action. The offer of indemnity related back to the plaintiffs promise and so was enforceable.

10

Illegality

Contracts can be rendered illegal by statute or under the rules of common law.

1 Statute

Contracts declared illegal by statute are void.

☐ Trevor Wit's accountancy practice deals with numerous small businesses. When they have cash flow problems Trevor lends them money at the minimum lending rate. Although this commences as a favour to one client it becomes a significant part of his business. Wit is not a licensed moneylender. Under the Moneylenders Act (1927) money lending contracts made by unlicensed moneylenders are illegal.

Failure to observe the provisions of a statute does not automatically render the offending contract illegal. It depends on the intention of Parliament as expressed (or implied) in the statute.

☐ Barl Enterprises require the services of an accountant. George Reedy, a partner in Dolittle and Plunder, is recommended. They contact the partnership and because they are promised that Reedy will personally supervise their affairs, they appoint them as accountants. They later discover Reedy never intended to supervise their accounts which have been the sole responsibility of Trevor Wit. The partnership is in breach of the Trade Descriptions Act but the contract is not void or unenforceable (s. 35).

Parliament has declared that certain contracts are void and unenforceable although they are not illegal. One example is the Gaming Act 1845 s. 18, which states that:

a) Gaming or wagering contracts are null and void, and
b) that no action can be brought to recover money won in a wager.

The Act's application is often complicated but a simple example is a 'bet' with a turf accountant (bookmaker) on a horse.

☐ Wit has financial problems because he cannot enforce his money-lending contracts. He therefore decides to gamble on the horses. Being a respected member of the community he is allowed credit. Wit places £500 on a horse at 10 − 1. It loses. It is a gaming contract and the bookmaker cannot bring an action to recover the £500.

AR Dennis & Co Ltd v. *Campbell* (1978)
A customer in the plaintiffs' betting shop, whose weekly bets totalled several thousands of pounds, on one occasion requested a £1000 bet on credit. Although contrary to company rules that only cash bets should be accepted, Campbell (the shop manager) permitted the bet. The customer lost but refused to pay the £1000. The plaintiff's contract with the customer fell within section 18 of the Gaming Act 1845. The contract was null and void and unable to sustain any action. The plaintiffs, therefore, sought to recover £1000 from their manager. The plaintiff's claimed

(i) they had won £1000 from the customer,
(ii) due to Campbell's breach of his contract of employment in allowing credit they had not received this sum,
(iii) they could not sue the customer for it because of s. 18,
(iv) that damages for Campbell's breach of contract should be assessed at £1000. The court held this was an indirect attempt to recover money won on a wager and was covered by the second part of section 18 which states 'no suit shall be brought or maintained ... for any sum of money to be alleged to be won upon any wager'.

2 Common law

Amongst contracts illegal at common law are:

(i) Contracts to commit a crime or civil wrong

☐ Many of Wit's clients possess market stalls and deal in cash. When preparing their tax returns he knowingly excludes many cash transactions. There is an attempt to defraud the revenue. The contracts between Wit and his clients are illegal and Wit cannot sue them for his fees. The bookmaker, in an attempt to recover the £500 hires Rough to 'persuade' Wit to pay. The contract between Rough and the bookmaker is to commit a tort (assault and battery) and therefore illegal. Neither party can sue on the contract.

Napier v. *National Business Agency Ltd* (1951)
A company paid an employee £13 per week plus £6 expenses. The latter figure exceeded his actual expenses but was designed to avoid paying tax. The plaintiff was summarily dismissed and sued for salary in lieu of notice. The contract was illegal, hence no action could be brought.

(ii) A contract promoting sexual immorality

☐   His financial problems cause Wit to become irritable. His married life suffers. He and his wife agree to a separation. He offers his attractive secretary £200 to spend the weekend with him in Brighton. She agrees. Their contract is promoting sexual immorality and illegal.

(iii) Contracts prejudicial to the status of marriage
These are contracts likely to produce 'bad' marriages or encourage the breakdown of existing marriages. It would include an agreement between spouses providing for a future separation (this might encourage spouses to separate if marital problems arise rather than seeking a solution.)

☐   Wit is divorced. He contacts a 'personal introductions' bureau who agree to introduce him to prospective brides upon payment of £500. An additional £500 is payable if marriage follows the introduction. Marriage brokage contracts are illegal because the brokage organization has an interest in arranging marriages, even if unsuitable.

(iv) Contracts promoting corruption in public life

☐   Wit closes his practice and obtains employment in local government organizing tenders for authority contracts. A builder agrees to pay him £500 for information on competitors' tenders. This contract is illegal.

The above is not an exhaustive list of contracts illegal at common law.

Effects of illegality

This depends on whether the contract is obviously illegal from the outset or whether the contract appears legal.

1   Obviously illegal
The legal maxim 'ex turpi causa non oritur actio' means neither party possesses any right under the contract. Neither party can commence an action to recover money paid under the contract or to enforce it.

☐   Wit's secretary received the £200 before the weekend in Brighton. On Thursday she decided not to go. Wit cannot recover the £200.

This may appear unfair but the principle discourages illegality and is based on the maxim 'in pari delicto potior est conditio defendentis' (where there is equal wrongdoing the position of the defendant is the stronger). It follows from this maxim that the court will allow one party to sue on an obviously illegal contract where:

a)   The parties are not in pari delicto ie they are not equally guilty. The innocent party can recover money paid or goods supplied to the defendant. A party is not in pari delicto if for example he was induced to enter the contract following misrepresentations or duress.

b)   One party repents before the commission of the illegality. The repenting party can recover money paid etc providing the repentance is genuine and does not arise from an inability to commit the wrongful act.

☐   Wit has paid his secretary £200 for their weekend. If he cancels the weekend on Thursday to attempt a reconciliation with his wife he can recover the £200. If, however, he makes the decision because he has broken his leg he cannot recover this sum. His repentance stems from an inability to sin.

c)   The action to recover property does not rely on the illegal contract. In *Bowmakers Ltd* v. *Barnet Instruments Ltd* (1945) the plaintiffs supplied tools to the defendants under an illegal hire purchase agreement. The defendants sold some of these to a third party. The plaintiffs sued the defendants for conversion. They recovered damages because their action was based, not on the illegal hire purchase contract, but upon their rights as owners of the goods.

2   *Contracts apparently legal*

The sale of a screwdriver is apparently legal but if the purchaser is using it for housebreaking it becomes an illegal contract. The guilty party cannot sue on the contract but the innocent party may, providing he or she repudiates it on discovering its illegality, sue on a quantum meruit for work performed prior to repudiation. The innocent party must however satisfy the court that he or she possessed no knowledge (actual or constructive) of the illegality to succeed.

☐   Wit eventually remarries and successfully rebuilds his practice. Being successful he takes a mistress, renting her a flat near his office. The contract between Wit and the landlord is illegal, it encourages immorality. Wit cannot enforce it. Providing the landlord is unaware of Wit's use of the flat he can sue for the rent. If he discovers the facts he must repudiate the contract or be remediless.

3   *Marriage brokage contracts*

These are exceptional in that money paid over is recoverable. Wit can recover the £500 paid to the 'personal introduction' bureau.

Contracts in restraint of trade are also illegal at common law but because of their importance and their different treatment by the courts they are considered separately.

Restraint of trade

Contracts in restraint of trade are those in which one party seeks to prevent another from carrying out his or her particular trade or profession. The law dislikes clauses that restrict individuals from earning a living in the way they choose. Restraint of trade clauses are therefore assumed to be void and the party seeking to enforce them must prove the clause is reasonable. He or she must satisfy the court that a good reason exists for the restraint.

The doctrine of restraint of trade is applicable to many situations but two of the most important are:

1   *Restraints between employer and employee*

A clause is illegal if its only function is to prevent an employee from setting up in competition with his ex-employer. Similarly a clause whose only object is to prevent an employee working for another competitor is void. To successfully enforce a restraint the employer must prove the employee possesses something of his, thereby allowing him some control over his employee; he is only seeking to retain what is his. What can an employee possess belonging to his employer? The court's answer is goodwill or trade secrets.

a) Goodwill

An accountant on joining a firm deals with a number of clients, as will a solicitor, salesperson, etc. These clients 'belong' to the firm and he only obtains them because of his employment. Assuming he is efficient he will eventually develop a good relationship with them. They will come to respect him and value his advice. His employer will be grateful; satisfied clients are good for business.

When the accountant, solicitor, salesperson, etc leave there is the possibility the satisfied clients will wish to remain with them. If they start their own businesses they might acquire these clients; if they work for another firm those clients may transfer their accounts to that employer.

The customers' goodwill initially belonged to the ex-employer but, due to the relationship of client-accountant, etc it may transfer to the employee. The court considers it reasonable that the employer can restrain the employee until the goodwill can be regained.

Marion White v. *Francis* (1972)

A hairdresser was not allowed to work as a hairdresser for one year within half a mile of her employer's premises. The clause was valid, being necessary to protect goodwill. As Lord Justice Buckley said, 'It is obvious that in an establishment such as a ladies hairdresser's establishment the assistants who actually deal with the customers, who dress their hair, wash their hair … provide a very important part of the personal contact between those engaged in the business and their customers. That constitutes an important element of the goodwill of the business; and that is an interest which the employer is entitled to have protected.' The court decided that as the clients lived within half a mile of the hairdresser such a restraint was valid, the area of restraint covering the catchment area from which customers were drawn.

A restraint must be reasonable in area and also time. Once the accountant, solicitor, etc resign the clients transfer to their replacement. After a certain time, depending on the nature of the business, the goodwill should transfer. The ex-employee can then commence business next door; that is competition and it is encouraged. If the ex-employer's clients transfer it is not because of the goodwill element but because the ex-employee is more efficient or possesses superior skills. The duration of the restraint depends on the nature of the business and the regularity of the contract between customer and employee.

b) Trade secrets

Trade secrets are possessed by certain employees and the employer can protect these by imposing reasonable restraints. The length of the restraint will vary, it will last until the employee's knowledge ceases to be useful to a competitor. In a period of rapid technological change this may be a very short period. Whatever the duration of the restraint it must only extend to a firm where the employee's secret knowledge would be useful.

Commercial Plastics v. *Vincent* (1964)

The employee possessed secret knowledge relating to the production of sheeting for PVC tape. The restraint stated he would 'not seek employment with any of our competitors in the PVC calendering field for at least one year after leaving our employ'. It was held that the restraint was invalid because it related to the whole of the PVC calendering field and not merely the small part in which he possessed secret knowledge.

Any restraint is only valid if reasonable in all the circumstances. Relevant circumstances include the area, duration and scope of the

restraint, the nature of the employer's business and the status of the
employee, (see table below).

	Business	Position	Restraining clause	Reasonable	Reason
1	Accountants	partner	Not to work as an accountant within a five mile radius for two years	√	necessary to protect goodwill
2	Accountants	partner	Not to work as an accountant for two years	X	unreasonable no area mentioned
3	Accountants	articled clerk	Not to work for an accountants within a five mile radius	X	unreasonable; no time limit mentioned
4	Accountants	typist	Not to work as a typist for an accountant within a five mile radius for one year	X	a restraint is unnecessary, the typist possesses neither goodwill nor trade secrets
5	Office equipment manufacturer	salesman	Not to solicit orders from his ex-customers for two years	X	restriction of competition because not limited to the type of goods supplied by his ex-employer.
6	Office equipment manufacturer	salesman	Not to sell to his ex-customers goods that compete with those of his ex-employers for 5 years	X	restraint longer than necessary to recover the goodwill
7	Office equipment manufacturer	Managing director	Not to canvass orders from ex-customers for goods that compete with those of his ex-employers for 5 years	√	the senior position of the employee would justify the longer restraint to protect goodwill

Most clauses take effect on the termination of employment but the
court may declare a clause to be in restraint of trade although it operates
during the existence of a contract. In *Instone* v. *A Schroeder Music
Publishing Co Ltd* (1974) the defendant songwriter gave Schroeder (a
powerful music publishers) an exclusive right to publish his songs for
five years with an extension to ten if his songs were successful. The publishers did not have to publish his songs and could terminate the agreement at any time. It was held the agreement was an unreasonable
restraint of trade.

Historically courts objected to restraint clauses, hence the burden of
proof resting on the employer. The courts' attitude was also reflected in
the interpretation of clauses; most employees could be exploited and

some restraint clauses effectively turned employees into slaves. If the court could interpret the clause to render it unreasonable it did so. This discouraged employers from inserting dubious clauses and so assisted the exploited worker. By 1970 the employee was no longer exploited; the trade union ensured the employee obtained legal rights. A strict interpretation was unnecessary and today the courts apply common sense when interpreting clauses.

☐ A firm of accountants inserts the following standard clause into all its partners contracts. 'For two years after leaving our employment you will not work for any firm of accountants within a five mile radius'. If a partner challenged the clause's validity, claiming it would stop him or her working for an accountants in any capacity eg secretary, he would lose. The court would interpret the clause to only relate to the task of accountancy.

Home Counties Dairies v. *Skilton* (1970)
A clause stated 'the employee expressly agrees not at any time during the period of one year after the termination of his employment under this agreement ... to serve or sell milk or dairy produce to, or solicit orders for milk or dairy produce from any person or company who at any time during the last six months of his employment shall have been a customer of the employer and served by the employee in the course of his employment.' The employee claimed the clause was unreasonable because it prevented him working in any grocer's shop visited by his ex-customers. A clause attempting such a restraint would have been void. The judge interpreted the clause in the light of the circumstances; clearly the restraint only intended to stop his soliciting orders from his ex-customers in his capacity as a milk roundsman. Interpreted thus, it was valid.

Severance
The courts' new attitude is also reflected in questions of severance. A restraint may consist of several clauses, some valid and others not. Severance is possible if, having struck out the bad, the remainder is a sensible and complete clause. Once the test was severely applied but today courts approach their task in a more realistic manner.

Scorer v. *Seymour Jones* (1966)
The employers were estate agents with offices in towns X and Y. The restraint clause stopped employees working as estate agents within a five mile radius of either town for a certain period. One employee had only worked in town X, hence the restraint on town Y was unreasonable. The court struck out the reference to town Y and enforced the remainder.

2   *Restraints between vendor and purchaser of a business*

In addition to contracts of employment restraint clauses are found in contracts involving sales of businesses. The purchase price includes a payment for goodwill; the purchaser buys the customers. If the vendor commenced business next door the goodwill would be lost. To safeguard his purchase the buyer inserts a clause restraining the vendor from working in a similar capacity for a number of years within a certain radius. The distance and time varies depending on the business. In one case (*Maxim-Nordenfelt Guns and Ammunition Co v. Nordenfelt*) a world-wide restraint was declared reasonable as the vendor's business was world-wide. The area of the restraint can cover the catchment area of the business, if it is wider it will be void.

Its duration must also be no longer than necessary for the new owner to establish the old customers' goodwill. (See the table below.)

	Business	Restraining Clause	Reasonable	Reason
1	Accountants	not to commence business as an accountant for 2 years within a twenty mile radius	√	no longer than necessary to protect goodwill and only covers catchment area.
2	Accountants	not to commence business as an accountant within a twenty mile radius	X	no time limit
3	Local hairdressers	not to commence business as a hairdresser for one year within a forty mile radius	X	the area exceeds the business's catchment area, it is too wide
4	Paris fashion house	not to commence a fashion business anywhere in the world for three years	√	as customers come from all over the world the restraint can be world wide.

In any restraint situation if the clause is void the employee or vendor can act as he or she wishes. A clause in an accountant's contract stipulating he or she will not work as an accountant within a ten miles radius is void (no time limit). He or she can set up in competition next door the day after leaving the employer and it is immaterial that a correctly worded restraint clause could have prevented this.

Past examination questions

1   Describe the effects of 'illegal contracts', giving four illustrations of such agreements.   C A May 1980

11

Privity and assignment

Privity of contract

The doctrine of privity of contract means that any person not a party to the contract cannot enforce any benefits conferred on him or her, and is immune from obligations imposed on him or her by that contract.

☐   Jackson wishes to establish his newly wed daughter in business. He agrees to give her £20 000 if her father-in-law does the same. Jackson pays the £20 000 but the other party refuses. Jackson can enforce the contract but his daughter cannot.

Tweedle v. *Atkinson* (1861)
T married G's daughter and G promised T's father he would pay T £200 if T's father paid him £100. G died before paying the £200. It was held T could not bring an action against the estate to enforce the contract.

There are exceptions to mitigate the harshness of this rule. These include[1]

a) Certain contracts relating to *land*. If either party to a lease transfers his or her interest to another party the obligations or benefits contained in the original lease are transferred.

☐   Jackson decides to promote his daughter's new business career by transferring to her the remainder of his office lease at a nominal rent. Although no privity of contract exists between Jackson's daughter and the original lessor the obligations and benefits contained in the original lease continue for the benefit (or otherwise) of the daughter.

When selling land it is common practice to insert into the contract *restrictive covenants* which limit the use to which the land may be put. These covenants also 'run' with the land, binding the owner and the owner's successors in title providing they have notice of them[2].

[1] Students might find it easy to remember these by the mnemonic **LAST** (land, agency, statute, trust).
[2] This can be ensured by registering them.

b) *Agency* As seen on page 136 a third party may sue a principal although the contract is made with the agent.

c) *Statute* ·

☐ Mrs Mitchell is involved in a car accident caused by Ali's negligence. Her husband, who is driving, is killed outright and she suffers severe injuries. Assuming the husband is insured she can sue the insurance company (although not a party to the contract) to recover the insurance money under the Married Women's Property Act 1882. She can also sue the other driver's insurance company, although she is a third party, under the Road Traffic Act 1972.

A similar provision is found in the Bills of Exchange Act 1882 which permits a person who is not a party on a bill to sue on it. Finally under the Resale Prices Act 1976 where goods are sold by a supplier subject to a legal price maintenance condition[3] he may enforce this against any trader who later purchases the goods for resale.

d) *Trusts* A beneficiary under a trust may sue to enforce it although not a party to the original contract.

Assignment

Jackson wishes to establish his daughter in business but because of cash flow problems he cannot give her a lump sum. He therefore decides to transfer (assign) to her certain rights, including:

a) a contractual debt for £15 000 owed to him by Hughes,
b) he also wants to take over one of his daughter's debts amounting to £1000,
c) the right to a legacy from a deceased uncle,
d) a Bill of Exchange.

How can he do this?

a) *Contractual debt*
This is a *legal chose in action* ie a right of property which can only be enforced through a court action and cannot be obtained by physically taking possession (when it would be a chose in possession). The easiest way to assign a *legal chose in action* is by *a legal assignment*.[4] To do this the assignor must comply with s. 136 of the Law of Property Act, 1925. The assignment must be:

a) absolute – the assignor must transfer all his interest,

---

[3] Under the Act such conditions are prohibited unless exempted by the court because they comply with certain conditions eg sale of books.
[4] It is not possible to transfer contractual rights of a personal nature either in law or equity.

b) in writing and signed by the assignor, and
c) written notice must be given to the debtor.

There is a valid assignment although the assignee does not furnish consideration.

Once the formalities are complied with the legal rights in the property are transferred to the assignee who can therefore sue the debtor in his or her own name and give a good discharge. The assignee nevertheless takes the property subject to any claims or defences which the debtor has against the assignor at the date on which the debtor receives notice of the assignment.

Where s. 136 is not complied with there cannot be a legal assignment but providing the intention to assign is clear there is an assignment in equity. An *equitable assignment of a legal chose in action* involves no formalities. Notice to the debtor is not essential but should be given because the debtor can raise any defences or claims he has against the assignor until the date of notice and it also furnishes protection should the assignor assign the same rights to another party. It also differs from a legal assignment because to commence an action the assignee must join the assignor, he or she cannot sue in his or her own name.

b) *To transfer the £1000 debt*
This is also a legal chose in action but, unlike the above, Jackson is not transferring property to his daughter but seeking to take over one of his daughter's liabilities (ie a debt). This can be achieved by *novation*. This differs from a legal assignment because it involves making a new contract between the parties in which the creditor, at the debtor's request, agrees to a third party taking the debtor's place (eg Jackson taking over his daughter's debts). The nature of the transaction means that, unlike a legal assignment where the debtor's consent is not required, a contract of novation requires the consent of all the parties.

c) Transferring the rights of the legacy
The rights of a legatee against an executor is an example of an *equitable chose in action* (ie a right which prior to 1873 was only recognized by equity.)[5] It is impossible to transfer an equitable chose in action by legal assignment and to transfer it in equity requires compliance with statutory requirements (it is therefore different from an equitable assignment of a legal chose in action.)

Under s. 53(1) of the 1925 Act an *equitable assignment of an equitable chose in action* must be in writing and signed by the assignor. The debtor need not be informed (but should be for reasons outlined above) and, unlike a legal assignment, it may be partial. If it is the assignee must join the assignor in any action but

---

[5] Another example is a claim by a beneficiary against his trustee.

where the transfer is absolute he or she may sue in his or her own name.

d) *Bill of Exchange*

Under statute certain assignments must be conducted in specified ways and s. 136 is inapplicable. Thus share transfers must comply with the Companies Act and to assign his rights under the Bill of Exchange Jackson must comply with the Bills of Exchange Act 1882.

The above relates to voluntary action by one party but property may be transferred by operation of law. When somebody dies all contractual rights and obligations (except those involving a personal element) pass to that person's personal representatives and on bankruptcy they vest in the trustee in bankruptcy.

Past examination questions

1   Explain what is meant by the doctrine of 'privity of contract'. What are the established exceptions to this doctrine?

A C A December 1979

2a)   Describe what is meant by privity of contract.

b)   A wishes to give his wife a car for her birthday. On 1 January A buys a car from B, who knows the purpose for which A is buying the car. As part of the contract B agrees to repair the car free of charge if it breaks down during the ensuing twelve months. In February A leaves his wife and lives abroad. In June the car broke down and B refuses to repair it. Advise Mrs A.   C A May 1980

12

Discharge of contract

☐ A new business, Barl Enterprises, hire Gabittas (who has recently set up his own accountancy practice) to keep their books and submit an annual tax return. Their agreement is for five years and Gabittas is to receive £1000 pa. They also engage Lennard Eyre, a local solicitor, to form them into a limited company and to purchase their new offices.

The above contracts can be discharged, with the parties' rights and obligations ceasing, in the following four ways:

1 Performance

The general rule is that each party must precisely perform their obligations to be discharged,

☐ Gabittas discharges his contractual obligations on completing the books and submitting the tax return. Eyre is entitled to Barl's performance (ie require payment) on conveying the property and forming the limited company.

Until there has been complete performance the other party is under no obligation to pay.

☐ Eyre has completed the enquiries, exchanged contracts but dies before completion of the conveyance. Because performance is incomplete no fee is payable.

As illustrated above this rule could create unfairness and hardship, hence exceptions to the common law rule developed:

a) *Divisible contracts* Whether a contract is entire or divisible is a matter of construction. That with Gabittas is divisible therefore he would be entitled to £2000 if he only completed the first two years of his contract although his performance is incomplete.

b) *Substantial performance* Where one party 'substantially' performs the contract (the defects or omissions are minor) he receives the agreed price less a deduction to remedy these.

☐　Eyre prepares the memorandum and articles of association but fails to despatch them. He receives his fee less the costs Barl Enterprises incur in having the incorporation completed.

In determining whether there has been substantial performance the court considers the cost of remedying the defects, expressed as a percentage of the total price, and their nature.

> *Hoenig* v. *Isaacs* (1952)
> The plaintiff agreed to furnish and decorate the plaintiff's flat for £750. Minor defects cost £55 to remedy. There was substantial performance and the plaintiff received £695. In *Bolton* v. *Mahadeva* (1972) the plaintiff installed a central heating system which provided inadequate heat and fumes causing sickness. The defects cost £174 to correct. The plaintiff had not substantially performed the contract and so received nothing.

c) *Partial performance*　With partial performance (less than substantial performance) if the other party, given freedom of choice, voluntarily accepts it he must pay a reasonable price.

☐　Gabittas completes Barl's books for six months but then refuses to finish them. Barl Enterprises must have their books completed, they have no choice but to accept his work. It does not amount to substantial performance hence Gabittas receives nothing.

> *Sumpter* v. *Hedges* (1898)
> The plaintiff agreed to build two houses for H. He abandoned the property half completed and because H completed the work he said this indicated his acceptance of his partial performance. As the half completed buildings constitute a nuisance H had no option but to finish the work. S received nothing.

d) *Prevention of performance*　If the other party prevents performance of the contract the innocent party can claim on a quantum meruit for work done.

☐　If Barl Enterprises refuse Gabittas access to their trading figures for the twelfth month he will receive a reasonable sum for the first eleven months work.

2　Agreement

When the contract is executory (ie neither party has performed the consideration) the '*bilateral*' agreement to discharge or modify the contract is supported by consideration, *both* parties forgoing their legal right to compel the other's performance. Where '*unilateral*' discharge arises (ie *one* party has performed his obligations under the contract) the release of the other party is not, subject to the doctrine of equitable estoppel, binding. The promisee has not furnished consideration. There is accord (agreement) but no satisfaction (consideration) which is essential unless the agreement is under seal.

☐ Gabittas and Barl Enterprises mutually agree to terminate their contract. This agreement is enforceable but if Eyre, having conveyed the property, waives his fee the waiver is unenforceable for lack of consideration (unless under deed, or estoppel operates).

3 Frustration

A contract is discharged through frustration if, through no fault of the parties, after the contract has been made its performance becomes illegal, impossible or fundamentally different from that envisaged by the parties.

☐ *Illegality*
Eyre is struck off for professional misconduct. As it is illegal for him to perform the conveyancing the contract is frustrated.

Frustration also arises where legislation is passed rendering performance unlawful. If an unqualified person was preparing Barl's books and legislation was passed stating this function must be performed by a member of a recognized accountancy body the contract would be frustrated.

☐ *Impossibility*
Professional pressures cause Gabittas to have a fatal heart attack and Eyre a severe nervous breakdown necessitating one year's complete rest. Both contracts with Barl Enterprises are therefore incapable of performance and frustrated.

Taylor v. *Caldwell* (1863)
The defendant agreed to hire his music hall to the plaintiff for a series of concerts. Before they could be held the hall was destroyed by fire. The contract was frustrated.

☐ *Fundamentally different*
Gabittas is convicted of fraud regarding another client and imprisoned for five years. Although the contract could be performed it would be frustrated because its performance would be fundamentally different. Barl Enterprises engaged an honest accountant!

Krell v. *Henry* (1903)
The defendant hired the plaintiff's flat to view the coronation procession. This was cancelled due to the King's illness. The sole purpose of letting was to view the coronation. The contract was frustrated, its foundation being destroyed.

Where however performance is possible, although less beneficial to one party, it will not be frustrated.

☐   After two years Gabittas realizes that inflation means his £1000 fee will not cover his expenses. The contract is not frustrated.

Davis Contractors Ltd v. *Fareham UDC* (1956)
D contracted to build 78 houses for £92 000 but due to unforeseen circumstances their completion cost exceeded £100 000. D argued this frustrated the contract and claimed on a quantum meruit for work done. His claim failed.

Although the contract may become impossible or illegal it will not be frustrated if the 'frustrating act' was induced by one of the parties. In *Maritime National Fish Ltd* v. *Ocean Trawlers Ltd* 'D' chartered P's vessel for fishing. He required a licence. As he owned four trawlers he applied for five licences. Only three were granted. He allocated these to his own vessels. It was therefore illegal to use the chartered vessel. The contract was not frustrated because D possessed a licence but chose not to use it for P's vessel. The frustrating event was self-induced.

Effects of frustration
In addition to terminating the contract the Law Reform (Frustrated Contracts) Act 1943 also stipulates that:
1   Payments made before the frustrating act are recoverable and sums owed are no longer payable.
2   If money *has* been paid or is *owed* to the other party before the frustrating event then he can retain or claim a reasonable sum to cover expenses already incurred.
3   Where one party has received a benefit under the contract the other is entitled to a reasonable sum in payment.

☐   Barl Enterprises pay Gabittas £1000 in advance. The accountant dies but has spent £50 commencing work although no benefit has been conferred on Barl Enterprises. His estate must repay the £1000 less the £50 for expenses. Eyre is to be paid after performance. Prior to his nervous breakdown he spends £70 but no benefit is conferred on Barl Enterprises. He cannot recover this £70. If however there had been a benefit to Barl Enterprises a reasonable sum is recoverable under 3 above.

4 Breach

The innocent party can terminate the contract where there is a serious breach (see page 30). This usually arises when the guilty party refuses to perform his obligations at the due date. Sometimes he notifies the other party of his intention to break the contract. He commits an *anticipatory* breach of contract. The innocent party possesses a choice. He can sue immediately *or* ignore the breach hoping the contract will be performed at the appropriate date. If it is not he can then sue. If he chooses this course the contract remains open for the benefit of both parties.

☐ Gabittas informs Barl Enterprises at the beginning of their financial year that he will not complete their tax returns. They decide to wait until the end of their financial year, in the hope he will change his mind. Before then Gabittas has his fatal stroke. This frustrates the contract and Barl Enterprises are remediless.

Avery v. *Bowden* (1885)

B agreed to load A's ship with wheat at Odessa. Due to shortages B informed A, before the date for performance, he would be unable to comply. A ignored the anticipatory breach because if on the day for performance B broke the contract A could then sue for damages which, because the price of wheat was rising, would be greater than at the time of the anticipatory breach (A would have gained). By refusing to accept the anticipatory breach the contract continued in existence. Before the date for performance arrived the Crimean war commenced frustrating the contract. A lost the right to sue.

Past examination questions

1 What is meant by an anticipatory breach of contract? What steps may be taken in this event by the innocent party? A C A June 1976

2 Explain what is meant by an anticipatory breach of contract, and discuss the remedies available to the party not in default.

A C A December 1977

3a) State and explain the circumstances in which a contract may be frustrated.

b) S, an exporter, and B, an importer, make a contract whereby S will supply a large quantity of palm oil to B. Before the contract was executed, S is prohibited by a government decree from exporting palm oil because of a serious shortage of oil in S's country. B sues S for non-delivery. Advise S as to his legal position.

What would be your advice if S had failed to deliver the oil because the price of oil had quadrupled within the last month?

A C A December 1978

4a)   Define 'frustration' in the law of contract. In what circumstances might a contract be frustrated on the ground that the labour required to carry it out was not available?

b)   Swift Builders Ltd agreed to install a central heating system in Jacqui's flat for £600, the price to be paid on completion of the job. Swift Builders had spent £300 in obtaining labour and materials for the work but before the work could begin, the flat was accidentally destroyed by fire.

Advise Jacqui whether she is liable to pay the whole or any part of the contract price to the builders.   I A S 1979

5   **a)**   What is meant by 'discharge of contract', and how, briefly, may it be achieved?

   b)   Consider the following situations:

   (i)   A agrees to build a house for B, but abandons the work half completed and wishes to claim for the value of the work done.

   (ii)   C, a music concert promoter, hires from D a hall to stage a concert. Two days before the performance, D, to defraud the insurers of the hall, sets fire to it. Consequently the hall is not usable for C's concert and he suffers financial loss.

C A October 1980

6   **a)**   Describe the effect of frustration in a contract.

   b)   Discuss the following situations:

   (i)   George agrees to buy the Dragon Public House from Roger. However, the local magistrates refuse to transfer the licence to George because of his previous criminal convictions. George therefore claims to set aside the sale.

   (ii)   Jones agrees to purchase Blackacre from White. Contracts were signed but before the sale was completed the local authority made a compulsory purchase order in respect of the land.   C A 1980

13

Remedies for breach

1 Damages

This is the common law remedy and attempts to compensate the plaintiff, as far as this is possible, by placing the plaintiff in the same position as if the contract had been performed. They are not usually intended to punish the guilty party, therefore if no loss arises from the breach, only nominal damages are recoverable.

☐ George Reedy, an accountant, is engaged on a three year contract at £24 000 pa in Saudi Arabia. Before he commences his contract it is illegally terminated. He takes alternative employment at £11 000 pa. He is entitled to £39 000 damages. He agrees to purchase a second hand car for £6000 but the vendor refuses to complete. He obtains a similar car for £5800. His losses are non-existant (he made a £200 profit) hence he receives nominal damages.

Most contracts are silent on the amount of damages payable in the event of their breach but some contain clauses specifying the sum payable if the contract is broken. Such a clause is advantageous to the parties because the sum recoverable in damages is certain, and a costly court action to ascertain the amount payable following breach is avoided.

☐ A law lecturer moving from London to Devon is due to commence employment there on 1 April. He purchases a new house which will be ready for occupation on that day. He calculates that if there is a delay the cost of storing furniture, hotel bills, etc will be £170 pw. The contract therefore contains a clause stipulating that £170 will be paid for every week's delay in completing after 1 April. This is not a penalty but liquidated damages (see below).

The sums agreed are enforceable at law providing they genuinely attempt to pre-estimate the possible losses stemming from a breach of the contract. The sum stipulated is called *liquidated* damages. As, however, the function of damages is compensatory if the sums stipulated exceed any losses that may arise, the object of the clause cannot be compensatory and it will not be enforced by the court. The clause is then called a *penalty*. It may have been inserted to penalize the other party or to terrorize him into performing his contractual obligations. The innocent party is not, however, remediless but damages payable will not be those specified in the contract but will be assessed by the court.

Whether a clause is a penalty or liquidated damages depends not on the contractual description but on the parties' intention as ascertained from the terms and circumstances of each case. Guidelines can however be obtained by reference to past cases. Therefore:

1   It will be a penalty if the sum exceeds the greatest loss that could flow from the breach.

☐   If a clause in Reedy's contract states that in the event of a wrongful termination of the contract by either party liquidated damages of £80 000 will be payable this is a penalty. The greatest loss the accountant can suffer is £24 000 × 3 = £72 000.

2   It will be a penalty if the breach consists of not paying money and the sum stipulated is greater than the sum due to be paid.
3   It is presumed that it is a penalty where one sum is payable on the occurrence of one or more or all of several events, some of which may cause serious and others minor damage.

☐   If Reedy's contract contains a clause stating that damages of £4000 will be payable for *any* breach of contract this will be a penalty. The breaches possible can range from wrongful dismissal (a loss of possibly £72 000) to being late for work (nominal damages).

Where a contract provides for liquidated damages it is this sum which is payable on breach. If actual losses are less this is for the plaintiff's benefit but he or she cannot claim more where they exceed the stipulated sum.

☐   The house the law lecturer has purchased is unfinished. A colleague discovers this and offers him free accomodation in his flat. Because the damages clause was a genuine pre-estimate of possible losses £170 pw is payable although actual losses are considerably less.

Cellulose Acetate Silk Co Ltd v. *Widnes Foundry* (1925) *Ltd* (1933)
The appellants agreed to pay 'by way of penalty the sum of £20 per week for every week we exceeded eighteen weeks' in the delivery of certain machinery. The machinery was thirty weeks late and the respondents sued for their actual loss of £5850.

Despite the description of the sum as a penalty the court decided that it was liquidated damages. The respondents were awarded £600 (£20 × 30) as agreed in the contract although this was totally inadequate.

Where the clause is a penalty or the contract is silent on the extent of damages, these must be assessed by the court (unliquidated damages). The basic rule provides damages for all losses that were foreseeable when the contract was made (not at the time of breach). Unforeseeable losses are too remote and irrecoverable. What is foreseeable depends on the defendant's knowledge at the time of contracting. Losses that normally flow from that type of breach are always foreseeable because the defendant possesses *imputed* knowledge of their occurrence. Where losses arise because of 'special circumstances' the defendant is only liable for these if he or she knew of the special circumstances when the contract was made, ie possessed *'actual'* knowledge.

a) Imputed knowledge

☐ The accountant dismissed from his lucrative post in Saudi Arabia takes another position at a lower salary. This 'type' of loss flows from such a breach, hence his ex-employers are deemed to have knowledge of it. They cannot contest his claim for damages by saying this loss was unforeseeable.

'The Heron' (1969)
The defendants agreed to transport sugar from Constanza to Basrah. Instead of proceeding direct they visited other ports in breach of their contract which meant the journey to Basrah took an additional ten days. During this period the price of sugar fell, losing the plaintiffs over £4000. The defendants did not foresee this loss and so claimed it was unforeseeable.

Lord Justice Salmon said, Foreseeability may be established by showing that on the facts, presumably within the knowledge of the parties at the date of the contract, such damage was in the ordinary course of things, liable to occur as a result of the breach. ... On the facts of the case, it seems plain to me that at the time the charter party was signed, the shipowners must be presumed to have known that sugar markets, like all other commodity markets, are liable to fluctuation. Accordingly, as a reasonable man, he must have foreseen that, if he broke his contract and thereby delayed delivery, there was a serious possibility of a real danger that the market might fall and that the plaintiffs would suffer a loss. The loss would be the difference between the price at the time of delivery and the price at the time delivery would have been effected but for the breach. Damages of £4183 were awarded.

b) Actual knowledge

☐   Reedy agrees to work in Saudi Arabia because the high salary will enable him to purchase a partnership in Dolittle, Plunder & Grabbit. After his wrongful dismissal he cannot afford to purchase the partnership. This loss does not normally flow from such a breach, hence the employers are only liable if they knew (had actual knowledge) he was using his salary for this purpose.

Cottrill v. *Steyning & Littlehampton Building Society* (1966)
The plaintiff possessed an option to purchase land which the defendant knew he required for redevelopment. The defendant sold the house to another individual. The judge was asked to include the loss of profit from the development in the damages. In the course of the judgment he said, 'It is clear ... that if the defendants are shown to have known that the plaintiff intended to develop the land for profit, special circumstances are established which entitle the plaintiff to have the damages assessed by reference to the profits which both parties contemplated they would make. There cannot be the slightest doubt here that the defendant knew what the plaintiff's intentions were.' Damages, therefore, included the loss of profit referable to the development.

Both 'actual' and 'imputed' knowledge were involved in *Victoria Laundry (Windsor) Ltd* v. *Newman Industries Ltd* (1949). The plaintiff ordered a large boiler from the defendants to enable expansion of their business to cope with increased demand. Instead of arriving in June it arrived in November. Damages claimed fell under two headings: (1) £16 per week lost profit from their inability to take on new customers; and (2) £262 per week because they were unable to fulfil a lucrative Government contract. Given the lack of laundry facilities available just after the war it was common knowledge that if a laundry increased its capacity it could obtain new customers. Knowledge of the first loss was, therefore, imputed; it was foreseeable and thus recoverable. The second loss stemmed from special circumstances, the Government contract. As the defendants were unaware of this the loss was unforeseeable and irrecoverable.

When assessing damages the court includes compensation for any mental distress or unhappiness suffered providing this is foreseeable.

☐   The accountant working in Saudi Arabia had undertaken to purchase a partnership because of his high salary. His employers were aware[1] of this when they dismissed him. Because he could no longer afford the partnership he became depressed. A sum to compensate him for this is recoverable.

[1] Hence the loss was foreseeable.

Cox v. *Phillips Industries Ltd* (1976)
The plaintiff was demoted in breach of his contract and given no details of his new duties. As a consequence he became depressed and ill. The damages awarded included a sum for his distress and frustration because his firm should have foreseen this when demoting him.

Even foreseeable damages may be irrecoverable if the plaintiff has not attempted to *mitigate* (minimize) losses by acting reasonably. Losses which could reasonably have been avoided are irrecoverable.

☐   Reedy was dismissed from his position in Saudi Arabia and must seek other 'reasonable' employment. If he is offered a similar job at £14 000 he must accept it. His damages would be £72 000 (estimated earnings) minus £42 000 (actual earnings) which equals £30 000.[2] If he refuses reasonable alternative employment and does nothing for three years he can only recover £30 000 because he failed to mitigate his losses.

Yetton v. *Eastwoods Froy Ltd* (1967)
The plaintiff, the defendant's joint managing director, was dismissed in breach of contract but offered employment as assistant managing director at a similar salary. He refused this and sued. Should he have taken the post offered to mitigate his loss? The court held that his action was reasonable in the circumstances and he had mitigated his losses by searching for similar alternative employment. Damages were assessed at £30 000.

In considering mitigation it is necessary to distinguish between an action for damages for breach of contract and an action for a sum of money payable under the contract (ie the consideration for your promise). Where the plaintiff is claiming a debt due the rules regarding mitigation are inapplicable, the plaintiff is not obliged to minimise losses.

This was illustrated in *White and Carter (Councils) Ltd* v. *McGregor* (1962). The appellants were contractors who arranged for the advertising carried on council litter bins. They agreed to advertise the respondent's garage for three years. The day the contract was signed the respondents attempted to repudiate it; they committed an anticipatory breach of contract. The appellants rejected this unilateral repudiation and performed their part of the contract. After three years they sued for the contract price. The respondents argued this was a claim for damages for breach, hence the mitigation rule applied. The plaintiffs failure to seek an alternative advertiser meant there had been no mitigation hence

---

[2] The actual figure would be less because of tax.

their damages should be reduced. The appellants claimed their action was for a contractual debt and therefore mitigation was irrelevant. By a majority of three to two the House of Lords accepted the latter argument and awarded the appellants the full contractual price.

This decision allows the innocent party to continue with a contract to increase the sum recoverable. It is, however, restricted in application to cases where performance is possible without the active co-operation of the other party.

2   Quantum meruit[3]

This is a claim to compensate the plaintiff for work done. In *Planché* v. *Colbourn* (1831) the defendant hired the plaintiff to write a book. The former broke the contract. The plaintiff had researched part of the book and successfully claimed on a quantum meruit for this work.

3   Specific performance

This is an equitable remedy which compels a person to perform his contractual obligations and, being equitable, it is only awarded where this would be fair. It arose because the common law remedy of damages was inadequate, hence it is unavailable where they are adequate.

☐   Trevor Wit has prospered and purchases one of the few 1908 Rolls Royces in existence. The vendor breaks his contract by refusing to deliver the car. If another 1908 model is available damages will be awarded (the difference between the prices of the two cars) but if no 1908 Rolls is obtainable the court will award specific performance.

Specific performance is available where goods or land are 'one-off' items not available elsewhere. It will not be granted in certain circumstances, for instance, in contracts of personal service or where it would require the constant supervision of the court to ensure the decree of specific performance was observed.

☐   After his trials and tribulations Wit eventually finds an excellent secretary. He therefore gives her a three year contract with a high salary and a percentage of the profits. To his annoyance she decides, in breach of her contract, to work for a competitor. He consults his solicitor about obtaining a decree of specific performance. He is advised against this course of action.

[3] In the example the plaintiff's action is contractual but it becomes quasi-contractual where there is no contract between the parties and he merely claims the value of a benefit conferred on the defendant. To succeed he must show the defendant, being in a position to reject the benefit, chose to accept it. (Thus it is similar to the doctrine of partial performance on page 72.)

4 Injunction

This restrains a party from committing a breach of contract and is only available where damages are inadequate. In *Sky Petroleum Ltd* v. *VIP* (1974) the plaintiffs sought an injunction to prevent the defendants breaking their contract to supply petrol. If there has been an alternative source of petrol (even at a higher price) damages would have been adequate but, due to a petrol crisis, no alternative source was available, hence the injunction was granted.

An injunction, unlike specific performance, may be available in contracts of personal service. If the defendant agrees *not* to work for anyone else (an express negative stipulation) an injunction may be granted preventing a breach of contract. A professional footballer agreeing not to play for another club during his contract *may* be restrained from doing this by an injunction, provided he possesses another reasonable method of earning his living. If the decree 'forces' him to continue with his original employer it will be refused. An injunction can 'encourage' but not force.

☐   In his secretary's contract Wit included a clause that she would not work for anyone else during the three years of her contract. Assuming her only earning capacity is as a secretary, the court will not grant an injunction preventing a breach. Wit's only remedy is damages.

Page One Records Ltd v. *Britton* (1967)
The plaintiff was a pop group's sole agent and they agreed not to use anybody else for five years. The court refused an injunction restraining them from appointing another agent because their only earning capacity was as a pop group and its award would force them to retain their manager. If the group had all possessed university degrees an injunction might have been granted. The plaintiff's only remedy was damages.

Past examination questions

1a) What principles will the court apply in assessing unliquidated damages for breach of contract?

b) A boards an express coach to London to finalize an important contract which will bring him a profit of £50 000. The coach breaks down and reaches London very late, and A loses the contract. Discuss the liability of the coach company.   A C A December 1976

2a) What is specific performance? Explain the principles on which the court awards or withholds the remedy of specific performance.

b) Harry, a student, signs in March 1976 a contract with XYZ, a foreign language school promising that, during his summer vacation he will work exclusively for the company as a teacher of English. In April 1976 Harry is offered a better paid job by another company and writes to XYZ cancelling the contract. XYZ seek your advice as to their legal rights.   A C A June 1977

3a) What are the rules which govern remoteness of damage in a contract?

b) What is a penalty clause in a contract? How does a penalty differ from liquidated damages?   A C A June 1978

4a) Distinguish between penalties and liquidated damages. Explain the importance of this distinction.

b) Speedy Ltd, a construction company, has agreed to build an oil terminal for Gulp Ltd, an oil exploration company operating in the North Sea. The contract contains a clause under which Speedy undertakes to complete the terminal in sixty weeks and in the event of it taking longer, Speedy agrees to pay Gulp Ltd £1,000 per week as liquidated damages. Due to bad weather and strikes the work is delayed and it takes Speedy Ltd eighty weeks to complete the terminal. Gulp Ltd is now claiming £20 000 liquidated damages from Speedy Ltd. Advise Speedy Ltd.   C A December 1979

5 Consider the contractual remedies available in the following situations:

    a) James is employed by Products Ltd as works manager on a service contract for two years. Within six months of the operation of the contract, Products Ltd terminates James' employment. James has been offered a similar job by Makers Ltd, but has refused that offer and is intent on suing Products Ltd.

    b) Mimi, a singer, is under contract to Artistes Ltd to give a series of concerts for them, and during that period not to take any other public engagements. Mimi refuses to give the concerts and is singing in public for a rival organization. C A May 1980

6 Describe the following terms as they relate to contracts:
    (i) Rescission
    (ii) Liquidated damages
    (iii) Specific performance.   C A 1980

14

Types of contract

Partnership contract

THIS DEED OF PARTNERSHIP made the _____ day of _____ BE-
TWEEN A. B. of etc. of the one part and C. D. of etc. of the other
part WITNESSETH that it is hereby mutually agreed that the said
A. B. and C. D. shall become partners in the trade or business of
_____ upon the following terms:—

1. The partnership shall commence [or shall be deemed to have
commenced] on the _____ day of _____ and shall continue [for the
term of _____ years from that date and thereafter] until determined
as hereinafter provided.

2. The name of the firm shall be "B. and D."

3. The business of the partnership shall be carried on at _____ in
the County of _____ or at such other place or places as the partners
shall from time to time agree upon.

4. The bankers of the firm shall be _____ Bank Limited _____
Branch and all cheques shall be signed by both partners [or and each
partner shall be at liberty to draw cheques upon the firm's account
for payments on account of the business of the partnership].

5. The capital of the partnership shall be the sum of £ _____ and
shall be provided by and belong to the partners in equal shares. If at
any time hereafter any further capital shall be required for the
purposes of the partnership the same shall, unless otherwise agreed,
be contributed by the partners in equal shares.

6. The profits and losses of the business (including loss of capital)
shall be divided between and borne by the partners in proportion to
the capital for the time being credited to them in the books of the
partnership.

7. The lease [tenancy agreement] under which A. B. now holds the
premises situate at _____ at which the said business is now carried
on shall on demand by C. D. be assigned to the partners as tenants in
common to be held by them as part of the partnership property and

it is hereby agreed that all liability under the said lease shall during the continuance of the partnership or until the said lease [tenancy agreement] shall determine whichever shall first happen be discharged as debts of the partnership.

8. Each partner may draw out of the banking account of the partnership sums not exceeding £ _____ a month on account of his share of profits but if on taking the annual general account the drawings of either partner during any year shall be found to exceed his share of profits for the year he shall forthwith refund the excess.

9. All necessary and proper books of account shall be kept by the firm and on the _____ day of _____ 19___ and on the _____ day of _____ in each succeeding year a general account shall be taken of all the assets and liabilities and of the profits and losses of the partnership (including therein profits and losses earned or incurred but not actually received or paid) [*or* (but so that actual receipts and payments alone shall be taken into account)] for the preceding year and shall be signed by each partner. Such account when signed shall be conclusive and final between the partners as to all matters stated therein unless some manifest error shall be discovered within three months after the signing thereof in which case such error shall be rectified. So soon as the annual general account shall have been signed by the partners the net profits (if any) of the business shall be divisible between them in accordance with the provisions of this Deed.

10. Each partner shall—
(a) Devote his whole time and attention to the partnership business (except during holidays)
(b) Punctually pay and discharge his separate debts and engagements and indemnify the other partner and the partnership assets against the same and all proceedings costs claims or demands in respect thereof
(c) Be just and faithful to the other partner in all transactions relating to the partnership business and at all times give to the other a true account of all such dealings.

11. Neither partner shall without the consent of the other—
(a) Engage or be concerned or interested either directly or indirectly in any other business or occupation
(b) Engage make any contract with or dismiss any employee
(c) Enter into any engagement whereby the partners may risk the loss of or be made liable for one sum or any number of sums in respect of the same transaction amounting to £ _____ or upwards
(d) Forgive the whole or any part of any debt or sum due to the partners

(e) Except in the ordinary course of trade dispose by loan pledge sale or otherwise of any part of the partnership property.

(f) Become bail guarantor or surety for any person or do or knowingly suffer anything whereby the partnership property may be endangered

(g) Assign or charge his interest in the firm or

(h) Draw or accept or endorse any bill of exchange or promissory note on account of the partnership.

12. [After the expiration of the said term of _____ years] the partnership may be determined by either party giving to the other not less than [three] months' notice in writing [expiring on any anniversary of the commencement of the partnership] and on the expiration of such notice the partnership shall determine accordingly.

13.—(a) If during the continuance of the partnership either partner shall die or become bankrupt or become a patient under the Mental Health Act 1959 the surviving or solvent or other partner shall have the option [to be exercised by notice in writing to the personal representative of a deceased partner or to the trustee in bankruptcy of a bankrupt within [one month] after the death or bankruptcy or to the receiver of the patient duly appointed] to purchase the share of the other partner as at the date of his death or bankruptcy or becoming a patient as aforesaid in the capital and assets of the partnership.

(b) The purchase price shall be—

  (i) A sum equal to the amount standing to the credit of the deceased or bankrupt partner as his share in the capital of the partnership and as undrawn profits belonging to him in the last annual general account prior to the death or bankruptcy or becoming a patient as aforesaid or if such event shall occur before the taking of the first annual general account the amount credited to him as his share in the capital at the commencement of the partnership;

 (ii) A sum equal to the amount of any further capital brought by him into and credited to him in the books of the partnership after the taking of the last annual general account or commencement of the partnership as the case may be;

(iii) A sum equal to one [half] of the excess (if any) in the value of any freehold or leasehold property vested in the partnership over that shown in the said last annual general account and for this purpose the said property shall be valued by a professional valuer of such property to be agreed on by the personal representatives of the deceased partner or the trustee in bankruptcy or the receiver as the case may be and the surviving or other partner (*i*).

(iv) A sum in place of current profits equal to interest on the

said share of capital and further capital (if any) of the
deceased or other partner at the rate of _____ per cent. per
annum from the date of the last annual general account or
from the commencement of the partnership as the case may
be or in the case of further capital from the date when such
capital was credited to such partner in the books of the
partnership up to the date of the death or bankruptcy or
becoming a patient as aforesaid.

after deducting from the total of the said sums any drawings by the
deceased or other partner during the current year of the partnership
such drawings being taken in satisfaction so far as possible the sum
payable in respect of current profits.

(c) The purchase price shall be paid as to the sum payable in place
of current profits on the exercise of the option and as to the balance
of [twelve] equal instalments at intervals of [three] months from the
date of the exercise of the option.

(d) The said purchase price or the balance thereof for the time
being remaining unpaid shall carry interest at the rate of _____ per
cent. per annum from the date of the exercise of the option until
payment and all interest due to date shall be paid on each date on
which an instalment becomes payable.

(e) PROVIDED ALWAYS that if default shall be made in the
payment of the sum payable in place of current profits or any of the
said [twelve] instalments or of any part thereof [one month] after the
same shall have become due and payable then the whole of the said
purchase price or the balance thereof for the time being remaining
unpaid shall forthwith become payable and be paid by the
purchasing partner with interest thereon as aforesaid.

(f) Further upon the exercise of the said option the surviving or
solvent or sane partner shall enter into a proper covenant to
indemnify the representatives of the deceased partner or the insolvent
partner and his trustee in bankruptcy and the estate of the deceased
or insolvent partner or the receiver and the estate of the partner so
becoming a patient as aforesaid against all proceedings costs claims
and expenses in respect of the partnership.

14. Subject and without prejudice to the express provisions
contained in this Deed on the dissolution of the partnership hereby
constituted the same shall be wound up and the assets thereof sold as
provided by the Partnership Act 1890 or any statutory modification
or re-enactment thereof for the time being in force but so that each
partner shall be at liberty to bid at any sale of any partnership assets.

15. Any notice required to be given hereunder shall be duly given if
the same shall be delivered personally to the person to whom the
same is intended to be given or left for him at or sent by post by

registered letter to his usual or last known place of address in the United Kingdom or in the case of a notice to a partner left for him at the office of the partnership.

16. Any dispute or question in connection with the partnership or this Deed shall be referred to a single arbitrator [to be appointed by the _____ Chamber of Commerce] under the provisions of the Arbitration Act 1950 or any statutory modification or re-enactment thereof for the time being in force.

IN WITNESS, etc.

Figure 5 Partnership contract

SECURICOR FREIGHT & PARCELS OPERATION
(PARCELS SECTION)

CUSTOMER COPY   SPS 23 (5/80)

To: SECURICOR MOBILE LTD.
Registered in England with No. 816887
Registered Office — 24 Gillingham Street, London SW1 1HZ

VAT Registration No. 238 5602 56
VAT Registered Address:
583, Fulham Road, SW6 5UE

T 430956

Receive and forward the consignment **SUBJECT TO THE STANDARD TERMS OF CONTRACT** of Securicor Mobile Limited ("the Company") a copy of which terms is available on request. An extract from such terms namely those relating to **limitation of the Company's liability to £50 per consignment** and to an indemnity by the customer, is printed overleaf.

CUSTOMER'S SIGNATURE

NAME OF SIGNATORY IN CAPITALS

FROM CONSIGNOR	TO CONSIGNEE	LABEL NUMBERS
		From _____
		To _____
POST CODE	POST CODE	inclusive

TICK			
TYPE OF	**A** ☐	* next working day by 1200	* for total distances of 250 miles or more, and for transits in either direction between England and Scotland involving locations north of a straight line passing through Glenrothes and Greenock, add one working day.
SERVICE	**B** ☐	* next working day	
	C ☐	* two working days	
REQUIRED	SAT A.M. ☐	by 1200 Saturday (if agreed)	

WORKING DAYS DO NOT INCLUDE SATURDAYS, SUNDAYS OR PUBLIC HOLIDAYS

NUMBER OF ITEMS	TOTAL WEIGHT	DATE	TIME	COLLECTING BRANCH
	kgs.			

COURIER'S SIGNATURE...   Order Number

Invoicing instructions if not charged to consignor _____

FOR SECURICOR OFFICE USE ONLY

Contract Number		Basic Charge	£	:
Excess Weight	kg	VAT at %	£	:
Temporary	Miles	Total	£	:
Account Number		Invoice Number	Invoice Date	

Figure 6 Freight and parcels contract

STANDARD TERMS OF CONTRACT

1.　(i)　"Consignment" means any article or articles of any sort which may be, or be intended to be, received by the Company from any one consignor at any one address for carriage and delivery at any one time to any one consignee at any one other address.

(ii)　"The Customer" means the person requesting the Company to transport the consignment.

(iii)　"The excepted risks" mean:—

(a)　War, invasion, act of foreign enemy, hostilities (whether war be declared or not), civil war, rebellion, revolution, insurrection or military or usurped power, or loot, sack, or pillage in connection therewith, and/or

(b)　Ionising radiations or contamination by radioactivity from any nuclear fuel or from any nuclear waste from the combustion of nuclear fuel, and/or

(c)　Radioactive, toxic, explosive or other hazardous properties of any explosive nuclear assembly or nuclear component thereof, and/or

(d)　Pressure waves caused by aircraft and other aerial devices travelling at sonic or supersonic speeds, and/or

(e)　The absence, failure or inadequacy of packing or packaging.

LIABILITY OF THE COMPANY

Note: Where the Customer deals with the Company as a consumer the provisions set out hereunder do not and will not affect his statutory rights.

2.　**WHEREAS:**

(a)　The value of the property intended to be carried and/or delivered under this Agreement and also the amount of any consequential loss which might arise from damage or loss to or of the said property are matters which are better known to and/or more readily ascertainable by the Customer than the Company; indeed to some extent they cannot be known to the Company, but are under the control of the Customer;

(b)　The potential extent of the damage (as defined in (f) below) that might be caused or be alleged to be caused to the Customer is disproportionate to the sum that can reasonably be charged by the Company under this Agreement;

(c)　The Company is not able to obtain insurance giving unlimited cover for its full potential liability to its customers under Agreements such as this and in any case even insurance giving limited cover for such liability is more difficult and more expensive to obtain than insurance in respect of any loss of or damage to his own property or of loss arising therefrom which insurance the Customer should be able to, and should, obtain;

(d)　The Company is concerned to keep down the costs of the services it provides to its customers under Agreements such as this;

(e)　In the circumstances the Company intends to limit its liability for any damage caused to the Customer (as defined in (f) below) to amounts which are not out of proportion to its charges hereunder, namely the amounts defined in (II) below;

(f)　In this Agreement "damage caused to the Customer" means any damage suffered by the Customer (including for the avoidance of doubt any loss of or damage to any Consignment and loss of any other kind whether direct or consequential), howsoever arising caused by any negligence, breach of duty or other wrongful act or omission (which phrase, wherever it appears in this Agreement, includes any deliberately wrongful act or omission and any breach, howsoever fundamental, of any express or implied term of this Agreement) on the part of the Company its servants or agents;

(g)　It is difficult to investigate claims received weeks after the loss or damage is alleged to have occurred.

THE COMPANY AND THE CUSTOMER AGREE TO THE FOLLOWING LIMITATION OF LIABILITY

(I)　**Provision as to liability of the Company, its servants or agents**

So far as concerns damage caused to the Customer the Company shall be liable to the Customer (and then only to the limited extent set out below) only if and in so far as such damage is caused by the negligence, breach of duty or other wrongful act or omission of the Company itself or its directors or servants acting within the course of their employment.

(II)　**Provision as to limitation of the amount of liability of the Company**

If, whether pursuant to the provisions set out herein or otherwise, any liability to the Customer shall arise on the part of the Company, its servants or agents (whether under the express or implied terms of this Agreement, howsoever fundamental, or in negligence or in any other way, however fundamental may be the breach of any duty) for any damage caused to the Customer, such liability shall in all cases whatsoever be limited to the payment by the Company on its own behalf and on behalf of its servants and agents by way of damages of a sum not exceeding £50 in respect of damage caused to the Customer in the case of any one Consignment and to a maximum sum of £10,000 in respect of all or any damage caused to the Customer during any one calendar year.

(III)　**Provision as to notification of claims**

The Company its servants or agents shall not be liable to the Customer in any circumstances or to any extent whatever in respect of damage caused to the Customer unless written notice is received by the Company at its Head Office (stated hereon) within 7 days immediately following discovery of any damage caused to the Customer but in any event within 14 days of the date upon which the Consignment was collected or received by the Company.

(IV)　**Special provision as to the excepted risks and as to strikes etc.**

(a)　The Company and its servants or agents shall not in any circumstances whatever be liable for any damage caused to the Customer arising directly or indirectly from or in consequence of any of the excepted risks, or for any expenses whatsoever resulting or arising therefrom.

(b)　If the Company shall at any time be prevented from or delayed in starting, carrying out or completing any service referred to overleaf by reason of strikes, lockouts, labour disputes, weather conditions, traffic congestion, mechanical breakdown or obstruction of any public or private road or highway or any cause whatever beyond the Company's control, the Customer shall have no claim for damages or otherwise against the Company its servants or agents for any consequential loss as a result thereof PROVIDED that in the case of mechanical breakdown of one of the Company's vehicles the Company shall use its best endeavours to provide a replacement vehicle with the minimum practicable delay.

(V)　**Special provision as to labelling**

The Company its servants or agents shall not in any circumstances whatever be liable for any late delivery or misdelivery or non-delivery caused or contributed to by any deficient or ambiguous labelling of the Consignment.

3.　**PROVISION FOR INDEMNITY BY THE CUSTOMER**

The Customer shall for all purposes be treated by the Company and its servants or agents as sole beneficial owner of any and every Consignment and it is agreed that if any other person shall in respect of any Consignment, or part thereof, make any claim against the Company its servants or agents arising out of the subject-matter of this Agreement whether arising out of any negligence, breach of duty or other wrongful act or omission by the Company its servants or agents or otherwise in respect of any loss or damage (including loss of any kind whether direct or consequential) outside or beyond the liability of the Company to the Customer, as limited herein, then the Customer shall indemnify the Company its servants or agents against any such claim (and all costs incurred therein) in respect whereof the Company is by this Agreement declared to be under no liability to the Customer, or in so far as any such claim shall cause the total liability of the Company to the Customer and all such claimants to exceed the limited sums set out above PROVIDED NEVERTHELESS that if any servant or agent of the Company shall have been guilty of any deliberately wrongful act or omission (relevant to such loss or damage in respect of which any such claim is made) such servant or agent shall not be, as between himself and the Customer, entitled to the benefit of this indemnity.

Accounts Clerk in a public undertaking

Dear

Following your interview, I am pleased to offer you an appointment as an accounts clerk in this office.

Your commencing salary will be £   per annum, payable monthly.
This progresses to £   and then by six-monthly increments to a
maximum which is at present £   per annum. Your duties and
responsibilities will be reviewed periodically with a view to
progression to a higher maximum of £   per annum.

The other terms and conditions relating to your employment are
set out in the attached appendix, and in certain reference
documents, up-to-date copies of which may be seen at our offices.
I am sorry that some of these conditions may seem lengthy and
complicated but this is necessary in order to fulfil our commit-
ments in connection with the Employment Protection (Consolidation)
Act 1978.

Would you please let me have your written acceptance of this
appointment.

It would be convenient if you could commence with us on the
and on that day you should report at 9.00 am to the Reception
Office, and ask for

Please bring with you this letter and appendix in order that the
commencement of employment can be officially inserted in
accordance with statutory requirements, and also your GCE/CSE
certificates for noting in my records, when available.

Yours sincerely

Figure 7 Contract of employment

APPENDICES

a) <u>Date of commencement of employment</u> _____

b) <u>Agreement</u>

   Your terms and conditions of employment will be as laid down
   in the National Agreement.

c) <u>Reference</u>

   The appointment is subject to satisfactory references as
   discussed at your interview.

d) <u>Hours of duty</u>

   Your normal hours of work are 38 per week, Monday to Friday.
   The office is closed on Saturdays. Time worked in excess of
   these hours will be treated in accordance with the provisions
   set out in the Agreement. A flexible working hours scheme is
   currently in operation.

e) <u>Holidays and sickness</u>

   Your entitlement to paid annual and public holidays and the
   terms and conditions relating to sickness absence, including
   entitlement to sick pay, are set out in the Agreement.

f) <u>Superannuation</u>

   On reaching the age of 20 years you will, if eligible, be
   required to join the Superannuation Scheme, details of which
   will be made available to you.

g) <u>Trade Union membership</u>

   Your attention is specifically drawn to the provisions of the
   Agreement under which you are required to become a member of
   one of the trade unions signatory to the Agreement within
   30 days of commencing employment.

h) <u>Grievance procedure</u>

   The grievance procedure relating to your employment is set out
   in the Agreement. If you have a grievance, you should raise
   it in the first instance, either orally or in writing, with
   your immediate supervisor. If the matter is not resolved by
   this means you may ask for it ot be referred to your Departmental Head. At both stages you may be accompanied and assisted by your Staff Committee/Trade Union Representative if you
   so wish.

Failing a settlement by these means you may, if you are a member of a recognised trade union, raise the matter with your union for further discussion and if a settlement is not then effected the matter may be referred to the Staff Committee.

i) Termination of employment

The appointment may be terminated by one calendar month's notice in writing from yourself or by the following notice in writing from the firm.

(i)   Less than 5 years
      continuous service
      in the firm   One calendar month

(ii) 5 years or more
      continuous service
      in the firm but less
      than 12 years   1 week for each completed
                                      year of service

(iii) 12 years or more
      continuous service
      in the firm   12 weeks

j) Disciplinary rules

A statement on disciplinary rules relating to serious misconduct is the Agreement referred to above.

NB The agreement referred to is too lengthy to be included.

Section 2

Mercantile law

15

Sale of goods

(All references are to the Sale of Goods Act 1979 unless otherwise indicated.)

Bernard Rayne, an accountant who is expanding his practice by taking on a new partner, will require extra office furniture for the additional office accommodation he has acquired. Whilst purchasing this he will probably be affected by the provisions of the Sale of Goods Act (1979) and the Unfair Contract Terms Act (1977).

The main act applies to 'contracts whereby the seller transfers or agrees to transfer the property in goods[1] to the buyer for a money consideration called the price.'[2] Where the transfer of property takes place immediately the contract is one of sale but where it occurs in the future it is an agreement to sell. It is therefore possible for the subject matter to be goods that exist (existing goods) or goods which are to be manufactured, or acquired, by the vendor (future goods).

☐ A written contract is issued commissioning a portrait of Rayne which is to adorn the committee room. Rayne also agrees to exchange his antique desk for a new four drawer filing cabinet and an electric photocopier.

Neither contract is covered by the Act. Although no special form is required (contracts can be oral, written, under seal or implied) the definition states 'money consideration.' If goods are exchanged this is barter although a part exchange with money involved falls within the act. The contract commissioning the painting is outside the scope of the act because the goods (the canvas and the frame) are secondary to the skill of the artist. Where however the main ingredient is the materials, and the workmanship is secondary, the act applies and in the former situation (contracts for work and materials) courts imply conditions and warranties similar to those specified in the act.

[1] Goods are defined as 'all chattels personal other than things in action and money'. This excludes anything naturally found on land unless it is detached from the land before sale.
[2] This can be specified in the contract, determined by a previous course of dealings or be fixed by a third party. Where a price is not agreed a 'reasonable' price is implied by the court.

Implied terms

The act has modified the caveat emptor rule (let the buyer beware) by implying conditions and warranties into relevant contracts.

1 Section 12

Unless the seller only intends to transfer a limited ownership a condition is implied that he or she possesses the right to sell the goods and if the seller is not the rightful owner the purchaser can recover the whole purchase price even though he or she enjoyed the benefit of the goods. There are also implied warranties that the goods are free from any charge or incumbrance not disclosed or known to the buyer before making the contract and that the buyer will enjoy quiet possession.

☐   Rayne decides to purchase a prestige car. He buys a five year old Rolls Royce from a lawyer friend for £25 000. Six months later he discovers it was stolen when the owner reclaims it. He also purchases office furniture from X who is an execution debtor. As these goods have been seized by the sheriff the title passed is not without a charge. He can sue X. He can also recover £25 000 from the lawyer even though the sale was not in the course of a business.

Microbeads AC v. *Vinhurst Road Markings* (1975)
The plaintiffs were sold road marking machines; unknown to either party another company was patenting a similar machine. After receiving the patent they sued the buyer who sued the vendors. There was no breach of condition because at the time of selling they had the right to sell but there was a breach of the warranty relating to quiet possession.

Under s. 11 a buyer may treat a breach of condition as a breach of warranty but, subject to a contrary intention, where the contract is non severable he or she can only sue for damages (ie treat the breach as one of warranty) if he or she has accepted the goods. Acceptance arises when the buyer expressly accepts them or, after they have been delivered, either performs an act which is inconsistent with the seller's ownership or fails to reject them within a reasonable time.

2 Section 13

Where there is a sale of goods by description there is an implied condition that the goods correspond with the description. The section applies when the buyer relies on the description even though he or she sees the goods, or, as in the case of self service, selects them. Goods not corresponding to their description can be rejected although of merchantable quality.

☐ To safeguard his client's records Rayne purchases a 'four drawer filing cabinet.' Four one drawer cabinets are delivered and although they can be stacked and cost the same as the four drawer version he can reject them.

Re Moore & Co (1921)
M sold L 3100 cases of fruit each containing 30 tins. M delivered the correct quantity of tins but many were packed in cases of 24. Although this did not affect their value L was entitled to reject the whole consignment.

3 Section 14(2)

Where goods are sold in the *course of a business*, there is an implied condition that they are of merchantable quality, except:
a) as regards defects specifically drawn to the buyer's attention before the contract is made, or
b) if the buyer examines the goods before the contract is made, as regards defects which he ought to discover.

Goods are of merchantable quality if they are fit for the purpose or purposes for which they are commonly bought having regard to all the relevant circumstances including their price. If goods have only one purpose they must be suitable for that purpose but where they are multipurpose they may be of merchantable quality if suitable for one purpose although unsuitable for that purpose for which they were bought (the vendor may however have broken s. 14(3).)

☐ Rayne purchases from another practice a desk infested with woodworm which he should have noticed when he examined it prior to purchase. No action lies because although a sale in the course of business (ie the sale is made by a business and not a private individual) the woodworm was apparent.

Rayne purchases a second hand electric typewriter for £ 250 for his secretary. It works but requires a full service after two months. The machine is of merchantable quality considering the price.

4 Section 14(3)

Where the goods are sold in the *course of a business* and the buyer, expressly or impliedly, indicates that the goods are required for a special purpose, there is an implied condition that the goods are *reasonably fit for that purpose*, except where the circumstances show the buyer is not relying, or it is unreasonable for the buyer to rely, on the skill or judgment of the other party.

☐   Rayne purchases two new fire extinguishers for his Rolls Royce car. They 'blow up' when used. They are not 'fit for their purpose' and a successful action lies.

Having returned the stolen Rolls Royce, Rayne requires another. He contacts a dealer and, having found a suitable model, has it tested by the Automobile Association. Although s. 14(3) applies to second hand sales it is excluded because the circumstances indicate the buyer is relying on the AA inspection and not the seller's skill and judgement.

5 Section 15(2)

Where there is a sale by sample:

a) the bulk must correspond with the sample,
b) the buyer must have a reasonable opportunity of comparing the bulk with the sample before acceptance, and
c) the goods must be free from defects rendering them unmerchantable which would not be apparent on reasonable examination of the sample.

☐   Rayne purchases fifty audio cassette tapes for his secretarial staff. He examined them by playing one on a machine; after one hour's use by his staff they start to break. He can sue under s. 15 because this defect was not apparent on his reasonable examination of the tapes.

Godley v. *Perry* (1960)
A young boy purchased a catapult from P's shop which due to faulty manufacture broke in use and damaged his eye. The catapult was bought after P's wife had tested a sample by pulling back the elastic. The wholesalers were liable for breach of s 14(2), s. 14(3) and s. 15(2).

Exclusion clauses

The vendor

cannot exclude	*cannot exclude where one party deals as consumer*	*cannot exclude as against a person dealing otherwise than as a consumer unless the clause is REASONABLE*
Section 12	Section 13	Section 13
	Section 14	Section 14
	Section 15	Section 15

A purchaser deals as consumer providing:

a) he or she does not make (or pretend to make) the contract in the course of a business where
b) the vendor *does* make the contract in the course of a business, providing
c) the goods are of a type ordinarily supplied for private use or consumption.

It is up to the vendor to prove the purchaser is not dealing as consumer.

In determining reasonableness the court considers all relevant circumstances. Does the seller have a monopoly? Was the buyer aware of the clause? Did the buyer receive a price reduction for accepting it etc?

Exceptions to nemo dat

Under s. 12 the seller is liable if the seller sold the stolen goods but, as explained above, the purchaser must return them to the rightful owner although he or she can recover sums spent improving the goods.[3] The remedy against the seller may however prove worthless if he or she is a 'rogue.'

☐ Rayne has returned the stolen Rolls Royce and sues his lawyer friend for £25 000. The lawyer has however emigrated to Bermuda because he knows he 'sold' more than one stolen Rolls Royce and there is no extradition treaty with Bermuda. Rayne's remedy is therefore worthless.

To assist innocent purchasers the law has therefore developed exceptions to the rule that no one can pass a better title than he or she possesses (nemo dat non quod habet). In limited circumstances an innocent purchaser can acquire a good title from someone whose title is defective.

S. 24 allows a person who has sold goods but continues in possession of them or the documents of title (for whatever reason) to pass a good title to an innocent purchaser. The logic underwriting this is that where goods are sold to numerous people the first to obtain ACTUAL possession obtains the best title.

☐ After his earlier experience Rayne decides to purchase an antique desk from a reputable company. Having paid for it he asks them to store it for him for two weeks until his new office is open. During this period another customer offers £1000 more for the

---

[3] This is another example of an action in quasi-contract; the innocent purchaser can recover sums spent improving the goods 'as if a contract' existed between the purchaser and the rightful owner.

desk. It is sold and delivered to him. As he is unaware of the earlier sale he obtains a good title. The accountant can recover the £1000.

Under *s. 22* where goods are sold in market overt the buyer obtains a good title if he acts in good faith without notice of the seller's defective title. Goods are sold in market overt if sold from:

a)		b)
WHERE	shop in the City of London,	market stall in a regularly constituted market,
WHEN	from Monday to Saturday, and are:	on market day during the hours of sunrise and sunset,
HOW	goods normally sold by that establishment.	according to the usages of the market.

☐   Rayne is still seeking an antique desk. Whilst walking home for lunch he is browsing around an antique stall looking for a desk when the neighbouring stallholder, who sells vegetables, tells him he has a suitable desk in his van. The accountant examines it very carefully for woodworm before agreeing to buy it. He later discovers it was stolen. It is not a sale in market overt because it is not according to the usages of the market. Desks are not sold from vegetable stalls. The desk must be returned to the original owner.

Under *s. 23* a seller with a voidable title (see page 48) which has not been avoided at the time of sale can pass a good title to an innocent buyer.

S. 25 refers to sales by a buyer (not hirer) who obtains possession. If a buyer obtains possession of the goods or documents of title with the owner's consent (even if this is obtained by deception), their delivery to an innocent purchaser transfers title. The original seller's conduct is more blameworthy than that of the innocent purchaser.

Cahn v. *Pockett's Bristol Channel Steam Packet Co Ltd* (1899) The seller transferred a bill of lading, endorsed in blank (ie a document of title), to a buyer with a draft for acceptance. When the buyer failed to accept the draft the seller tried to regain possession of the goods. By this time, however, they had been sold to an innocent third party. Under s. 25(2) he obtained a good title because the original buyer had obtained the documents of title with the seller's consent.

The other exceptions to nemo dat are more general and include:

a) sale by factor,

b) sales under common law or statutory power (this includes sales by repairers of uncollected goods),

c) estoppel − when the owner allows the buyer to believe the seller possesses the authority to sell he is estopped from proving otherwise.

☐ Rayne asks his secretary to advertise the second hand electric typewriter for sale as he intends to purchase a new one now business has improved. When a buyer arrives, the secretary, who has been told to pass all enquiries to her employer, ignores his instructions and tells the potential buyer it is her typewriter. Although Rayne overhears this statement he does nothing. Having sold the typewriter the secretary absconds with the proceeds. Although the secretary was not authorized to sell the machine the buyer obtains a good title because the accountant is estopped from denying her ownership of the machine.

Note: Merely giving someone possession of your goods is insufficient to create an estoppel.

Passing of property

Having bought or agreed to buy goods Rayne will need to know when to insure them. Should he become a trustee in bankruptcy he will need to know what goods belong to the bankrupt. Both questions depend on who possesses the property (ownership) in the goods; you insure immediately the property passes as the goods then belong to the buyer even though they may be held by the other party.

	Rayne agrees to purchase	specific	unascertained	ascertained when
1	Rolls Royce registration VNK 524S	√		
2	10 desks and chairs from a display of 200		√	10 chairs are selected buyer is notified
3	1 × 4 drawer filing cabinet being the only one in stock	√		
4	A colleague's desk	√		
5	Two new fire extinguishers selected out of a catalogue		√	2 are chosen by the supplier

N.B. UNASCERTAINED GOODS CAN NEVER BECOME SPECIFIC.

The time at which property passes depends on the parties' intention but where there is no agreement on this matter the answer is found in s. 18. The section distinguishes *specific goods* (those identified when the contract is made) from *unascertained* (those that become identified, ascertained, after making the contract.)

Specific goods

Where there is no agreement by the parties:

Rule one states: Where there is an unconditional contract for the sale of specific goods in a deliverable state the property in the goods passes to the buyer when the contract is made, and it is immaterial whether the time of payment or time of delivery, or both, be postponed.

☐   Rayne purchases for his office a length of carpet which is to be fitted. It is delivered in heavy bales but before being laid it is stolen. As the carpet is not in a deliverable state the property has not passed; the seller bears the loss. In addition he purchases an orange lampshade agreeing to pay for it when it is delivered. This is stolen when the vendor's shop is broken into but the loss falls on the buyer, the property in the goods having passed.

Rule two states: Where there is a contract for the sale of specific goods and the seller is bound to do something to the goods, for the purpose of putting them in a deliverable state, the property does not pass until such thing be done, and the buyer has notice thereof.

☐   Rayne purchases a stereo unit for his Rolls Royce but it requires modification before being fitted. The property passes once the unit is modified and Rayne is notified.

Rule three states: Where there is a contract for the sale of specific goods in a deliverable state, but the *seller* is bound to weigh, measure, test, or do some other act or thing with reference to the goods for the purpose of ascertaining the price, the property does not pass until such act or thing be done, and the buyer has notice thereof.

☐   Rayne buys a 'job lot' of cassette tapes (60 mins 50p and 90 mins 70p) for the audio machines. The vendor does not know the length of the tapes and has to play them through to calculate the price. Before he does this they are destroyed by an accidental fire. As the property has not passed the seller bears the loss.

Rule four states: When goods are delivered to the buyer on approval or 'on sale or return' or other similar terms the property therein passes to the buyer:
  (i) When he signifies his approval or acceptance to the seller or does any other act adopting the transaction.

(ii) If he does not signify his approval or acceptance to the seller but retains the goods without giving notice of rejection then, if a time has been fixed for the return of the goods, on the expiration of such time, and if no time has been fixed, on the expiration of a reasonable time.

☐ Rayne decides to buy his girlfriend a present after her frequent complaints regarding his late working hours. He obtains a £500 ring from J on seven days' approval. He shows it to her. She likes it and is allowed to keep it. The following day she informs Rayne she is breaking off their relationship but refuses to return the ring. Although seven days has not elapsed since he obtained the ring the property has passed to the accountant because by giving his girlfriend the ring he adopted the transaction.

Unascertained goods
The property in unascertained goods passes when

'Goods of that description and in a deliverable state are unconditionally appropriated to the contract (ie ascertained), either by the seller with the assent of the buyer, or by the buyer with the assent of the seller. Such assent may be express or implied, and may be given either before or after the appropriation is made. (s. 18 rule 5(1)).'

☐ One of Rayne's staff writes to Hertford Bookshop asking them to send a copy of *'Essential law for accountancy students.'* The moment the copy is selected the property in it passes. The goods become ascertained and the buyer has, by his conduct, impliedly assented to the appropriation.

Rights of the buyer

Having purchased his office requirements Rayne is entitled to their 'delivery'; this is a legal term which means *the voluntary transfer of possession from one person to another*. The term delivery does *not* mean their physical movement. The goods can be handed over (actual delivery) or the buyer can be handed the documents of title or the means of possessing the goods such as the key to the warehouse (constructive delivery).

Where the seller refuses to deliver (transfer possession) the buyer can request:
a) damages (for assessment see page 77),
or

b) specific performance (page 82).

If the buyer paid in advance this is recoverable because there is a total failure of consideration[4].

If the vendor delivers the wrong goods the buyer can:

Under delivery of correct goods	Over delivery of correct goods	Delivery of consignment containing correct and incorrect goods
reject consignment *or* accept consignment	reject consignment *or* accept consignment *or* accept quantity ordered and reject rest.	reject consignment *or* accept quantity ordered and reject rest

Rights of the seller

A buyer who refuses to accept delivery without good reason can be sued for damages plus storage costs and where the buyer's refusal is total the contract can be repudiated. If however the buyer is prepared to accept the goods at a later date this constitutes a breach of warranty and the seller cannot repudiate the contract and can only sue for damages.

Once the 'property' (ownership) has passed the seller can sue for the price. If however the buyer goes bankrupt the goods vest in his or her trustee in bankruptcy and the seller joins the other creditors and will receive so much in the £. To avoid this a contractual clause may stipulate that the property only passes when a condition is complied with, for example the price is paid (the rules in s. 18 being subject to a contrary intention). The seller has therefore expressly reserved the right of disposal and this right is impliedly reserved where:

a) goods are shipped and by the bill of lading they are deliverable to the order of the seller,

b) the seller sends a bill of exchange to the buyer with a bill of lading.

The property passes once the buyer accepts the bill of exchange.

Although an *unpaid seller* can sue for the price it is better (because of the bankruptcy rules) if he or she retains the 'property' in the goods. The unpaid seller can reserve the right of disposal (ie the property in the goods) as seen above but he or she may possess rights against the goods although the property has passed.

An unpaid seller in this latter instance has:

---

[4] Money paid on a consideration that has wholly failed is recoverable in quasi-contract. If however the failure is only partial the only remedy is an action for damages for breach of contract.

1 *A lien for the price* Although the property has passed the unpaid seller can *retain* possession of the goods until payment is made where

a) goods were sold without any stipulation as to credit,
or
b) goods were sold on credit but the time for payment has expired,
or
c) the buyer becomes insolvent (ie is unable to pay his debts).

As lien depends on possession it is lost when goods are delivered to a third party or the buyer (or his agent).

2 *A right of stoppage in transitu* The unpaid seller can stop the goods whilst in transit and retain possession until the price is tendered where

a) the buyer becomes insolvent
and
b) the goods are in transit.

Goods cease to be in transit once in the buyer's actual or constructive possession.

☐   Hurricane publishers send 500 copies of *Essential law for accountancy students* to three bookshops, each of which becomes insolvent.

   a) Hertford bookshop have already received the book; lien and stoppage in transitu is impossible.
   b) Hereford bookshop has not received the books which are still with BRS. The publisher can exercise his right of stoppage in transitu.
   c) Hampshire bookshop collected the books from BRS depot as term had started and students needed the book. The publisher cannot exercise the right of stoppage in transitu.

The exercise of lien and stoppage does not rescind the contract and the seller is only entitled to resell the goods if:

a) they are perishable,
or
b) the seller notifies the buyer of his or her intention to resell and payment is not made within a reasonable time,
or
c) the seller has reserved the right to resell.

A sale in any other circumstances, although passing a good title to the new buyer, renders the seller liable for breach of contract.

3. *A 'Romalpa' type clause*   The unpaid seller possesses additional rights against the goods if he or she incorporates a 'Romalpa' type clause in the contract.

> *Aluminium Industrie BV* v. *Romalpa Ltd* (1976)
> The sellers incorporated the following clause in their contract.
>
> 1 'The ownership of the material to be delivered by AIV will only be transferred to purchaser when he has met all that is owing to AIV no matter on what grounds.' (ie s. 18 rules are excluded.)
> 2 a) 'AIV and purchaser agree that, if purchaser should make (a) new object(s) from the material, mix this material with (an) other object(s) from the material or if this material in any way whatsoever becomes a constituent of (an) other object(s) AIV will be given the ownership of this (these) new object(s) as surety of the full payment of what purchaser owes AIV to this end AIV and purchaser now agree that the ownership of the article (s) in question, whether finished or not, are to be transferred to AIV and that this transfer of ownership will be considered to have taken place through and at the moment of the single operation or event by which the material is converted into (a) new object(s).'
>   b) 'Nevertheless, purchaser will be entitled to sell these objects to a third party within the framework of the normal carrying on of his business and to deliver them on condition that − if AIV so requires − purchaser, as long as he has not fully discharged his debt to AIV shall hand over to AIV claims he has against his buyer emanating from this transaction.'

The purchasers went into liquidation having sold part of the consignment of aluminium foil; as they were unpaid the seller recovered all the unsold aluminium and traced the proceeds of the sub-sale. They therefore obtained full payment prior to the distribution of the firm's assets to the other creditors.

An appropriately worded clause[5] allows the unpaid seller to recover possession of goods which have been delivered, (hence the rights of lien and stoppage in transitu have been lost) on the buyers insolvency. Such a clause might also allow the seller to reclaim unsold goods which have been paid for, providing other payments are outstanding.

---

[5] In *Re Bond Works* [1979] *and Borden (UK) Ltd* v. *Scottish Timber* (1979) the unpaid sellers' action failed because the clauses were not appropriately worded.

Past examination questions

1a) 'Under a contract for the Sale of Goods risk passes with title.' To what extent is this true?

b) Bunting, a farmer, orders from Sweetcorn, a seed merchant, five tons of corn seed. In addition he asks Sweetcorn if he will put the five tons on one side and store them for him until he (Bunting) is ready to take delivery. Sweetcorn accepts the order, complies with Bunting's request and writes to him informing him that 'five tons have been put aside and await collection.' Three days later the warehouse is burnt down and the seed destroyed. Advise Sweetcorn as to whether he is likely to succeed in recovering the price.　　　　　A C A June 1976

2 S. 55 of the Sales of Goods Act 1979 allowed complete freedom to contract out of any of the obligations implied by the Act. To what extent has this freedom been restricted by the Supply of Goods (Implied Terms) Act 1973?　　　　　A C A June 1977

3 State and explain the rules governing the passing of property under contracts for the sale of goods in cases where the parties have not indicated an intention that it should pass at any particular time.

A C A December 1977

4a) Rita sells a kitchen table to Irene to be collected in three days. The day after the sale Rita sells the table to Catherina. Irene wishes to recover the table from Catherina and seeks your advice as to her legal rights. Advise her.

b) Peter sells his motor car to Helen who pays by cheque. The cheque is dishonoured. As soon as Peter discovers the true position he informs the police. Meanwhile Helen sells the car to Nelly who buys in good faith. Peter seeks to recover the car or its value from Nelly. Advise Nelly.　　　　　A C A June 1978

5 In a contract for the sale of goods, outline the rights which are available to the unpaid seller against the goods. A C A December 1978

6 Discuss the rights of action which a seller has for breach of contract against the buyer personally.

7 James agreed to buy 100 tons of wheat from ABC Ltd at £50 per ton. James later refused to accept delivery of the wheat as the market price of wheat had fallen to £30 per ton. ABC Ltd are now claiming damages. Advise James.　　　　　A C A June 1979

8 What legal rules determine the passing of property in goods? Why may it be important to ascertain the time at which the property in goods passes from the seller to the buyer?　　　　　I A S June 1979

9a) Explain the rights of an unpaid seller against the goods sold by him. When will such rights be lost?

b) By a written agreement entered into in April 1979 Shanahan Ltd agreed to sell a boat to Jeff for £4000. A clause in the agreement reads:

☐   'Until the date of payment, the purchaser is required to hold the vessel in such a way that it shall remain the property of the seller and any fitments or other materials added to this vessel shall also become the property of the seller.'

After delivery of the boat, Jeff installed a new engine in it. However, he then went bankrupt before any payment was made to Shanahan for the boat. Advise Shanahan Ltd whether they are entitled to recover the boat, together with its new engine, from Jeff's trustee in bankruptcy.

I A S December 1980

10a)   What conditions and warranties are implied by the Sale of Goods Act 1979, in every contract of sale?

   b)   Dave is an accountant in practice on his own. He seeks your advice on the following matters:

   a)   He has purchased a new typewriter from a local shop which he has since discovered is faulty. The shopkeeper has refused to replace it with another one or to refund him his money.

   b)   He has purchased a second-hand car which he saw advertised in the local paper in the following terms, '1976 Vauxhall Viva de luxe in good condition £1200 ono. Apply to Joe Smith, 3 Railway Cuttings, Newtown'. Before purchasing the car he inspected it but failed to discover that it was only a standard model Viva and that it needed the steering to be replaced.

A C A December 1979

16

Negotiable instruments

(The words in italics are defined in a glossary at the end of the chapter.)

Instruments which are 'negotiable' possess the following characteristics:

1 Their title (ownership) passes on delivery or on delivery and *endorsement*.
2 The holder may sue in his own name.
3 The person liable on the instrument need not be informed of any transfer.
4 A *holder in due course* takes free from any defects in his predecessor's titles.

A document which is non-negotiable, like a cheque crossed 'not negotiable', is still transferable but it loses these negotiable qualities: the holder, for example, takes it subject to the defects in title of earlier transferors. The figure below indicates the negotiability of common business documents.

Negotiable instruments	*Non-negotiable instruments*
Bills of Exchange	Postal and money orders
Cheques	Share certificates
Promissory notes	Bills of lading
Dividend warrants	Dock warrants
Share warrants	Travellers' cheques
Exchequer bills	IOU's
Bankers drafts	

Negotiability is acquired through mercantile custom or statute

Bills of exchange

Section 3(1) of the Bills of Exchange Act 1882 (to which all references apply unless otherwise stated) defines a bill of exchange as:

☐ 'an unconditional order in writing, addressed by one person to another, signed by the person giving it, requiring the person to whom it is addressed to pay on demand, or at a fixed or determinable future time, a sum certain in money to or to the order of a specified person or to bearer.'

The three parties to a bill of exchange are:

1 *Drawer*   the person giving the order to pay;
2 *Drawee*   the person to whom the order to pay is given;
3 *Payee*   the person to whom payment is to be made.

The above definition is almost self-explanatory but students should note that:

a) The order must be unconditional and not require any act other than the payment of money. If the drawee is instructed to sign a receipt following payment, the instructing document cannot be a bill of exchange.
b) The term requiring means 'ordering.' If the drawee has a choice (eg 'authorized' to pay) the instructing document cannot be a bill of exchange.
c) If the bill is payable on a future event this must be certain (eg X's death); if it is an event which might never occur (eg X's marriage) the instructing document cannot be a bill of exchange.

X owes £10 000 to Y and may require Z to pay the debt on X's behalf. X can achieve this by drawing a bill ordering Z to pay £10 000 to Y or to Y's order (ie to anybody Y may specify).

£10 000   Plymouth. October 5th 1981

    On demand pay Y or order the sum of £10 000
    for value received

                              signed by X.
To Z

The above is an example of an *order bill*.

X could make the bill payable to bearer when it is called a *bearer bill*. The main feature of a bearer bill is that it can be transferred by mere delivery without endorsement. This is relevant because:

a) A person is not normally liable on a bill unless that person endorses (signs) it. As there is no need to sign a bearer bill the number of parties liable on it will be fewer than on an order bill which must be endorsed to transfer ownership.

b) A forged signature on an order bill 'breaks the chain' and a holder cannot usually sue parties who signed the bill before the forgery. With bearer bills, because an endorsement is unnecessary, the court ignores the forged endorsement and a holder can sue parties who signed the bill prior to the forgery.

For the purposes of the flow chart (see page 116) it is assumed the bill of exchange is an *order bill*. The drawer (X) presents it to the payee (Y) who can present it to the drawer (Z) for *acceptance*.[1] Presentation is optional except where the bill:

1   is payable elsewhere than at the drawee's business or domestic address,
2   stipulates that presentation is required,
3   is payable after sight. In this case it must be presented for acceptance within a reasonable time otherwise the drawer is discharged.

Presentment is always advisable because if the drawee refuses to accept, or makes a qualified acceptance which is rejected by the payee, the bill becomes dishonoured allowing the holder the remedies shown in the chart.

If Z refuses to accept the bill or gives a qualified acceptance which the payee rejects Y has three choices:

1   If there is a *referee or drawee in case of need* indicated in the bill he or she may be asked to accept it.
2   The payee may seek an acceptance for honour. This takes place after the bill has been *protested* for non-acceptance. The acceptance for honour supra protest is written on the bill and signed by the acceptor for honour. It is assumed this is to save the drawer's honour and the acceptor for honour agrees to pay the bill if the drawee does not do so when it is presented.
3   The payee may present the bill to the drawer requesting payment.

If the payee accepts a qualified acceptance or the bill is accepted by a third party it is treated as an accepted bill although with a partial acceptance the drawer is discharged from liability unless he authorizes the payee's actions.

The payee may wish to transfer (*negotiate*) the accepted bill to a third party to whom the payee owes money. Being an order bill the payee must endorse (sign) it before delivering it to the new holder. An endorsement can be either:

a) Blank endorsement   This turns an order into a bearer bill which can in future be transferred by mere delivery without endorsement.

---

[1] To simplify the explanation of a bill's life history it is assumed the bill is presented to the acceptor for acceptance before the payee endorses it to another party. In practice this may not be so.

As indicated in the chart, there is a forged endorsement on the bearer bill but for reasons outlined above this can be ignored and the holder may sue parties prior to the forgery. Where the bill is transferred by delivery the transferor's liability on the bill is very restricted (see chart).

b) Special endorsement   As the bill remains an order bill it must be endorsed before delivery and hence the forged endorsement is relevant. A later party to the bill cannot sue parties before the forged endorsement.[2] The order bill is endorsed by an accommodation party and sans recours (see chart) before reaching the holder who is presenting the bill for payment.

There are two types of holder. A *holder for value* is one who holds a bill for which value has been given, although not necessarily by him. If he gave value he can sue all endorsers (only after a forged endorsement if an order bill) but if he did not give value he can only sue endorsers prior to the last party to give value.

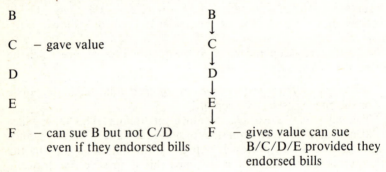

B	B ↓
C − gave value	C ↓
D	D ↓
E	E ↓
F − can sue B but not C/D even if they endorsed bills	F − gives value can sue B/C/D/E provided they endorsed bills

In the above F is a holder for value in both cases.

A holder in due course must have given value so he or she can sue all prior endorsers (subject to the forgery exception) and unlike a holder for value he or she is not affected by any defects in his or her predecessor's title.

The holder presents the bill for payment (subject to the exceptions). The bill is discharged when paid in full at the appropriate time to the right person by the acceptor. The acceptor is primarily liable. If the acceptor refuses to pay the bill the drawer must pay provided due notice of dishonour is given but he or she may sue the acceptor for damages as the acceptor has dishonoured the bill. Where any endorser is required by the holder to pay the bill the holder can claim against prior endorsers[3] and eventually the drawer (subject to forgeries).

[2] Unless estoppel operates.
[3] It is a rebuttable presumption that endorsements are made in the order in which they appear on the bill.

Note: Payment by the drawer or endorsers does not discharge the bill, merely discharges subsequent endorsers from liability.

Once the acceptor has refused to pay and the bill has been 'protested' for non payment a third party may make a payment for honour on the acceptor's behalf. This discharges the bill.

The other methods of discharging a bill are:

1 suing the drawer for damages,
2 renunciation,
3 cancellation,
4 merger,
5 alteration.

Life history of a bill of exchange

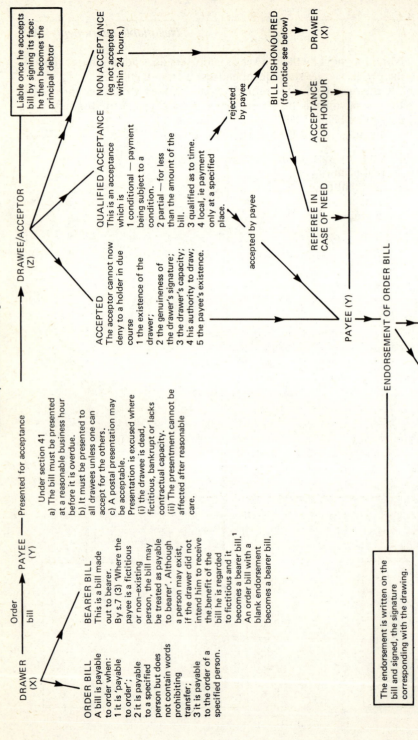

DRAWER (X) → Order bill → **PAYEE (Y)** → Presented for acceptance → **DRAWEE/ACCEPTOR (Z)**

Liable once he accepts bill by signing its face: he then becomes the principal debtor

ORDER BILL
A bill is payable to order when:
1 it is 'payable to order';
2 it is payable to a specified person but does not contain words prohibiting transfer;
3 it is payable to the order of a specified person.

BEARER BILL
This is a bill made out to bearer.
By s.7 (3) 'Where the payee is a fictitious or non-existing person, the bill may be treated as payable to bearer'. Although a person may exist, if the drawer did not intend him to receive the benefit of the bill he is regarded to fictitious and it becomes a bearer bill.[1]
An order bill with a blank endorsement becomes a bearer bill.

Under section 41
a) The bill must be presented at a reasonable business hour before it is overdue.
b) It must be presented to all drawees unless one can accept for the others.
c) A postal presentation may be acceptable.
Presentation is excused where (i) the drawee is dead, fictitious, bankrupt or lacks contractual capacity.
(ii) The presentment cannot be affected after reasonable care.

NON ACCEPTANCE
(eg not accepted within 24 hours.)

QUALIFIED ACCEPTANCE
This is an acceptance which is
1 conditional — payment being subject to a condition.
2 partial — for less than the amount of the bill.
3 qualified as to time.
4 local, ie payment only at a specified place.

ACCEPTED
The acceptor cannot now deny to a holder in due course
1 the existence of the drawer;
2 the genuineness of the drawer's signature;
3 the drawer's capacity;
4 his authority to draw;
5 the payee's existence.

BILL DISHONOURED (for notice see below) → **DRAWER (X)**

rejected by payee

accepted by payee

REFEREE IN CASE OF NEED

ACCEPTANCE FOR HONOUR

PAYEE (Y) → **ENDORSEMENT OF ORDER BILL**

The endorsement is written on the bill and signed, the signature corresponding with the drawing.

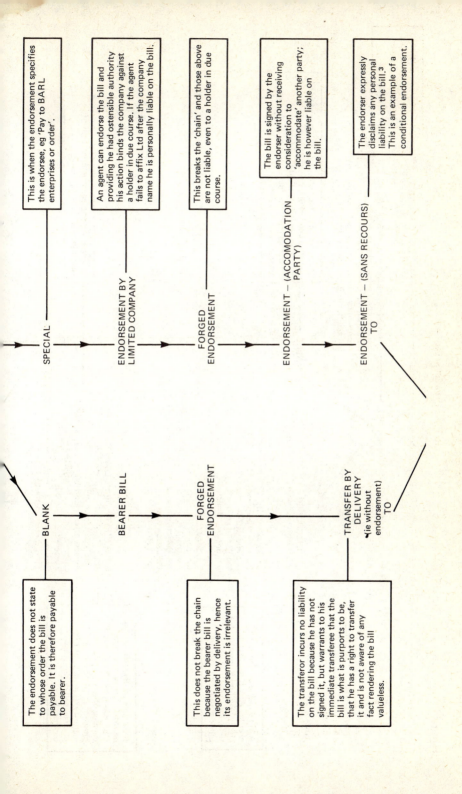

Figure 8 Life history of a bill of exchange

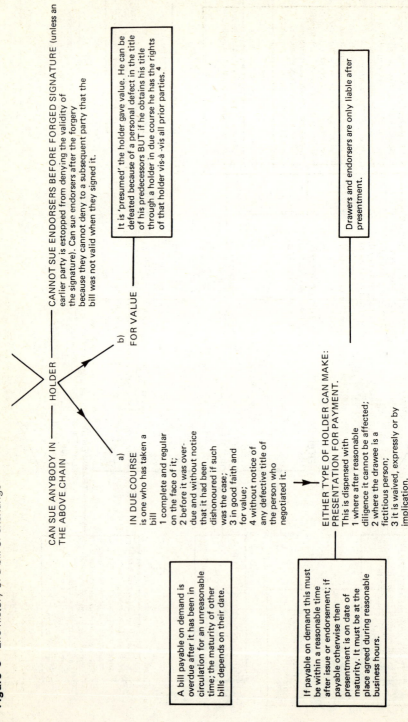

CAN SUE ANYBODY IN THE ABOVE CHAIN —— HOLDER —— CANNOT SUE ENDORSERS BEFORE FORGED SIGNATURE (unless an earlier party is estopped from denying the validity of the signature). Can sue endorsers after the forgery because they cannot deny to a subsequent party that the bill was not valid when they signed it.

a)

IN DUE COURSE is one who has taken a bill

1 complete and regular on the face of it;
2 before it was overdue and without notice that it had been dishonoured if such was the case;
3 in good faith and for value;
4 without notice of any defective title of the person who negotiated it.

b)

FOR VALUE

It is 'presumed' the holder gave value. He can be defeated because of a personal defect in the title of his predecessors BUT if he obtains his title through a holder in due course he has the rights of that holder vis-à-vis all prior parties. [4]

EITHER TYPE OF HOLDER CAN MAKE: PRESENTATION FOR PAYMENT.
This is dispensed with
1 where after reasonable diligence it cannot be affected;
2 where the drawee is a fictitious person;
3 it is waived, expressly or by implication.

A bill payable on demand is overdue after it has been in circulation for an unreasonable time; the maturity of other bills depends on their date.

If payable on demand this must be within a reasonable time after issue or endorsement; if payable otherwise then presentment is on date of maturity. It must be at the place agreed during reasonable business hours.

Drawers and endorsers are only liable after presentment.

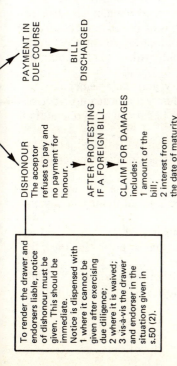

To render the drawer and endorsers liable, notice of dishonour must be given. This should be immediate. Notice is dispensed with

1 where it cannot be given after exercising due diligence;
2 where it is waived;
3 vis-à-vis the drawer and endorser in the situations given in s.50 (2).

DISHONOUR
The acceptor refuses to pay and no payment for honour.

AFTER PROTESTING IF A FOREIGN BILL

CLAIM FOR DAMAGES
includes:
1 amount of the bill;
2 interest from the date of maturity or presentation if payable on demand;
3 expenses of noting and any necessary protest.

BILL DISCHARGED

PAYMENT IN DUE COURSE

BILL DISCHARGED

PAYMENT FOR HONOUR (SUPRA PROTEST)
After being 'protested' any party may pay the bill for the honour of a party involved. He acquires the rights of the holder.

BILL DISCHARGED

A bill may also also be discharged by:

1 Renunciation. The holder at, or after maturity, renounces in writing (unless he delivers up the bill) his rights against the acceptor, or endorsers. Consideration is not required for the renunciation to be effective.

2 Cancellation. A deliberate cancellation by the holder discharges the person whose name is cancelled and all endorsers who could claim against him.

3 Merger. When the acceptor acquires the bill as holder.

4 Alteration. A material alteration avoids liability of any party who has not consented to it although subsequent endorsers will be liable on it.[2]

BILL DISCHARGED

NB
A person cannot be liable unless they signed the document except that a trade signature or use of an assumed name is equivalent to a personal signature.

1 In *Bank of England* v. *Vagliano Bros* (1891) a clerk drew up a bill in favour of a customer. He always intended to misappropriate the bill and cashed it having forged an endorsement. It was held that although the payee was an existing person, as the clerk never intended him to receive the benefit of the bill he must be regarded as "fictitious". The bill was therefore a Bearer Bill, the forged endorsement was irrelevant and the bank could not be liable for paying the bill.

2 In *Garrard* v. *Lewis* (1883) the defendant signed an acceptance, the amount being left blank. In the margin was the sum of £14-0-6. The drawer completed the bill for £164-0-6 and altered the other figure. As the marginal figures were not part of the bill there was no material alteration (ie date, time, amount and place of payment) of the bill.

3 If a bill is endorsed by a minor lacking contractual capacity the title is passed by his signature but is passed
  • 'Sans recours' to him.

4 The consideration to support a bill is either
  a) any consideration sufficient to support a simple (ordinary) contract; or
  b) any antecedent debt or liability (ie past consideration) of the drawer.
  Where value has been given at any time the holder is deemed to be a holder for value as regards the acceptor and all parties to the bill who become parties prior to such time.

Glossary

(All references are to the Bills of Exchange Act (1882)).

Acceptance: S. 17(1) defines acceptance as 'the signification by the drawee of his assent to the order of the drawer'. After acceptance the drawee is known as the Acceptor.

Bearer bill: A bill is payable to bearer when it is expressed to be so payable or when the only or last endorsement is an endorsement in blank. It can be negotiated by delivery without endorsement.

Drawee: The drawee must be named or indicated with reasonable certainty and is the person to whom the order to pay is given.

Drawer: This is the person giving the order to pay.

Holder in due course: Is one who has taken a bill complete and regular on the face of it before it was overdue in good faith and for value. He or she can sue in his/her own name and obtain a good title notwithstanding any defects in the title of his predecessors. Every holder is assumed to be a holder in due course until the contrary is proved.

Holder for value: This is a holder of a bill where value has been given at an earlier date. He or she can sue any party before value was last given subject to forged endorsement (where relevant) and defects in his predecessor's titles.

Endorsement: This is written on the bill and only operates if it endorses the whole bill. It is necessary to negotiate an order bill.

Negotiate: A negotiable instrument is negotiated when, if it is a bearer bill it is delivered and if it is an order bill it is delivered *and* endorsed. A transfer for value of an order bill without endorsement gives only such rights as the transferor had in the bill, with a right to require endorsement.

Order bill: A bill which requires delivery and endorsement to be negotiated. Without endorsement the transferee cannot acquire a better right to the bill than the transferor possesses (ie the bill lacks one of the attributes of negotiability).

Payee: The payee is the person to whom payment is to be made and unless the bill is payable to bearer must be named or clearly indicated in the bill.

Protested: This is a document certifying that the bill was duly presented for payment and that payment was refused. It must be signed and include details of:

a) The person at whose request the bill is protested,
b) The date and place of protest and the reason for protesting the bill,
c) The demand made and the answer given.

Referee in case of need: In the event of dishonour at acceptance and 'protest' for dishonour he may, with the holder's assent, accept the bill.

17

Cheques and promissory notes

(All references are to the Bills of Exchange Act unless otherwise indicated.)

Cheques

A cheque is defined as a bill of exchange drawn on a banker payable on demand (s. 73). The Bills of Exchange Act (1882) therefore applies (although cheques are not normally accepted by the drawee) alongside the Cheques Act (1957).

Duties of the banker
1   The bank must pay cheques presented within a reasonable time by the holder providing the drawer's account has sufficient funds.

A banker wrongfully dishonouring a cheque drawn by a trader automatically pays substantial damages but other customers only receive nominal damages unless special loss is proved. The banker's authority to pay is terminated by:
a) *receipt* of oral or written countermand of payment,
b) *notice* of the customer's death,
c) the *making* of a receiving order against the customer,
d) *notice* of a bankruptcy petition against the customer.
2   To obey the customer's lawful instructions, this includes making payments only on the customer's signature and according to his or her instructions (see below).
3   A banker owes a duty of care to the customer.

Liability of the drawer
The general rule, stated in s. 23, is that no one can be liable on a cheque as drawer (or endorser) unless they sign it in that capacity. It is subject to the following exceptions.

  (i) A person signing a cheque in an assumed or trade name is as liable as if that person's real name was used.
 (ii) A partner signing a cheque in the firm's name binds all the other partners providing the partner possesses express or implied

121

authority to sign that cheque. In trading partnerships, where the principal operations are buying and selling, partners always possess implied authority to sign cheques relating to these activities and all partners in professional partnerships (such as accountants) possess implied authority to draw and endorse ordinary cheques.

(iii) The signature of an authorized agent binds the principal although the authorized agent may incur personal liability on a cheque if he fails to indicate he signs as agent.

(iv) S. 108(4) of the Companies Act 1948 renders company officers personally liable on cheques which they sign, or authorize, where the company's name is not properly and legibly written, which includes omitting the word 'limited.' Liability is strict and not dependent on a party being misled by the mis-description.

The general contractual rule that signatures bind the signatory applies to cheques hence, unless there is fraud or misrepresentation, the drawer is liable on signature although unaware of the amount of the cheque or the name of the payee. Liability may, however, be avoided if the drawer (signer) successfully pleads non est factum (it is not my deed). This defence was originally available to assist blind or illiterate persons tricked into signing deeds and other documents but it has been extended to the aged or infirm. It is available to anybody who can prove that the document they signed was fundamentally different from the document they thought they were signing *and* that they have not been careless. The burden of proving that due care was taken is an onerous one and rests on the party seeking to establish the plea.

The leading authority is the House of Lords' decision in the following case.

Saunders v. *Anglian Building Society* (1971), often called *Gallie* v. *Lee*.

Mrs Gallie, an elderly widow, owned property. She wanted her nephew, Parkin, to have her house so he could obtain additional business capital by mortgaging it. To avoid paying anything to his estranged wife, Parkin arranged for the house to be assigned to Lee. The latter agreed to mortgage it and give the proceeds to Parkin. Mrs Gallie signed the assignment to Lee believing it was a deed of gift to Parkin. Lee mortgaged the property but absconded. When he failed to pay the instalments the society sought foreclosure. Was Gallie's signature binding? The court applied the above test and said yes. Mrs Gallie's intention was to give Parkin the house to enable him to raise money. The assignment was a method of achieving this, the documents were not fundamentally different. Even if they had been Mrs Gallie had been careless, not reading the document or seeking professional advice.

☐ Trevor Wit signed several cheques presented to him by his confidential secretary. Because he trusted her implicitly he did not read them. One was for £2000 payable to 'bearer.' The secretary's boyfriend, who was a company director[1], cashed it and they absconded with the proceeds. The bank can debit Wit's account. Non est factum is inapplicable because he has been careless.

United Dominions Trust Ltd v. *Western* (1976)

The defendant purchased a car on hire purchase signing blank hire purchase forms. Incorrect figures were later inserted by the sellers and, on discovering this, he refused to pay the instalments. His plea of non est factum failed because there was no fundamental difference in the documents (only a small difference in amount) and his action was careless. Nobody should sign a blank document.

Gallie v. *Lee* appears to restrict the availability of non est factum. This probably reflects the court's concern for innocent third parties who are unaware of the condition of the signatory. If the aged, infirm or the poorly educated could easily plead non est factum it would be impossible to rely on a signature without making further enquiries. This would introduce a commercially intolerable situation.

Once the cheque has been honoured the drawer can assume the payee has received payment.

Liability of bankers (see page 124)

The paying banker is the bank on whom the cheque is drawn (the drawee), whilst the collecting banker is the bank to whom the cheque is presented by the payee.

Paying banker

The relationship between banker and client is a contractual one which means the banker must comply with the customer's instructions as contained in the customer's cheques. At common law a failure to honour any instructions stops the banker debiting the customer's account with the amount of the cheque, no matter how careful the banker has been. This produces difficulties when there is a forged endorsement, where the cheque is cashed by a thief, where the payee alters the amount of the cheque or where a blank cheque is stolen and the customer's signature is forged. Legislation therefore exists to protect paying bankers.

---

[1] Hence there were no suspicious circumstances to put the bank on enquiry.

SUMMARY OF STATUTORY PROTECTION FOR PAYING & COLLECTING BANKERS

a) PAYING

Liable	*Not liable*	*Authority*
Uncrossed cheques		
Bearer		
1 for paying a cheque on which drawer's signature forged	If drawer ratifies signature or is estopped from denying its validity	s. 24
2 for paying on an altered cheque	if alteration due to drawer's carelessness	*London Joint Stock Bank* v. *MacMillan & Arthur* (1918)
3	if it pays on a forged endorsement	endorsement is unnecessary to negotiate a bearer bill
4	if it pays in good faith and without notice of any defect in the holder's title (subject to 1 & 2 above)	s. 59
Order		
5 for paying a cheque on which drawer's signature forged	If drawer ratifies signature or is estopped from denying its validity	s. 24
6 for paying on an altered cheque	if alteration due to drawer's carelessness	*London Joint Stock Bank* v. *MacMillan & Arthur* (1918)
7	if it pays on a forged endorsement in good faith and in the ordinary course of business	s. 60
8	if it pays in the absence of an endorsement or on an irregular endorsement in good faith and in the ordinary course of business	s. 1 (Cheques Act (1957))
Crossed cheques		
Bearer & order		
9 for paying a cheque on which drawer's signature forged	If drawer ratifies signature or is estopped from denying its validity	s. 24

10 for paying on an altered cheque	if alteration due to drawer's carelessness	*London Joint Stock Bank* v. *MacMillan & Arthur* (1918)
11	if it fails to pay the true owner (perhaps because of a forged endorsement) provided he or she acted in conformity with the crossing, in good faith and without negligence (subject to 1 & 2 above)	s. 80
12 for ignoring the crossing	if the crossing is obliterated or if the cheque appears not to be crossed and not to have been added to, or altered otherwise than in accordance with the Act and the banker acts in good faith and without negligence.	s. 79(2)
Order only 13	if it pays in the absence of an endorsement or an irregular endorsement in good faith and in the ordinary course of business.	s. 1 (Cheques Act (1957))
b) COLLECTING 1 if he or she collects a cheque crossed 'a/c payee only' for an account other than the person specified	if it collects a cheque for a customer who is not the true owner provided it acts in good faith and without negligence	s. 4 (Cheques Act)
2	if it collects a cheque and is a holder in due course (unless it obtains via a forged endorsement).	

Payment of a bearer cheque to the wrong party (eg a thief)
S. 59 states that a banker who pays a *bearer* cheque in good faith and without notice of any defect in the title of the holder (who may be a thief) is regarded as paying the cheque in due course and so can debit the customer's account (providing the customer has signed it). Any forged endorsement is irrelevant on a bearer cheque because the holder obtains title through delivery and not the forged endorsement.

Payment of order cheque with forged endorsement
With *order* cheques the bank is protected against a *forged* endorsement of a crossed or uncrossed cheque by s. 60. This states that when a paying banker pays in good faith and in the ordinary course of business the banker is deemed to have paid the bill in due course, although any endorsement has been forged or made without authority. The term 'ordinary course of business' means during banking hours and in the manner generally adopted by bankers.

Payment of order cheque with irregular endorsement
Bankers are protected against irregular or no endorsement by s. 1 of the Cheques Act 1957. Although this ostensibly protects banks paying cheques without endorsement, payments must be made in the ordinary course of business. A circular of the Committee of London Clearing Banks states that ordinary banking practice requires cheques cashed over the counter to be endorsed. It follows, therefore, that a bank not requiring an endorsement for a cheque which is cashed over the counter would be ignoring usual banking practice and s. 1 would be inapplicable.

☐   A client sends a crossed cheque, made payable to Wit, in settlement of his account. Wit received it but because of an urgent business meeting leaves it laying on his desk. His dishonest secretary steals it and forges an endorsement to X who receives the cheque in payment of a debt. He pays it into his account. The bank can debit the client's account, and Wit cannot require another cheque from the client in settlement (see below).

Payment of order cheque to the wrong party (eg a thief)
A banker paying a *crossed cheque* to a thief is protected providing the banker pays in good faith and without negligence, and the payment is made in accordance with the crossing (s. 80).

   If s. 80 applies the paying banker is placed in the same position as if he had paid the true owner and providing the cheque had reached the payee the drawer is similarly protected. To obtain the benefit of s. 80 the paying banker must comply with the crossing. Relevant ones include:

(i) A *general crossing* This consists of two parallel transverse lines (with the words 'and company' or 'not negotiable' possibly added) and instructs payment to be made into a bank account and not across the counter.

(ii) A *special crossing* is similar except that it specifies the collecting bank.

(iii) A *crossing 'not negotiable'* This is not an instruction to the banker. It merely limits the cheque's negotiable character. The person taking the cheque cannot obtain or give a better title than the transferor possessed (s. 81).

The crossing is a material part of the cheque and cannot be obliterated, added to, or altered except:

1 Where it is uncrossed the holder may cross it;
2 Where a cheque is crossed generally a holder may cross it specially or not negotiable;
3 A bank to whom the cheque is crossed specially may cross it specially to a collecting bank;
4 A collecting bank may cross a cheque specially to itself.

If the crossing is obliterated or the cheque appears uncrossed (and not altered or added to otherwise than in accordance with the Act) then any banker, in good faith and without negligence, treating the cheque as uncrossed is not liable (s. 79(2))[2].

Figure 9 Types of crossing

[2] S. 79(2) states that a banker failing to honour the crossing is liable to the cheque's true owner for any loss sustained.

Payment of an 'altered' cheque

The above sections provide no protection where the amount of the cheque is altered. A banker paying on an altered cheque can only debit the customer if the customer's carelessness made the alteration possible. If the customer fails to take the 'usual and reasonable' precautions against alteration and the cheque is altered then the customer must bear any loss and not the banker.

☐   Wit obtains a new secretary and asks her to buy a crate of dry sherry from the off licence. She asks for a cheque but suggests that the figure be left blank because she is unsure of the price of sherry. After his earlier experiences he is reluctant but agrees. He inserts the name of the payee, crosses it 'A/C payee only' and writes on the cheque in pencil — 'not to exceed £30'. The secretary erases this and writes out a cheque for £250 to pay existing bills with the off licence because, unknown to Wit, she is an alcoholic. Wit's account can be debited because his carelessness made the alteration possible.

London Joint Stock Bank v. *MacMillan and Arthur* (1918)

M's confidential clerk filled in cheques for the partner's signature. He prepared a bearer cheque, which he said was for petty cash, with the space for the amount in words left blank although £2 was written in figures. After the cheque was signed the clerk added a 1 before the 2 and a 0 after it and then wrote in One hundred and twenty pounds. The cheque was cashed and the firm's account was debited because they had not taken the 'usual and reasonable precautions' to prevent the forgery.

Whether the customer is in breach of his or her duty to take care depends on the facts of each case. In *Slingsby* v. *District Bank Ltd* (1931) the drawer left a space between the payee's name and the words 'or order.' A fraudulent solicitor inserted his firm's name and obtained payment. It was held the bank could not debit the firm's account but as it is now common practice to fill in the gap after the payee's name the case might be decided differently today.

Payment of a cheque where the customer's signature is forged

Where the drawer's signature is forged the position is covered by s. 24. This states that a forged or unauthorized signature is 'wholly inoperative ... *unless* the party against whom it is sought to ... enforce payment of the bill (cheque) is precluded from setting up the forgery or want of authority, provided that nothing in this section shall affect the ratification of an unauthorized signature not amounting to a forgery.' Thus a banker who pays a cheque which the customer has not signed or authorized cannot debit his account, no matter how skilled the forgery is, unless there is estoppel or ratification.

A customer's conduct may estop him or her from setting up the forgery, he or she is stopped from denying the validity of his or her signature. This would arise where a customer verified the signature and later discovered it had been forged or where he or she delayed informing the bank of a forgery of which he or she was aware. This was the situation in *Greenwood* v. *Martin's Bank Ltd* (1933) where a husband discovered his wife was forging his signature. Because he accepted her explanation for the forgeries he did not inform the bank because of the adverse publicity. On discovering his wife's explanation to be untrue he threatened to inform the bank. She committed suicide and he sued the bank for the return of the monies paid under the forged cheques. The husband's action meant the bank had, as the law then stood, lost the right to sue the wife. The House of Lords held that the husband's conduct estopped him from denying the validity of the signature. In the course of his judgment Lord Tomlin said, 'the deliberate abstention from speaking in those circumstances seems to me to amount to a representation to the (bank) that the forged cheques were in fact in order, and assuming that detriment to the (bank) followed, there were ... present all the elements essential to estoppel.'

The second exception to s. 24 is ratification. Where an unauthorized signature is later ratified by the customer the bank can debit his or her account.

Where neither exceptions apply the paying bank can, when it discovers the forgery, sue the payee (even though he may have acted to his detriment on reliance of the cheque being honoured-*National Westminster Bank Ltd* v. *Barclays Bank International Ltd* and *Another* (1974)) and the collecting bank for the sum paid. This right is of course lost if the paying bank is guilty of negligence.

Collecting banker

Most of the crossings affect the paying banker but one is an instruction to the collecting banker. A crossing containing the words, 'account payee only,' instructs the collecting banker to credit only the payee's account and payment to another person will probably render the bank liable in conversion. It avoids liability by proving proper enquiries were made regarding the authority of the person to whose account the cheque was credited. In other cases where a banker collects payment of a cheque for a person other than the true owner the banker is liable to the true owner in conversion unless he can rely on s. 4 of the Cheques Act 1957. This states that if a banker receives payment of a crossed or uncrossed cheque for a *customer* in *good faith* and *without negligence* he incurs no liability merely by receiving payment.

A customer is a person possessing a bank account, no matter how recently it was acquired, on which he or she draws cheques. A person who casually cashes a cheque at the bank is not a customer within this act.

Negligent	Not negligent
(i) To open an account without enquiring as to the customer's identity.	(i) To pay a large cheque to 'bearer' unless there are suspicious circumstances.
(ii) To receive payment of a cheque for a customer which is drawn in favour of the customer's employer without enquiries.	
(iii) To pay a cheque into a customer's private account without enquiries when the cheque is made out to him in his official capacity.	

A collecting bank not protected under s. 4 because it has been negligent cannot have the damages awarded reduced if the cheque's owner was guilty of contributory negligence because this is no longer a defence in conversion.

Proviso
A collecting bank can enforce payment against the drawer even if s. 4 is inapplicable if it is a holder for value (ie it gave value to the customer). This occurs where:

(i) There is an express or implied agreement to apply the cheque in reduction of an overdraft or allow the customer to draw against it before it is cleared,

or

(ii) The bank gives the customer cash for the cheque before it has been cleared,

or

(iii) The bank has a lien on the cheque because the customer is overdrawn.

If the bank satisfies the other requirements and becomes a holder in due course it takes free from defects of earlier holders. It therefore possesses a good defence to a claim in conversion even though s. 4 may be inapplicable because of negligence.

☐   To avoid a repetition of earlier problems, Trevor Wit, asks clients to cross all cheques 'A/C payee only.' His dishonest secretary obtains a bank account in the name of T. Wit with Midwest Bankers and pays in and draws cheques signing herself T. Wit. The bank does not obtain references prior to opening the account. She has a £1200 overdraft and steals cheques from her employer worth £1000 which she pays in to reduce this. Although the bank has been negligent it

a) gave value,
b) took cheques that appeared regular on their face,
c) took cheques that were not overdue,
d) possessed no notice of her defective title and so was a holder in due course. It obtains a good title against the true owner (Wit) and is not liable to him in conversion.

Postscript
Everybody hopes the bank will mistakenly credit their account with a large sum. If this happens the bank is only estopped from reclaiming this if the customer was unaware of the mistake and altered his or her position as a result of the error.

Promissory notes

S. 83 defines a promissory note as 'an unconditional promise in writing made by one person to another signed by the maker, engaging to pay, on demand or at a fixed or determinable future time, a sum certain in money, to, or to the order of, a specified person or to bearer.'

Plymouth
October 14 1982

I promise to pay on demand BW or order the sum of £200.

ARL

Figure 10 A promissory note

In the above ARL is the maker and BW the payee. Primary liability is on the maker (or makers) who, if the note is payable on demand, remain liable although the bill is not presented for payment within a reasonable time. Indeed presentment for payment is usually unnecessary to render the maker(s) liable. Where there is more than one maker liability can be joint or joint and several, depending on the note's wording. Liability however only commences once the note is delivered.

Once the payee endorses the note he or she becomes liable providing it is presented for payment within a reasonable time of his or her endorsement.

Bills of exchange & promissory notes — compared

Promissory notes	*Bills of Exchange*
1 Usually only two parties	Has three parties
2 Is not usually accepted	Acceptance necessary
3 Can become a holder in due course although an unreasonable time has elapsed between a note's issue and its negotiation to the holder.[3]	Cannot become a holder in due course if the bill of exchange is overdue.

[3] A promissory note is treated as a continuing security.

Past examination questions

1 What is a bill of exchange? In what ways, if at all, do cheques differ from other bills of exchange? A C A June 1976

2a) How far is the paying banker protected by law when paying a cheque to a person who is not the rightful owner of it?

b) How far is the collecting banker protected by law when collecting a cheque for a person who is not the rightful owner of it? A C A December 1976

3 Write notes on the following:
a) a cheque,
b) qualified acceptance of a bill of exchange,
c) transfer of a bill of exchange. A C A June 1977

4a) How would you define a negotiable instrument? State and explain the main characteristics of such an instrument.

b) William draws an uncrossed cheque on Bottomless Bank Ltd payable to Anthony. James steals the cheque, forges Anthony's endorsement and obtains cash for the cheque by presenting it to Bottomless Bank Ltd. Is the bank liable? A C A December 1978

5a) What are the essential characteristics of a negotiable instrument?

b) Explain the legal effect of crossing a cheque 'not negotiable'. I A S June 1979

6a) Define a 'holder in due course' of a bill of exchange. Why is it advantageous for the holder of an 'order bill' to be a 'holder in due course?'

b) John owed Robin £7 and settled the debt by drawing a cheque payable to Robin for that amount. When Robin received the cheque he altered the words 'seven pounds' to 'seventy pounds' and the figure '£7' to '£70' and then endorsed the cheque over to Tom, who paid him seventy pounds in cash. John now refuses to meet Tom's claim on the cheque for £70. Advise Tom. I A S December 1979

7 (i) Discuss the nature of negotiability and explain the difference between negotiability and transferability.

(ii) What is the effect of crossing a cheque and marking it 'not negotiable'?

(iii) Fred draws a cheque for £5 in favour of Bill and posts it to him. The cheque is stolen by Jim who forges Bill's endorsement and obtains cash for it from Charles, a local shopkeeper. Charles pays the cheque into his account at North Bank. The bank then collects the cheque from South Bank where Fred has his account.

Advise Bill as to his rights against Charles, Fred, and South Bank. A C A December 1979

8 What protection is given by Cheques Act 1957 to bankers collecting payment of cheques? C A May 1980

9　Define and distinguish between transferability and negotiability of a bill of exchange.　　　　　　　　　　　　　　C A October 1979

10　State, giving reasons, whether the following examples are valid bills of exchange:

    a)　Mr Harding will much oblige Dr Grantly by paying Josiah Crawley, or order, twenty pounds on his account.

    b)　Please let the bearer have seven pounds, and place it to my account and you will oblige.

    c)　Pay to Dean Arabin the sum of fifty pounds provided the receipt form at the foot hereof is duly signed and dated.

    d)　Pay to Mortimer Tempest the sum of seven thousand pounds thirty days after the arrival of the s.s. "Cardinham" at Falmouth.　　　　　　　　　　　　　　C A October 1979

11a)　When may a banker's authority to pay a cheque drawn on him be terminated?

 b)　Proudie and Roberts were both customers of the Bullhampton Bank. Proudie employed Roberts as the manager of his corn chandler's business. Roberts was authorized to draw cheques 'per pro' the business. Over a period of five years, in fraud of Proudie, Roberts drew 50 cheques on Proudie's business account, all of which were collected for and credited to Roberts' private account by the Bullhampton Bank. Proudie discovers the fraud and wishes to sue the Bank for conversion. Advise Proudie.　　　　　　　　　　　　　　C A May 1980

12　Thorne, a customer of the Barchester Bank, drew a cheque for £10 000 in favour of Silverbridge Builders Ltd. On hearing that a receiver had been appointed to the company, Thorne countermanded payment of the cheque before presentation. On the receiver presenting the cheque, it was paid in error and the receiver refused to repay the money.

    What advice would you give (a) Thorne and (b) the bank?　C A 1980

13　What is the general position of a banker who pays a cheque upon which the drawer's signature has been forged? What is the exception to the general rule?　　　　　　　　　　　　　　C A 1980

14　a)　What is a holder in due course?

    b)　Crawley receives a bearer cheque from Arabin. Crawley endorses the cheque and gives it to his daughter Grace. What is Grace's position as regards the cheque?　　　　　　C A 1980

18

Agency

Definitions

An *agent* is employed to bring his principal into contractual relations with a third party.

A *named principal* exists where the agent discloses his principal's identity when making the contract.

An *unnamed principal* exists where the agent discloses the principal's existence but not the name when making the contract.

A *disclosed principal* is one whose existence is known by the third party at the time of contracting, but not necessarily the name.

An *undisclosed principal* exists when the agent fails to disclose the existence of the principal and contracts as the principal.

A *del credere* agent guarantees the payments of the third parties.

A *mercantile agent* is an agent 'having in the customary course of business as such agent authority either to sell goods, or to consign goods for the purpose of sale, or to buy goods, or to raise money on the security of goods'.[1]

Agency is the relationship between two legal persons whereby a principal appoints an agent to conduct transactions, like making contracts, on the principal's behalf.

Because the real contract is between the principal and the third party the agent does not require contractual capacity. A minor can make a contract on behalf of an adult principal for the purchase of non necessary goods providing the principal possesses full contractual capacity. A minor however cannot avoid incapacity by employing an adult principal.

☐   A sixteen year old is asked by her father to purchase a Rover for his business. Although the minor could not make a valid contract on her own behalf she can bring her principal into contractual relations with the car dealers.

[1] Factors Act 1889, s. 1

After the contract

The basic rule is that once the agent has made an *authorized* contract with a third party *for a disclosed principal* then the agent disappears and incurs no rights or liabilities under the contract, the contractual relationship is between P and T. The agent only incurs rights and liabilities under the contract if:

a) The agent expressly or impliedly agrees to be liable on the contract. An agent signing a contract in his own name without clearly signifying he is signing as agent is presumed to be contracting personally and so is liable.
   An agent signing as 'broker' still remains personally liable.
   An agent signing as 'manager' still remains personally liable.
   An agent signing 'on behalf of' is not personally liable.
b) The alleged principal is mythical.   Under s. 9(2) of the European Communities Act (1972) 'where a contract purports to be made by a company or by a person or agent for a company at a time when the company has not been formed then subject to any agreement to the contrary the contract shall have effect as a contract entered into by the person purporting to act for the company, or an agent for it, and he shall be personally liable on the contract accordingly.'
c) The contract is by deed and the agent signs it in his own name. He remains liable although he clearly signs as agent.
d) Trade custom requires agent liability.
e) The Partnership Act (1890) applies. Under s. 5 a partner remains jointly liable with the other partners on any contract made.

☐   A is a partner in an accountancy firm. A appoints X as an articled clerk at a salary of £2500 pa. A's action binds the other partners but A also remains personally liable on the contract.

Where an agent makes an *authorized* contract *for an undisclosed principal* the third party may sue agent *or* principal (once he discloses his existence). Once he elects to sue the principal he cannot sue the agent and vice versa (their liability is alternative not joint). Any unequivocable act showing an intention of holding one of them liable automatically discharges the other.

☐   An accountant agreed to act as X's agent in financial matters. He incurs £500 expenses and his commission amounts to £3000. He then discovers X was acting as P's agent, hence he sends a bill for £3500 to P. When P refuses to pay, the accountant commences legal proceedings. Both actions raise the presumption that he has elected to deal with the principal. The agent avoids liability on the contract.

The agent alone can be sued where he contracts *on the basis of* being the only principal. In *Humble* v. *Hunter* (1848) an agent represented himself as the owner of a ship. This impliedly excluded the existence of a principal, therefore T could not sue the real P.

The undisclosed principal may sue T but to protect innocent third parties the undisclosed principal cannot sue:

1 where he lacked contractual capacity when the contract was made,
2 where the contract prohibits the intervention of an undisclosed principal,
3 if T can prove the agent's personal qualities were crucial in making the contract,
4 if T can establish that he would not have contracted with P.

☐ An accountant, Thomas Wist, is dismissed as financial director from XYZ Co Ltd and is suing them for unfair dismissal. Whilst awaiting the hearing he is approached by A who wishes to purchase his land for redevelopment. After agreeing to sell to A he discovers he is XYZ Co Ltd's agent. In these circumstances an action brought by XYZ Co Ltd to enforce the contract would probably fail.

If the principal sues T he can be met with any defence which the third party could have brought against the agent before discovering the principal's existence.

In the above the principal is automatically liable on *authorized* contracts. The authority of an agent depends on his method of creation.

Express

☐ An accountant verbally engages an estate agent to rent business premises for him. Although the contract the agent makes must be in writing, the verbal agency agreement is enforceable.

The agency contract can take any form except that agents who make contracts under seal must be appointed by deed.

The agent's *actual authority* consists of that conferred by law or by the principal, expressly (ie in the contract) or impliedly. Thus a shop manager possesses implied authority to order goods, to receive payment from customers and give receipts. An estate agent authorized to sell property has implied authority to sign memorandum to comply with s. 40 of the Law of Property Act (1925).

☐ A, a partner in a firm of accountants, accepts a client's cheque in payment of an account. A's action binds the partnership because he possesses implied authority to receive payments from clients.

Panorama Developments Ltd v. *Furnishing Fabrics Ltd* (1971)
X, the defendant's company secretary, hired cars from the

plaintiffs in the firm's name although he was using them for private purposes. Although this was unauthorized his contracts bound the company, who therefore had to pay for the cars, because company secretaries have implied authority to hire cars for company purposes.

Supplementing actual authority may be *ostensible* (apparent) authority, this often coincides with actual authority but may exceed it. Ostensible authority is authority as seen by a third party. If that type of agent normally possesses authority to make certain contracts, third parties can assume such contracts are authorized by the principal. A principal who limits an agent's actual authority may still be contractually bound to T if the agent is acting within apparent (ostensible) authority.

☐ George Rope, a partner in a firm of accountants, has a liking for attractive young secretaries and has been known to appoint staff possessing these qualities but lacking secretarial skills. The other partners therefore forbid him appointing new staff. Miss X, who is unaware of this restriction, is appointed by A. His act binds the partnership being within his ostensible authority.

Watteau v. *Fenwick* (1893)
H managed a public house for Fenwick. He had been expressly forbidden to purchase cigars on credit. Despite this he purchased them on credit from Watteau. As managers in public houses can normally purchase cigars on credit W could sue F. H possessed ostensible authority and the secret limitation of which Watteau was unaware could not affect the agent's authority.

When a principal acts in a way that appears to vest certain powers with the agent he is said to be *estopped* from denying A's act was authorized.

One example of ostensible authority has been incorporated into statute. Under s. 2(1) of the Factors Act (1889) where 'a mercantile agent is, with the consent of the owner, in possession of goods or other documents of title to goods, any sale, pledge, or other disposition of the goods, made by him when acting in the ordinary course of business of a mercantile agent shall, subject to the provision of this Act, be as valid as if he were expressly authorized by the owner of the goods to make the same, provided that the person taking under the disposition acts in good faith and has not at the time of the disposition notice that the person making the disposition has not authority to make the same.' This means the mercantile agent possesses, in certain circumstances, ostensible authority to pass a good title to goods he possesses (this is an exception to the nemo dat rule).

For s. 2(1) to apply, the agent must be a mercantile agent and satisfy all the above requirements. The section is inapplicable unless the agent obtains possession of the goods to sell them.

☐ A businessman delivers a car for repair to a garage owner, who is also a mercantile agent. After repairing it the garage owner sells it to X. The car still belongs to A because the garage owner is not in possession of goods in his capacity as a mercantile agent.

This can be contrasted with the following case.

Folkes v. *King* (1923)
F delivered his car to H, a mercantile agent, for sale at not less than £575. He sold the car to K for £340 and disappeared. K obtained a good title as H obtained possession of the car with F's consent for the purposes of sale.

The sale must also be made in the ordinary course of business. This means, does the transaction appear satisfactory to the transferee? Provided it does and the buyer is acting in good faith, a good title is obtained because the mercantile agent possesses ostensible authority to make a valid contract on behalf of the person who entrusted the goods.

If the agent is acting within his ostensible authority the contract is *authorized* and binds the principal but because the agent is exceeding his *actual* authority he can be sued by the principal.

Implication/conduct
An implied contract of agency can arise from the relationship of the parties or be implied from their conduct. If a person, by words or conduct, holds out another as his agent he is estopped from denying the existence of the agency.

☐ P's wife always runs out of housekeeping money before the end of the month. To remedy this P takes over the responsibility of buying household necessaries, giving his wife a small allowance to cover her personal needs. Unknown to him she continues to buy household items on credit from the local department store. As a wife has implied authority to pledge her husband's credit for necessaries her contracts bind him.

The reason P's wife cannot pay her food bills is that she cannot resist purchasing expensive hats. Her husband, a prominent lawyer, is concerned about the scandal attached to unpaid bills and so always pays them. Finally he decides not to pay them and informs his wife accordingly. She continues to purchase them on credit from her milliner's. P must pay the bills, he is estopped from denying the existence of the agency because he has always paid her hat bills in the past.

Lloyd v. *Grace Smith & Co Ltd* (1912)
A solicitor's managing clerk, whilst dealing with a client's property, fraudulently obtained her signature on documents which transferred the estate to him. The solicitors were liable because by allowing the clerk to deal with similar matters they had represented that he possessed the authority to arrange the transfer of client's property.

In the first example the wife is presumed to be her husband's agent[2] in the purchase of 'necessaries'; to rebut the presumption the husband must prove:

1   he forbade his wife buying goods on credit,
or
2   he told the supplier not to sell goods on credit,
or
3   his wife had sufficient funds to purchase the goods for cash.

In the second example there is agency by estoppel and liability on his wife's bills can only be avoided by expressly informing the supplier the wife's authority is revoked.

Agents under this heading possess implied and ostensible authority.

Necessity

Agency of necessity arises where a person is entrusted with another's property and action becomes necessary to preserve that property. The former becomes an agent with the implied authority to take the necessary steps on behalf of the other party. This type of agency only arises where it is impossible to obtain the principal's instructions, where the action is prompted by commercial necessity and where the act is in the principal's interest.

Springer v. *Gt Western Railways* (1921)
Tomatoes were being sent from Jersey. Owing to strikes when the tomatoes were unloaded at Weymouth they were found to be bad. The railway company sold them locally. It was held they were not agents of necessity because they could have communicated with S.

A principal is only bound by an *unauthorized* contract when he *ratifies* it. Where an agent exceeds his actual or ostensible authority or possesses no authority, the principal, once he possesses full knowledge of the facts[3], can within a reasonable period of time ratify the *whole* contract. He can do this expressly or impliedly, for example by suing on

[2] Provided the parties are living together.
[3] Unless he expressly ratifies the acts 'whatever they are'.

the contract. <u>Ratification is only possible where:</u>

(i) <u>the agent contracted on behalf of a disclosed principal,</u>
(ii) <u>the principal was in existence and possessed contractual capacity when the contract was made,</u>
(iii) <u>the principal possesses capacity when he wishes to ratify,</u>
(iv) <u>the contract is not void,</u>
(v) <u>the principal has a choice.</u> If A wrongly allows a garage to respray P's car the latter cannot reject the contract; P will want the car returned.

Once a contract has been ratified the ratification dates back to the time of the original contract.

☐ Sidney Harp employs a stockbroker to prepare a share portfolio for him. The stockbroker prepares the portfolio and then, without consulting the principal, accepts an offer to purchase the shares. This is an unauthorized contract. The shares double in price the following day because of takeover rumours. The vendor then discovers the stockbroker's action was unauthorized and claims to revoke his offer. Harp discovers the position and because of the increase in share prices ratifies the contract to purchase the shares. This dates back to the vendor's offer. The revocation is ineffectual because the offer to sell has been accepted.

<u>Where the agent enters into an *unauthorized* contract which P refuses to ratify the third party (and not the principal) can sue A for breach of implied warranty (even though the loss of authority was caused by facts of which he was unaware) because by making the contract the agent</u> implies he possesses the necessary authority.

☐ An accountant employs an estate agent to acquire an office lease for him. The accountant dies from a heart attack brought on by overwork. Later the same day the estate agent, who is unaware of the heart attack, acquires the lease. The lessor does not have a contract with the accountant's personal representatives but can sue the estate agent for breach of implied warranty.

The agent can however exclude his liability in the contract; in addition he is not liable if his lack of authority was known to the third party at the time of contracting. The damages paid by the agent must place the third party in the same position as if a contract had been formed with the principal. If such a contract would have been valueless the third party therefore receives nothing.

To avoid liability an agent must therefore remain within his actual authority and obey any lawful instructions. An agent failing to carry out instructions is liable for any losses suffered, even if not his fault, but providing he obeys instructions he cannot be liable for losses arising.

☐ An accountant is retained to negotiate a client's tax liability with the Inland Revenue. He is instructed to settle once the inspector agrees a figure of £30 000. He settles at this figure although by further negotiations it could have been reduced. A is not liable because he carried out P's instructions.

If instructions are ambiguous the agent avoids liability to either party if his interpretation of them is reasonable.

☐ A businessman asked an estate agent to acquire the lease of certain premises for 'about £2500 pa for around ten years'. The agent acquired the lease for eight years at £2500. Providing the agent was acting in good faith his actions, being reasonable, will bind the principal.

Other duties of the agent include:

(i) _The exercise of due care and skill_   A gratuitous agent[4] is not liable for a failure to act but if he acts he will be liable for 'gross incompetence,' although if he is a 'skilled' or 'professional person' he must exercise a greater degree of competence. A paid agent is liable for inaction and must exercise reasonable care. What is reasonable depends on the circumstances, the professional person being required to show a higher level of competence.

☐ A, an accountant by training, is occasionally used by P to purchase businesses on P's behalf. Because of A's professional knowledge P allows A complete freedom in negotiating the price. A purchases T's business for £250 000. Six months later the £30 000 profit forecast is revised to a loss of £30 000 because of an accounting error in T's books. If A had exercised professional skill in a competent manner A would have discovered this error. A is liable to P for failing to exercise due care and skill.

The exercise of due care also means notifying the principal of any information which would influence the principal in making the contract.

Woolcott v. *Excess Insurance Ltd* (1978)
Insurance contracts are of utmost good faith therefore the party seeking insurance must disclose any relevant information. If he fails to do this the contract can be avoided. Mr Woolcott completed a proposal form and replied in the negative to the question 'Are there any other matters you wish to be taken into account'.

[4] One who is unpaid.

Although convicted for robbery in 1960 he considered this irrelevant. The court held that this was a 'material' fact and should have been disclosed. Mr Woolcott had however obtained insurance through brokers who were the company's agents. They knew of his conviction and their knowledge was imputed to their principals. His contract with the insurance company was binding and he obtained £32 500. Because the agents had failed to disclose relevant information to the principals they had to pay £32 500 damages to them.

(ii) *Non delegation of duties* (delegatus non potest delegare) Because the principal and agent have a personal relationship the agent can only delegate if this is expressly or impliedly authorized by the principal. The court implies the power to delegate if this is necessary to perform the agency (perhaps because of an unforeseen emergency) or delegation is customary in that trade.

☐ An accountant in North Devon engages a local solicitor to act as his agent in purchasing a London business. The local solicitor arranges for a London solicitor to act on his behalf. This is permissable because it is customary for country solicitors to use town agents.

(iii) *To render an account* The agent must account to the principal for money received; the principal's money cannot be mixed with the agent's.

(iv) *Not to let interest conflict with duty to the principal* This duty arises from the fiduciary relationship between the parties; the agent must always act in good faith. He must not disclose confidential information entrusted to him by his principal and if his interests conflict with his duty, any contract he enters into is voidable at the principal's discretion (unless full disclosure was made).

☐ Wist is the financial director of his wife's company. He also runs a professional practice. A client asks him to negotiate a takeover of his wife's company. The takeover terms are fair but because Wist does not disclose his interest P, who is unaware of his contact with the company, can avoid the contract.

The rule's application means that the agent cannot make a secret profit out of his agency. He is entitled to commission but any profit made from the agency or the principal's property without the principal's consent belongs to the principal who may also refuse to pay commission, dismiss the agent and repudiate the contract.

☐ A is the Far East agent of XYZ Co Ltd. In this position A obtains lists of customers. A contacts these when he wishes to market goods supplied by XYZ's competitors. He must account to XYZ Co Ltd for any profits made.

The rule applies even though the agent has acted honestly and the principal incurs no loss. A bribe, a type of secret profit, also gives the principal the remedies outlined above. In addition the principal can also recover the bribe from the agent *or* sue the third party and/or the agent for damages sustained as a result of the bribe. The claim to recover the bribe and damages for loss are in the alternative.

☐   A retail organization employs an agent to acquire building sites. He purchases five sites from XYZ Co Ltd for £2 500 000 when their market value is £2 000 000 after receiving a bribe of £150 000. The principal can recover £150 000 from the agent *or* £500 000 from XYZ Co Ltd/agent. He cannot recover both amounts.

Note: This is based on a privy council decision in *Maheson S/O Thambiah* v. *Malaysia Government Officer's Co-operative* (1978) which disapproved of *Mayor of Salford* v. *Lever* (1891). The former is only a persuasive precedent.

In addition an offence has been committed under the Prevention of Corruption Act (1906).

Rights of the agent

The commission received depends on the contract. If no clause indicates the amount of the payment then, providing no clause indicates commission is not payable, the agent will receive what is customary in the trade or else 'reasonable' remuneration. Similarly the moment commission becomes payable depends on the contract.

On a sale being completed commission is payable only on completion and if the vendor refuses to complete no commission is payable even though the purchaser is anxious to complete.
On introducing a person ready, able and willing to purchase commission is payable once an unqualified offer to purchase is made.
On finding a prospective purchaser commission is payable when someone is found who seriously contemplates purchasing.

The right to commission usually ceases on the termination of the agency.
The agent is also *indemnified* for any losses or liabilities legally incurred during the agency.

Christoforides v. *Terry* (1924)
C employed X to make speculative purchases of cotton for him. Cotton prices fell, X was personally liable on the contracts and having sold C's cotton, was substantially out of pocket. He was

entitled to be indemnified against these losses by C.

The right to an indemnity is lost if the agent acts beyond the scope of his duty or is negligent.

Termination of agency

In addition to normal methods of terminating contracts a contract of agency can be terminated by the unilateral action of either party. The principal can revoke the agent's authority to make further contracts, either expressly or impliedly, even if this is in breach of contract. New contracts made by the agent cannot bind the principal (subject to the rules re 'ostensible authority') but the agent can sue the principal if the termination of the agency was in breach of their contract (eg it failed to give the appropriate period of notice).

☐ A is engaged as an agent to sell textbooks published by P. A receives a 10% commission on sales and the agency agreement lasts for five years. After one year P becomes bankrupt. As the agent cannot perform the job his agency has been terminated by P's conduct. Depending on the contract A may be able to sue P.

The power to revoke the agent's authority is limited:

a) under the powers of Attorney Act (1971)   Section 4 states that a power of attorney expressed to be irrevocable and given to secure a proprietory interest of the donee cannot be unilaterally removed by the donor,

or

b) if the agent is given an authority coupled with an interest.

☐ P approaches an accountant asking him to represent him in negotiations with the Inland Revenue. Because of liquidity problems P cannot pay for this but A agrees to act as his agent in the sale of his business and recoup his fees out of the purchase price. A has authority coupled with an interest and it cannot be revoked.

Smart v. *Sanders* (1848)
An agent was to sell goods for his principal. He made advances to the principal on the security of the goods. The principal could not revoke the agency.

Agency contracts can also terminate by operation of law. The agent's authority ends when the principal dies, even if the agent is unaware of this. The insanity of either party terminates the agency although the agent can still make binding contracts after the principal's insanity if the third party is unaware of the insanity.

☐   P, the lawyer, whose wife is prone to overspending is so concerned about his reputation he becomes mentally disordered. His wife continues to purchase hats from the milliner who is unaware of her husband's illness. The husband is still bound by the contracts.

The principal's bankruptcy is also a terminating factor but a bankrupt agent may be able to continue depending on the nature of the agency.

Past examination questions

1   What is the effect on a principal of a contract made on his behalf by his agent where the agent has not disclosed to the third party the identity of the principal?
In such a case, has the third party any rights against the agent?
A C A December 1976

2a)   Explain the circumstances in which an agent's act which is initially unauthorized may be subsequently ratified by his principal so as to become binding.

b)   Fred offers to sell his house to Sidney whom he knows in the past has acted as Jim's agent in the business of selling furs. Sidney says that he does not want the house but he is sure that Jim, who knows nothing at all about this, would like it. Sidney accepts Fred's offer.
Next day Fred, who has got a better offer from Ted, writes to Sidney saying the offer is revoked. The same day Fred receives a letter from Jim saying: 'Sidney has told me about your house. When would you like a deposit?'
Fred writes back saying that he no longer wishes to sell the house to Jim and has told Sidney so, Jim then brings an action for specific performance. What are his rights?
A C A June 1976

3a)   Describe the duties which an agent owes to his principal.

b)   Philip instructs Steven to sell his house and agrees to pay him £200 commission on completion of the sale. Steven sells the house and on completion is paid his commission by Philip. Philip subsequently discovers that Steven has also been paid a commission of £100 by the purchaser. Advise Philip.
A C A June 1979

4a)   Distinguish between actual and ostensible authority of an agent.

b)   Percy appointed Arthur as an agent to buy quantities of goods for him from John and a number of other suppliers. Later Percy became dissatisfied with Arthur's work and wrote to him on 1 May telling him that he did not wish Arthur to continue buying goods for him. On 1 June Arthur buys goods on credit from John and Percy refuses to pay John for these goods. Advise John.
I A S June 1979

5   What terms are implied in the contract of agency because of the confidential nature of that relationship?
C A 1980

6   'The personal and confidential nature of the relationship is illustrated by the duties which an agent owes his principal.' Discuss.
C A October 1979

7   Define the following terms as used in the principal/agency relationship:
a) ostensible authority,
b) breach of warranty of authority,
c) indemnity.
C A May 1980

19

Principles of insurance

An accountant starting his own practice may be concerned that in the event of his death his family will lose their main breadwinner. He also faces the risk that if his offices are damaged, perhaps by fire, this will have an adverse effect on his practice as well as involving him in considerable expenditure. To cover himself against these misfortunes he may effect insurance. An insurance policy either indemnifies the insured against losses arising out of the insured event or, in the case of personal accident or life policies, makes a certain sum of money payable on the occurrence of a specified event, (ie injury or death).

Insurance contracts differ from gaming contracts (which are void) because the insured has an *insurable interest* in the matter to be insured. Expressed simply, the insured possesses a financial interest in the subject matter of the policy (ie suffers loss if the event insured against occurs). In a wager there is no interest other than the stake money.

An accountant would have:

An insurable interest in		*No insurable interest in*	
1	his debtors' lives to the extent of the debt (loss: if the debtor dies the debt may be irrecoverable)	1	a competitor's life
2	his own life	2	his son's life (in normal circumstances)
3	his spouse's life (loss: if she dies he will require a housekeeper)	3	his mother's house
4	his property (loss: he will have to rebuild or repair)		
5	the lives of his employees (loss: cost of retraining of staff)		
6	the contents of his office (loss: he will have to replace the destroyed contents)		
7	his personal health		

Where he has an insurable interest he may take out insurance but by law certain insurance is compulsory. Under the Employers Liability (Compulsory Insurance) Act 1969 he must insure against liability arising for injuries sustained by his employees during the course of their employment. In addition, as a motorist, the Road Traffic Act 1972 compels him to insure against liability to third parties.

The accountant (Bernard Rayne), being by nature cautious, takes out policies of

life insurance
personal accident
motor vehicle
employers liability
office contents (£6000 with company X and £6000 with company Y)
fire (for £20 000) with a consequential loss policy.[1]

To obtain insurance a proposal form is completed; this provides sufficient information for the insurer to calculate the premiums (the regular payments to the company) and is Rayne's application for a policy. He does this by paying the first premium and once the insurance company accept this there is a binding contract.

As only the proposer possesses the information the company requires to calculate the premium all relevant information must be disclosed to the insurance company. The contract is a contract umberrimae fidei. Because of this:

a) the insured owes a duty to disclose every *material* fact, ie one relevant in calculating the premium. Material facts include:
that another company has refused a policy,
a criminal conviction,
previous accidents in an application for a motor policy.

Where a material fact is not disclosed the contract is voidable at the insurer's option.

☐   Rayne wants a 'fidelity guarantee'[2] policy covering his staff. The proposal form asks if any of his staff have criminal convictions. He replies in the negative because although his articled clerk has several motoring convictions he considers these irrelevant. This information is material, hence the insurer can avoid the contract on discovering the truth.

(See page 142 for *Woolcott* v. *Sun Alliance*.)

But

---

[1] A consequential loss policy insures against any loss of profit caused by the business interruption following the fire.
[2] A fidelity guarantee policy insures the holder against losses arising from staff dishonestly whilst handling his client's funds.

b) If the non disclosure is not material the contract remains valid.

☐   Rayne is increasing his life insurance because of inflation. The proposal form asks if he has consulted a doctor in the previous two years. He replies no, although a doctor friend gave him a full medical six months ago. This indicated he was in excellent health. This non-disclosure is not material and the contract remains valid.

Mutual Life Insurance Co of New York v. *Ontario Metal Products Co* (1925)

The proposal form asked if the proposer had consulted a doctor in the past five years. He replied no because although he had seen a doctor and received tonics he had not been absent from work. The insurers' doctor stated that this fact would not have affected his decision to recommend issuing a policy at the ordinary premium. The contract was therefore valid.

Unless

c) The contract is conditional on all the answers being correct (ie the insured warrants the correctness of his answers); if any are wrong the contract is void (NB void not voidable).

   In addition a fraudulent or innocent misrepresentation by one party gives rise to the usual contractual remedies (see page 46).

☐   Rayne's offices are badly damaged by fire causing £10 000 of damage and part of the contents valued at £6000, are completely destroyed. The next day, whilst driving his car, he is reflecting on his misfortune when, because of his lapse of concentration, he hits a brick wall totally destroying his car.

   Apart from life and personal accident insurance where the insurer pays out the sum stipulated in the policy, insurance contracts exist to indemnify (compensate) the insured against losses incurred when the insured event happens. He receives the sum necessary to compensate him and not the amount specified in the policy. Rayne therefore recovers £10 000 (his loss) on his fire insurance and not £20 000.

   The above assumes:

a) the fire policy does not contain a subject to average clause,
or
b) that although such a clause exists the property is insured for its market value.

   Where such a clause exists and the property is not insured for its full value (under insured) the insured recovers such proportion of the loss as the value the property bears to the value of the insurance cover. Where the property is underinsured the whole loss, even though less than the insurance cover, cannot be recoverable.

Rayne's property is worth £40 000 but only insured for £20 000. He can only recover £40 000 ÷ £20 000 = ½ of any losses, ie £5000 in the above example.

Value of property	Insured for	Loss	Amount received
100 000	75 000	30 000	
75 000	50 000	21 000	
50 000	40 000	10 000	
50 000	25 000	30 000	

Policies which are index-linked automatically rise to compensate for inflation thereby avoiding the above situation.

Assuming he is not underinsured Rayne receives £6000 on his contents policy (because of the principle of indemnity) not £12 000 and can claim £3000 from each company or £6000 from one. If he chooses the latter option, the company paying can, under the principle of *contribution*, require a contribution from the other company. Each must contribute to the loss in proportion to the amount for which they are liable under the contract.

Contents value £12 000

Company X insures for	Company Y insures for	Claim is paid
6000	6000	50:50
9000	3000	75:25
4000	8000	33.3:66.6

and if either company pays more than its share this is recoverable from the other.

In an indemnity contract (ie all insurance contracts except life and personal accident) the insurer, once he has paid on the policy, is entitled under the principle of subrogation to any other benefits received by the insured in compensation and to any rights the insured possessed against third parties.

☐ Rayne loses his right hand due to X's negligence. His personal accident policy insures his hands for £50 000 each. He receives £50 000. He could have sued X for negligence; the principle of subrogation means the insurance company can sue X instead.

If the insured renounces rights against a third party this binds the insurer but the latter can recover from the insured any sums he could have otherwise recovered from the third party.

Past examination questions

1a)   In relation to contracts of insurance distinguish between (i) subrogation, and (ii) contribution.

b)   Steven's house is valued at £15 000. He has insured it for £10 000 against fire with Wong Insurance Co. He has also insured it against fire with Shah Insurance Co for £5000. The house is damaged by fire to the extent of £5000.
Steven sues Wong Insurance Company for indemnity. Advise Wong Insurance Company as to their rights and liabilities.

A C A December 1976

2a)   'A contract of insurance is a contract of the utmost good faith.' Discuss this statement.

    b)   David is insuring his house. He completes the proposal form issued by the insurance company and the company issues the policy. Some months later the house is seriously damaged by fire and David tries to recover on the policy. However, the insurance company refuses to pay and claims that David failed to advise them that he had been imprisoned for theft eight years ago. Advise David.

    c)   Would your advice be any different if David had insured his house through an agent, acting for the insurance company, who knew of his conviction for theft?   A C A June 1979

20

Consumer Credit Act

(The words in italics are defined in a glossary at the end of the Chapter.)

The Consumer Credit Act 1974   protects individuals who hire goods or purchase them on credit. It covers most forms of consumer credit, providing a basic skeleton to which flesh can be added through statutory instruments. It is supervised by the Director General of Fair Trading who:

(i) administers the licensing system,
(ii) supervises the Act's enforcement (primarily the responsibility of the local authority who possess wide ranging powers),
(iii) issues occasional reports and advises the relevant government minister on matters of consumer credit.

Most of the Act's provisions can be divided into those possessing national application and those only applying to *regulated* agreements.

National provisions

1   Licensing

The Consumer Credit Act established 'for the protection of consumers a system ... of licensing and other controls of traders concerned with the provision of credit, or the supply of goods on hire and hire purchase, and their transactions.'

This is probably the most original part of the act. Basically almost everybody involved in credit requires a licence[1]. This licence initially lasts for three years and is obtainable on satisfying the Director General that you are a 'fit person' according to the criteria specified in the Act.

Any circumstances thought relevant are considered; in particular any evidence that the applicant or applicant's employees or associates have committed any offence involving fraud or dishonesty, have contravened the Act or any other Act relating to business (for example, Sale

---

[1] Certain bodies are exempt from the licensing provisions, eg local authorities, and a business will not require to be licenced if its business does not comprise of or relate to regulated consumer credit or consumer hire agreements (eg it only provides credit to companies).

of Goods Act 1979, Trade Descriptions Act 1968), practised dis-crimination (by sex, colour, race or ethnic origin) or engaged in practices appearing to the Director to be deceitful, unfair or improper whether unlawful or not.

If a licence is refused an appeal can be made to the Secretary of State and, on points of law, to the High Court. Anybody trading without a licence, where one is necessary, will be guilty of a criminal offence punishable by a fine, imprisonment or both. In addition, the agreement is not enforceable against the borrower or hirer without the Director General's consent. Even if the lender or hirer is allowed to enforce the agreement he remains guilty of the criminal offence.

Licences are required by:

(i) Businesses lending money to the public (for example by hire-purchase, cash loans, budget accounts, credit cards,) to enable them to purchase goods or services where the credit price does not exceed £5000.

(ii) Businesses leasing or renting goods for a period exceeding three months where the amounts of the payments come to no more than £5000 (for example renting of television sets).

(iii) Businesses arranging credit from a third source for their clients; this is called credit brokerage. If a client requires a loan and the accountant arranges it with company X the accountant requires a licence (subject to the exception below). A retailer who arranges finance for a customer from a finance company also requires a licence as do mortgage brokers.

(iv) Businesses (such as accountants) advising clients how to deal with their debts or pay off specific debts (ie debt counselling) will require a licence providing the extent of the debts does not exceed £5000. Solicitors therefore require licencing and the Law Society has obtained a group certificate.

(v) Businesses collecting other firms' debts not exceeding £5000, (ie debt collectors).

(vi) Credit reference agencies.

Businesses in categories (i)-(v) do not require licences if they deal only with limited companies. A licence is required, however, even if the credit activity is only a small part of the business, for example, if an accountant's credit brokerage activities amount to only 5% of his busi-ness he still requires a licence. A licence is not required if you enter into transactions involving licences only 'occasionally'; the transaction must be exceptional and not in the course of normal business. Doing something very infrequently as part of your business is not 'occasional' and a licence is required; it is irrelevant how small a part of your total business it is or how infrequent an occurrence.

☐ Wit, anxious to increase the profitability of his practice, offers to arrange loans for clients (he receives a commission from the lender). Very few clients use this service and it is a minimal part of his business. He does not apply for a licence. His credit brokerage activities are not 'occasional' (as defined by the Act) and by failing to obtain a licence he has committed a criminal offence.

Any consumer can discover if a firm he or she is dealing with is licenced by examining the public register maintained by the Office of Fair Trading. Anybody guilty of malpractice may have the licence withdrawn by the Director General.

2 Advertising

The Act covers advertisements of businesses offering consumer credit (or the hire of goods) and adverts offering credit on the security of land (eg adverts of building societies). In addition the Act applies to adverts by credit brokerage, debt adjusting or counselling businesses. Adverts offering more than £5000 credit or relating solely to companies are not covered. A criminal offence is committed if the advert contains false or misleading information, fails to indicate the cash price of the items or infringes any other regulation the Secretary of State makes.

To canvass *debtor-creditor agreements* (eg loan, second mortgage) off trade premises unless this follows a written request from the debtor is a criminal offence. Where the canvassing relates to a *debtor-creditor-supplier agreement* (eg sale of double glazing with a loan arranged via a finance company) then providing the canvassing firm is licensed it is legal.

A criminal offence is also committed if the services of a credit broker, debt adjuster or counsellor are canvassed off trade premises. Further criminal offences are committed by sending minors circulars offering them credit or by sending unsolicited items, such as credit cards, through the post.

3 Extortionate credit bargains

The court can grant relief to debtors who have entered into extortionate credit transactions. This power covers **all** credit transactions, even those exceeding £5000, where the debtor is an individual and the creditor need not be in the business of providing credit, (a loan to a friend can be extortionate). Credit covers all forms of credit provision (cash loans, credit sale, etc) but the provisions do not cover rental or hiring agreements.

In deciding whether to reopen the credit agreement the court must consider the **credit bargain**. This is defined as the credit agreement plus any other transactions which are included in the calculation of the *total charge for credit*. Simply stated, the court considers the total cost of the credit to the consumer; the credit agreement is often only part of the total cost.

Subject to certain exceptions the 'total charge for credit' consists of any charges paid by the debtor (or his relative) which arise under:

(i) the credit agreement,
(ii) any transaction entered into to comply with the credit agreement,
(iii) any contract for security relating to the credit agreement,
(iv) any other contract which the creditor insists is made before the credit is granted.

If X purchases a typewriter on credit from company Z, paying £300, and the cash price is £250 then the interest charges total £50 (see (i)).

If X is required to sign a service contract costing £20 with the company this falls under (ii) even though the charge does not specifically relate to the credit and the debtor receives other benefits for his payment. If the credit is only available if the servicing contract is taken out it will be caught by the section. There may be a £5 delivery charge but if this is made both to cash and credit customers it is **excluded** from the total charge for credit. The total charge for X's credit (the credit bargain) is £70 (£50 interest and £20 service contract). If the servicing contract could have been taken out with any company or was optional it would not form part of the credit bargain.

Having calculated the cost of the credit the court decides if the bargain is extortionate. If it requires the debtor (or a relative) to make grossly exorbitant payments or grossly contravenes the ordinary principles of fair dealing it is exorbitant. When a debtor seeks the court's assistance the creditor must prove the bargain was not extortionate.

The debtor can either seek to reopen an agreement **or** raise the question of extortionate provisions in any proceedings brought against him by the creditor, such as where he is sued for interest owing on the credit agreement. The extortionate credit provision can also be utilised where the creditor sues on a *linked transaction*, which is a transaction linked with the credit agreement although it may be irrelevant when calculating the *total charge for credit*.

☐   A businessman purchases a car from R's showroom. The sale is financed by a local garage, C. If R suggests C tests the car prior to purchase, any contract with C to test the car becomes a linked transaction. Because the loan was not conditional on the test its cost is ignored when calculating the 'total charge for credit'. If C sues the businessman for the test fee the latter can claim the credit bargain relating to the car's sale was extortionate.

If the credit bargain is considered extortionate the credit agreement may be reopened. The court can reduce the rate of interest payable and require repayment of part of the sums received by the creditor. It can also amend the provisions of any related agreement and require the creditor to repay sums the debtor paid to another party, even though this places an unfair burden on the creditor.

How does the court decide if a credit bargain is extortionate? In addition to the general guide lines it must consider certain specified factors such as the level of interest rates and the nature of any linked transactions. Some of the specified factors seek to ascertain the vulnerability of the debtor, hence age, health and experience become relevant. In addition the financial pressures on the debtor to enter into an agreement are relevant. A person facing bankruptcy may be more easily persuaded to make an unwise bargain.

Provisions relating to regulated agreements

Under s. 173 parties cannot contract out of the protection provided by the act for debtors and hirers.

1 Entry into a regulated agreement[2]

The Act requires compliance with certain formalities when consumer credit and consumer hire agreements are formed.

Disclosure To enable the debtor or hirer to discover the true cost of the agreement, the creditor or owner must indicate the total charge for credit, the percentage interest rate charged and the item's cash price.

Content The agreement must be in a written document containing all the express terms (unless reference is made to another document containing them) when presented for signature and these must be legible. Information provided must include rights of cancellation (if any), names and addresses of the parties, the amounts and dates of payments, the true cost of the credit and the right of early settlement. The agreement is only enforceable when signed by the debtor or hirer and by, or on behalf of, the creditor or owner.

Copies Where the agreement is executed in the debtor's presence a copy of the agreement is presented at that time. Where however the creditor or owner signs the agreement later the debtor or hirer receives one copy on signing it and a second copy within seven days of the creditor signing it.

Cancellation With a *cancellable agreement* the debtor must receive notice of his rights. If only entitled to one copy of the agreement this must be within seven days of making the agreement. Where a second copy is sent, his rights of cancellation are incorporated in that document. The customer can cancel his agreement by serving a written notice to the appropriate party within the 'cooling off' period (within five clear days of receiving the second copy or within five days of

---

[2] The formalities do not apply to non-commercial and certain small agreements.

notification of his cancellation rights where no second copy is sent). Cancellation terminates the agreement and any linked transaction.

Note: Cancellation is valid on posting and not receipt.

Agreements such as hire-purchase, credit or conditional sale allow the debtor to recover any payments made but the goods must be available for return. The creditor must collect them within twenty-one days of a written request from the debtor; after this time the debtor is not obliged to take reasonable care of the goods. If, however, the goods cannot be returned the debtor must pay for them despite cancellation.

In agreements such as loans the customer must repay the credit received plus interest unless the customer repays the loan within one month of cancellation.

Non-compliance with the above formalities means the creditor or owner requires the court's permission before enforcing the agreement. This **cannot** be granted where, for example, the customer did not sign the agreement or was not informed of the rights of cancellation but in most cases the court does what is fair in the circumstances.

During the agreement the debtor or hirer is entitled, with certain exceptions, to require a copy of the executed agreement and a statement of his outstanding balance. If the creditor or owner fails to comply with any request he cannot, whilst the default continues, enforce the agreement and after one month, commits a criminal offence.

2   Variation
Where the agreement is varied by the creditor or owner in accordance with the contract the alteration usually becomes effective after the debtor or hirer has received seven days notice.

3   Enforcement & termination
By creditor/owner (see flow chart page 168)
A   Enforcement
The creditor/owner may sue for arrears of interest without issuing a default notice. If the agreement allows interest to be charged on the arrears this must be no higher than that charged on the main contract.
B   Termination
  (i)   **By death of debtor or hirer**   Where the debtor or hirer dies and the agreement is fully secured the creditor or owner cannot
      terminate the agreement;
      demand earlier payment of any sum;
      recover possession of any goods or land;
      treat any right conferred on the debtor or hirer by the agreement as terminated, restricted or deferred;
      enforce any security;
      because the deceased's executors or personal representatives

assume his rights and obligations under the contract. Where the agreement is not fully secured the creditor or owner can perform the above acts where he proves nobody will take over the deceased's agreement. The above is inapplicable in certain situations, for example, where the contract stipulates that on the customer's death any outstanding debt will be paid out of a specified life policy.

(ii) **By mutual agreement**   Normally an agreement will be replaced by a new agreement: this is a 'modifying agreement' and must comply with the statutory formalities outlined above.

(iii) **In accordance with the contractual terms**   Prior to a creditor or owner terminating a contract (or taking certain other actions) the customer must be informed. Where the creditor's rights arise because the customer has broken the agreement the creditor issues a default notice containing specified information. The customer has seven days from the date to remedy the default. If the customer does so the breach is regarded as never having arisen. A failure to comply with the notice means the creditor or owner can pursue contractual remedies unless the customer seeks the court's assistance.

Where the creditor or owner wishes to enforce contractual rights and there is no breach of the contract then the creditor must notify the debtor/hirer of his intentions. This enables the latter to apply to the court. Notice is **only** necessary where the agreement has a specified period of duration (eg hire-purchase).

☐   A businessman obtains a £5000 overdraft from his bank repayable on demand. Because of a government instruction requiring banks to reduce their lending they require immediate repayment. The overdraft is not for a specified period, the section relating to notice is inapplicable.

After receiving either of the above notices (or in any court action by the creditor or owner) the customer can apply to the court for assistance. It can grant the orders indicated in the chart, the most important being a **time order**. This provides the customer with time to remedy the breach, perhaps by paying off arrears. Where a time order is awarded the court can make the payments 'payable at such times as the court, having regard to the means of the debtor or hirer and any surety, considers reasonable,' but the order cannot refer to future payments unless the agreement is one of hire purchase or conditional sale. In those cases the time order can relate to future payments thereby allowing the court to rewrite the instalment plan.

The other orders are the **suspended and conditional**. These may be linked to a time order.

☐   Gerald Rope purchased a Rolls Royce on credit and has fallen in arrears with the repayments. The creditor commences an action to recover possession. The court could grant a time order giving Rope time to pay off the arrears and also order him to return the goods. The latter order could be suspended, to take effect only if Rope fails to comply with the time order.

Where an order is refused or not complied with the creditor's and owner's remedies depend on the type of agreement and whether the contract has been broken.

Remedies where the customer has broken the contract:

(i)   The innocent party can treat any breach as one of warranty and sue for arrears (see above).

(ii) There is usually an express term enabling the owner or hirer to terminate the contract after any breach however trivial. After termination the owner or hirer can pursue other contractual remedies. In certain agreements, of which hire purchase is the most important, this will include:

recovery of the goods

The owner or hirer cannot enter premises to seize them without the occupier's or court's permission and where the goods are 'protected' (see flow chart for definition) they cannot be repossessed from the debtor without a court order. Repossession from the debtor without an order terminates the agreement, all payments made are returnable and the customer is relieved of any further liability under the agreement. A court order is unnecessary if the debtor has disposed of the goods to a third party.

☐   Rope is in arrears with the payments on the Rolls Royce and sells it to a friend. The finance company seize it from the friend. This is legal, the goods are not being seized from the debtor.

For the same reason an order is unnecessary where abandoned goods are seized or where the debtor voluntarily hands them over.

Note: The 'protected goods' provision is inapplicable to regulated consumer hire agreements although that relating to entry of premises applies. The owner can reclaim the goods immediately the contract is terminated (ie when the notice to the hirer expires) but the court may grant the hirer such financial relief as appears 'fair'. It can reduce any arrears or even order payments to be returned to the hirer. In determining its action the court considers 'the extent of the enjoyment of the goods by the hirer'.

Damages

After the contract is terminated and the creditor obtains a return order, or otherwise legally obtains the goods he can claim financial compensation from the debtor. If the contract contains a 'minimum payments clause' ie on termination the debtor must pay a stipulated amount, this may be enforced, declared void as a penalty or rendered ineffective through the extortionate credit bargain provisions. In the latter cases the court assesses the extent of the compensation payable as if no minimum payments clause exists.

The court's assessment of damages depends on whether the **debtor** repudiated the contract or whether the **creditor** terminated it in accordance with an express clause (for example he might possess the right to terminate for a breach of warranty). In the former case the creditor is entitled to be placed in the same position as if the contract had been performed.

☐ Rope purchases a £20 000 Rolls Royce.

Deposit	£3 000	
Total hire purchase price	£25 000	
Therefore owing		£22 000
Less instalments paid	£6 000	
Plus value of returned Rolls	£13 000	
		£19 000
Damages		£3 000

Where the creditor terminates the contract damages are restricted to arrears of payments; because the debtor has not broken contract the creditor cannot claim damages for breach.

☐ In the above example if Rope had not repudiated the contract but the creditor had terminated it because the debtor was £800 in arrears (this might only be a breach of warranty) the damages awarded would be £800.

Financings Ltd v. *Baldock* (1963)
The debtor was in arrears with the repayments but informed the finance company that he would pay these. Despite this they exercised their right to terminate the contract. It was held the company was only entitled to the arrears of repayments.

Remedies where the customer has NOT broken his contract:

The creditor can
  (i) recover the goods. These are not 'protected' but the restrictions on entering premises applies.
 (ii) Recover arrears but not damages.

By debtor/hirer
With cancellable agreements the customer can terminate the agreement within the 'cooling off period'. Otherwise:

1   A debtor under a regulated agreement can end the contract by paying the instalments early after giving written notice to the creditor. The debtor obtains ownership and a rebate on interest payable because of the prior repayment.
2   A debtor, if involved in hire-purchase, credit or conditional sale agreements can terminate the agreement at any time by notifying, in writing, the creditor or any other person authorized to receive payment. The goods must be returned, any arrears paid off, compensation paid for any damage resulting from any failure to take reasonable care of the goods. In addition the debtor pays:
    (i)   the amount stipulated in any minimum payments clause;
    (ii) the difference between his payments and half the total hire purchase price
or
    (iii) the amount of the creditor's loss,
whichever is the least. The maximum liability is therefore usually half the total hire purchase price plus any arrears.

With a hire agreement the hirer must usually wait until the agreement has run for eighteen months before the hirer can terminate. The notice required is the shorter of three months or the intervals between payments. If these are weekly only one week's notice is required to terminate the agreement.

☐   A businesswoman hires a telephone answering machine. The rental is paid monthly. After one year she wishes to terminate the agreement. She must wait for another six months when she may give one month's notice of termination.

Control and liability of third parties

Control
In addition to the licensing provisions, the Act's sections affect the activities of:

a) Credit reference agencies
The Act defines a credit reference agency as 'a person carrying on a business comprising the furnishing of persons with information relevant to the financial standing of individuals, being information collected by the agency for that purpose' (s. 145(8)). It allows a consumer to obtain their file from the credit agency providing the negotiations for credit related to 'regulated agreements'.

Retailer or creditor   The person selling goods or providing the credit is the person who usually consults the agency for a credit report. S. 157, therefore, requires the retailer or creditor, if he deals directly with the consumer, to provide him with the name and address, in writing, of the credit reference agency within seven working days of a written request from the consumer. The obligation ceases if no written request is received within twenty eight days of the conclusion of their business. The retailer or creditor need not give details of the report he received or whether it affected his decision. If credit or hire facilities are rejected and the creditor or retailer was approached via a credit broker then, when refusing the application, he must send the broker details of any agency consulted.

Credit broker   Following a written request from the consumer he must provide, within seven working days, details of agencies consulted by himself and the retailer or creditor.

Credit agency   On receipt of a written request from a consumer the agency must supply him with a written copy of his file. This is defined by s. 158(5) as 'all the information about him kept by a credit reference agency, regardless of how the information is stored'. The section specifically states all information (even if not included in the report) and if information on another party, for example his wife, is relevant to his financial standing this must be included in his 'file'. This must be sent within seven working days (or the consumer informed no file exists) and be in plain English. A document stating the consumer's rights must accompany the file. Failure to comply with these requirements is punishable by a fine.

Consumer   To obtain his file the consumer sends a **written** request to the agency plus a nominal fee. If he agrees with the information on file no further action is involved.

If certain information is incorrect and will adversely affect his chance of obtaining credit he may request, in writing, the agency either remove or amend the entry. He is not required to give reasons for this request.

The agency, within twenty eight days of receiving the consumer's notice, can:

(i)   Remove the offending entry from the file. In addition the agency must notify this change, in writing, to anyone given a credit reference on the consumer in the previous six months. This must be done within ten working days.

(ii)   Amend the entry and then notify the same parties as in (i).

(iii)   Inform the consumer it does not intend to take any action (this is assumed if no reply is received within twenty eight days). If the consumer receives the above reply (or is dissatisfied with the amendment to the file) a notice of correction can be written. This must not exceed two hundred words. It is sent to the agency with a request it be added to the file. The letter of correction must be sent within twenty eight days from the receipt of the agency's letter indicating which of the three courses of action it has adopted. The agency may accept the correction and inform past enquirers as with (i) and (ii).

If the agency fails to accept the letter of correction within twenty eight days the matter is referred to the Director General of Fair Trading. The agency's refusal will be accepted if based on one of the specified grounds (because it unjustly defames some body, or is incorrect, frivolous, scandalous, or for any other reason unsuitable). If no specified reason exists the Director General is empowered to make such order as he thinks fit. A failure to comply with the order can result in a fine.

S. 160 and 'Business consumers'   The credit agency may treat business consumers (individuals carrying on a business such as a sole trader or partnership) as ordinary consumers and follow the above procedure. It may, however, consider it undesirable to have to disclose the whole file to the business consumer and apply to the Director General, under s. 160, for permission to disclose only certain specified information to their 'business consumers'.

An order will be made under Section 160 if the Director General is satisfied the agency's service would be adversely affected by full disclosure *and* that 'business consumers' would probably not be prejudiced by such a direction.

If permission to shield behind Section 160 is given, the agency must, when sending the file, inform the business consumer of this fact and indicate his rights. This must be done within seven working days of receiving the consumer's request for his file.

If the business consumer is dissatisfied with the limited information received and the agency refuses further disclosure he can appeal to the Director General. After consulting with the agency he can order further disclosure of information. If the agency refuses to comply with the order they can be fined.

b) Credit brokerage firms
A customer seeking a broker's assistance in obtaining credit cannot be charged more than £1 if he does not receive the credit within six months and if he has paid more this must be refunded. If the broker obtains the credit his commission is subject to the extortionate credit provisions.

2 Liability
a)   Where the creditor and the supplier are the same person.

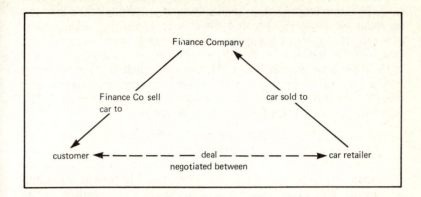

In the above the finance company provide the credit but (because they legally purchased the car from the retailer) they are also the supplier. The contract is between the customer and the finance company who are therefore liable for any breaches of the implied terms under the Sale of Goods Act. The retailer who negotiated the sale is not liable if the car is of unmerchantable quality. He can also avoid liability for misrepresentations inducing the customer to purchase the car. At common law the creditor/supplier, (finance co) would be liable where the retailer was their agent. Under s. 56 of the Act the negotiator in antecedent negotiations is now automatically the creditor/supplier's agent. This covers the dealer in hire purchase, conditional or credit sale agreements.

☐ The garage who negotiated the sale of the Rolls Royce to Rope told him it would be worth more in two years time than he paid for it. Although the contract is between the finance company and the accountant the latter may sue them for misrepresentation if the garage owner's statement was untrue.

Note: S. 56 only applies to regulated agreements.

b) *Debtor-creditor-supplier agreements* where the creditor and supplier are different persons.

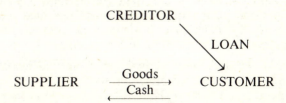

A customer wishes to purchase double glazing but cannot afford cash. The supplier suggests a finance company; although their loan can be spent on anything, because there is a pre-existing arrangement between the creditor and supplier to lend money to potential customers, there is a 'business connection' between them. It is a debtor-creditor-supplier agreement covered by s. 75. This states that a customer having 'any claim against the supplier in respect of a **misrepresentation** or a **breach of contract** shall have a claim against the creditor'. The customer can sue the creditor, supplier or both.

☐   XYZ Co Ltd are installing central heating in Rayne's office. He requires a loan. The company introduce him to a finance company with whom they frequently deal. They lend Rayne £3000. He uses this to pay XYZ Co Ltd. The central heating is noisy and emits obnoxious fumes; it is of unmerchantable quality. Rayne can sue the finance company for XYZ's breach of contract.

This section (s. 75) is wider than s. 56 because in addition to misrepresentation the creditor is liable for any breaches of contract committed by the dealer.

S .75 operates providing four conditions are satisfied:

 (i)   The credit grantor is in the business of granting credit and the credit agreement is made in the course of that business. A loan to a friend would not involve liability.
 (ii)   The cash price of the item being supplied is between £30 and £10 000.
(iii)   The credit is advanced under arrangements between the credit grantor and supplier. If X purchases £800 of double glazing from Z who arranges an £800 loan, the company supplying the loan falls within s. 75. The section is inapplicable if the customer obtains the finance himself and not through the retailer. If X obtained an £800 bank overdraft to purchase the double glazing this does not involve the bank in any liability. A bank is also not liable if it lends money to the double glazing company to finance its operations and the company operates its own credit scheme. The section only applies where suppliers arrange for the credit grantor to directly finance their customers' purchases.
(iv)   The final requirement is that the credit agreement is regulated. Normal trade credit arrangements are not regulated and certain agreements otherwise covered are deemed 'exempt', one of the most important being building society mortgages.

The liability of credit grantor and supplier is joint and several. Where an action lies, the customer (debtor) can sue either or both parties for the whole amount of the claim. The credit grantor cannot contract out of his obligations under s. 56 and s. 75 and any attempt to do so is void.

Credit grantors affected by s. 75 require a licence issued by the Director General of Fair Trading. When giving or revoking licences, he must consider business practices which appear deceitful, or oppressive or otherwise unfair or improper, whether unlawful or not. A notice excluding liability from s. 56 and s. 75 would be an attempt to deceive the consumer which could lead to revocation of the licence.

The effect of these sections is to render the credit grantor liable for certain actions of the supplier. If the former is sued by the customer he can either have the supplier made a party to the proceedings or claim an indemnity from the supplier if he loses. If, however, the supplier has 'vanished' or gone into liquidation the credit grantor will be unable to recover any money.

Enforcement & termination of regulated agreements

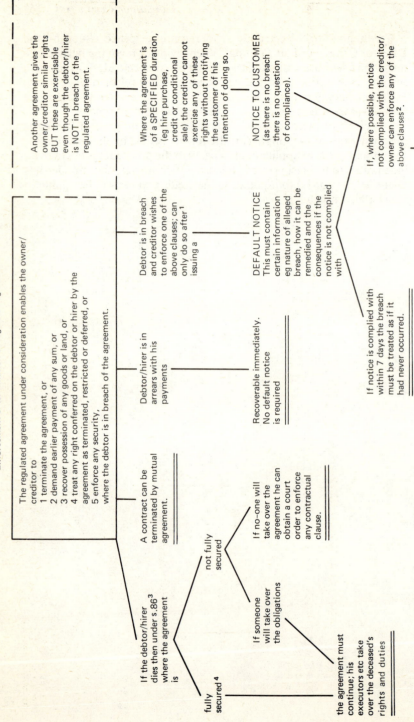

The regulated agreement under consideration enables the owner/creditor to
1 terminate the agreement, or
2 demand earlier payment of any sum, or
3 recover possession of any goods or land, or
4 treat any right conferred on the debtor or hirer by the agreement as terminated, restricted or deferred, or
5 enforce any security, where the debtor is in breach of the agreement.

Another agreement gives the owner/creditor similar rights BUT these are exercisable even though the debtor/hirer is NOT in breach of the regulated agreement.

Where the agreement is of a SPECIFIED duration, (eg hire purchase, credit or conditional sale) the creditor cannot exercise any of these rights without notifying the customer of his intention of doing so.

NOTICE TO CUSTOMER (as there is no breach there is no question of compliance).

If, where possible, notice not complied with the creditor/owner can enforce any of the above clauses[2].

Debtor is in breach and creditor wishes to enforce one of the above clauses; can only do so after[1] issuing a

DEFAULT NOTICE This must contain certain information eg nature of alleged breach, how it can be remedied and the consequences if the notice is not complied with

If notice is complied with within 7 days the breach must be treated as if it had never occurred.

Debtor/hirer is in arrears with his payments

Recoverable immediately. No default notice is required

A contract can be terminated by mutual agreement.

If the debtor/hirer dies then under s.86[3] where the agreement is

not fully secured

fully secured[4]

If no-one will take over the agreement he can obtain a court order to enforce any contractual clause.

If someone will take over the obligations

the agreement must continue; his executors etc take over the deceased's rights and duties

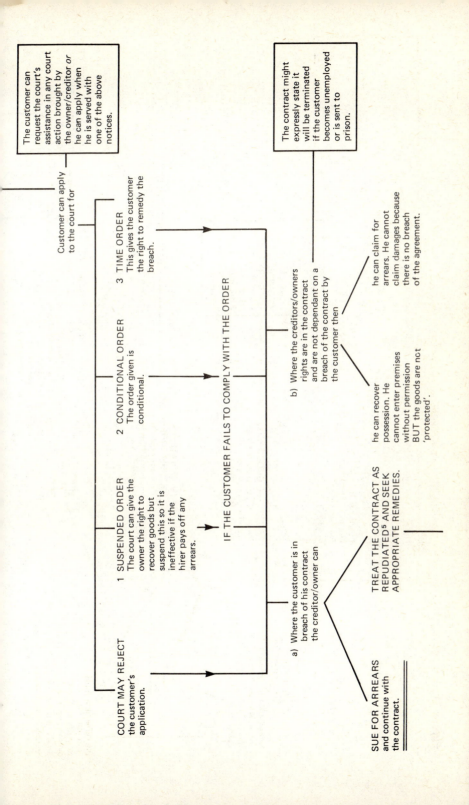

The customer can request the court's assistance in any court action brought by the owner/creditor *or* he can apply when he is served with one of the above notices.

The contract might expressly state it will be terminated if the customer becomes unemployed or is sent to prison.

Customer can apply to the court for

COURT MAY REJECT the customer's application.

1 SUSPENDED ORDER
The court can give the owner the right to recover goods but suspend this so it is ineffective if the hirer pays off any arrears.

2 CONDITIONAL ORDER
The order given is conditional.

3 TIME ORDER
This gives the customer the right to remedy the breach.

IF THE CUSTOMER FAILS TO COMPLY WITH THE ORDER

a) Where the customer is in breach of his contract the creditor/owner can

SUE FOR ARREARS and continue with the contract.

TREAT THE CONTRACT AS REPUDIATED[5] AND SEEK APPROPRIATE REMEDIES.

he can recover possession. He cannot enter premises without permission BUT the goods are not 'protected'.

b) Where the creditors/owners rights are in the contract and are not dependant on a breach of the contract by the customer then

he can claim for arrears. He cannot claim damages because there is no breach of the agreement.

Figure 11 Enforcement and termination of regulated agreements

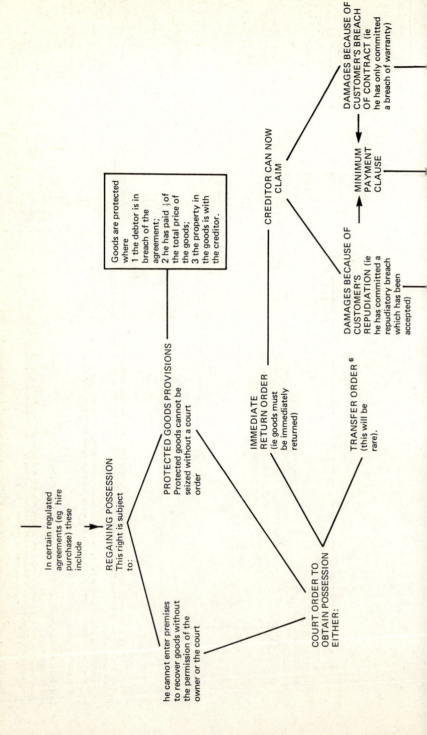

In certain regulated agreements (eg hire purchase) these include

REGAINING POSSESSION
This right is subject to:

he cannot enter premises to recover goods without the permission of the owner or the court

PROTECTED GOODS PROVISIONS
Protected goods cannot be seized without a court order

Goods are protected where
1 the debtor is in breach of the agreement;
2 he has paid ⅓ of the total price of the goods;
3 the property in the goods is with the creditor.

COURT ORDER TO OBTAIN POSSESSION
EITHER:

IMMEDIATE RETURN ORDER
(ie goods must be immediately returned)

TRANSFER ORDER [6]
(this will be rare).

CREDITOR CAN NOW CLAIM

DAMAGES BECAUSE OF CUSTOMER'S REPUDIATION (ie he has committed a repudiatory breach which has been accepted)

DAMAGES BECAUSE OF CUSTOMER'S BREACH OF CONTRACT (ie he has only committed a breach of warranty)

MINIMUM PAYMENT CLAUSE

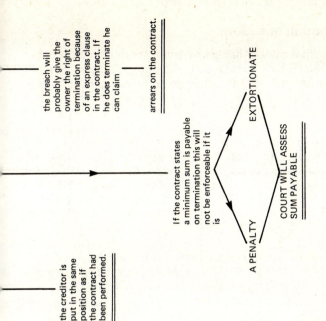

the breach will probably give the owner the right of termination because of an express clause in the contract. If he does terminate he can claim

arrears on the contract.

the creditor is put in the same position as if the contract had been performed.

If the contract states a minimum sum is payable on termination this will not be enforceable if it is

EXTORTIONATE

A PENALTY

COURT WILL ASSESS SUM PAYABLE

1 He does not automatically possess the rights in clauses (1-5); they only arise if expressly stated in the contract. The Act does not confer any rights on the creditor/owner, merely restrains him from pursuing certain remedies.

2 A default notice is not required before the creditor can restrict the debtor's right to draw on any credit, eg if you exceed your credit limit on an Access card the bank can immediately refuse further credit.

3 Subject to certain specified exceptions.

4 The creditor/owner has securities which cover outstanding sums.

5 This is because if it is a serious (repudiatory) breach the law of the contract gives the other party the right to terminate the agreement. In addition most agreements contain an express clause allowing the owner/creditor to terminate in the event of any breach of contract.

6 The court orders the debtor to return part of the goods but allows him to keep the remainder without further payment. The goods must be divisible and the debtor must have paid a minimum sum.

Past examination questions

1 To what extent is a dealer liable to a debtor for mis-statements concerning goods which have subsequently become the subject of a hire-purchase agreement between the debtor and a finance company? What is the legal position of the finance company if the debtor then discovers the goods are faulty?   I A S June 1979

2 Jim, a client of yours, wishes to introduce hire-purchase facilities for customers of his clothes shop.

Explain to him what formalities are necessary for the creation of a valid hire-purchase agreement under the Consumer Credit Act 1974, and what are the financial limits for an agreement to be covered by the Act?

I A S December 1979

Glossary:

Cancellable agreement: a regulated agreement is cancellable if
1   during negotiations oral representations are made **in the presence** of the debtor or hirer by, or on behalf of, the negotiator and
2   the debtor or hirer does not sign the agreement at the place of business of the
a)   creditor or owner, or
b)   negotiator, or
c)   party to a linked transaction (other than the debtor, hirer or their relatives).

Consumer credit agreement: 'A consumer credit agreement is an agreement between an individual (the 'debtor') and any other person (the 'creditor') by which the creditor provides the debtor with credit not exceeding £5000.' (s. 8)

Consumer hire agreement: 'a non-exempt agreement made by a person (the 'owner') with an individual (the 'hirer') for the bailment of goods to the hirer which is
1   not a hire purchase agreement,
2   capable of lasting for more than three months,
3   does not require the hirer to make total payments exceeding £5000

Credit: 'includes a cash loan and any other form of financial accomodation' (s. 9). Examples exclude hire-purchase, conditional sale, credit sales, credit cards, bank overdrafts.

In determining whether the credit exceeds £5000 the court considers the sum lent to the debtor and not the amount repaid.

☐   An accountant obtains a bank loan of £4500 for two years to purchase an £8000 car. As interest rates are high he repays £5500, (£4500 loan + £1000 interest). The transaction is a 'consumer credit agreement' because the credit provided is £4500. The court ignores the cost of the car and the interest repayments.

Debtor-creditor agreements: all consumer credit agreements which are not *debtor-creditor-supplier agreements*.

Debtor-creditor-supplier agreements: This describes those agreements where there is a business connection between the creditor and supplier of goods or services or where they are the same person (ie the seller gives the credit).

Exempt agreements: listed in the act (although the secretary of state may alter the list) these include building society mortgages, credit agreements to finance foreign trade, hire of telephones, gas and electricity meters.

Linked transaction: one which is related to a **regulated** agreement.

Regulated agreement: 'a regulated agreement is a *consumer credit agreement* or a *consumer hire agreement* other than an *exempt agreement*.'

Total charge for credit: the 'true cost' of credit to the debtor including certain secondary transactions he must enter before obtaining the credit.

Section 3

Law of tort

21

Negligence

To successfully sue in negligence the plaintiff must prove:

1 The defendant owed him a duty to take care

To assist understanding, this element will be examined under four headings:

a) *Where the defendant's ACT causes the plaintiff to suffer PHYSICAL damage* (with or without economic loss).

☐ A couple purchased a 999 year lease on a property built on a plateau adjoining a steep slope. During their tenancy a landslide occurred on the adjoining slope (which was owned by the company who built the houses) damaging their garden and reducing the life expectancy of their house to ten years. A negligence action against the company falls within the above category, their act being their failure to examine the stability of the neighbouring land.[1]

Where the defendant's act causes physical damage how does the court decide whether a duty of care is owed? In many instances the facts are similar to decided cases. These are a precedent and must be followed. Thus:

Situation	Duty	Authority	Facts
Does a manufacturer owe a duty of care to the ultimate consumer?	Yes	*Donoghue* v. *Stevenson* (1932)	A manufacturer of ginger beer sold a bottle to a retailer who resold it to X. He gave it to his friend to drink. The bottle contained a decomposed snail − she was ill. She successfully sued the manufacturer.

[1] These are the facts of *Batty* v. *Metropolitan Property Realisations Ltd* (1978).

177

Situation	Duty	Authority	Facts
Does a barrister owe a duty of care to his client when acting for him in court?	No	*Rondel* v. *Worsley* (1969)	
Does the Home Office owe a duty of care to the public in the vicinity of prisons in supervising prisoners?	Yes	*Home Office* v. *Dorset Yacht Co* (1970)	Several borstal boys were camping overnight on Poole Island. A group escaped during the night and stole a boat. The Lords held the Home Office owed a duty of care to the island's inhabitants.
Does a local authority owe a duty of care to householders when inspecting house foundations?	Yes	*Anns* v. *Merton London Borough* (1977)	The plaintiff's flats had been built on inadequate foundations causing them to slope and crack. They claimed the council had been negligent in checking the foundations. It was held that if this were true they would succeed as the council owed them a duty to take care.

Where however no precedent exists the court proceeds in three stages.

1   It applies the neighbour test as expounded by Lord Atkin in *Donoghue* v. *Stevenson*. 'In English law there ... is some general conception of relations giving rise to a duty of care ... The rule ... in law (is that) you must not injure your neighbour; and the lawyer's question, Who is my neighbour? receives a restricted reply. You must take reasonable care to avoid acts or omissions which you can reasonably foresee would be likely to injure your neighbour. Who, then, in law is my neighbour? The answer seems to be – persons who are so closely and directly affected by my act that I ought reasonably to have them in contemplation as being so affected when I am directing my mind to the acts or omissions which are called in question.'

If the plaintiff is not a neighbour as defined above there can be no duty. In *Bourhill* v. *Young* (1945) a pregnant fishwife was descending from a tramcar when it was overtaken by a motor-cyclist. He collided with a car and died. The tramcar obscured her view of the accident but after the body had been removed she saw some blood. She suffered a miscarriage but could not sue the motor cyclist's estate because she was not his neighbour (ie he could not reasonably foresee his action would affect her).

2 If the test produces a positive answer the court presumes the defendant owes the plaintiff a duty to take care. As Lord Reid said, 'the well-known passage in (Donoghue v. Stevenson) ... ought to apply unless there is some justification or valid reason for its exclusion'.

3 The defendant can attempt to rebut the presumption by showing public policy grounds exist which negative the duty of care.

The practical application of the above is seen in the following case.

Saif Ali v. *Sydney Mitchell* (1978)[2]
The plaintiff was a passenger in a car involved in an accident with another car being driven by a Mrs Sugden. The second car was insured by Mr Sugden and because his wife was taking her daughter to school in the car the plaintiff's solicitor, having consulted counsel, advised him to sue Mr Sugden as being vicariously liable. Following this advice the House of Lords decided *Launchberry* v. *Morgans* which allowed the husband to avoid liability. The plaintiff's solicitors consulted the barrister again, suggesting an action be commenced against Mrs Sugden and the driver of the other car. Counsel advised the plaintiff to continue his action against Mr Sugden. By the time it was realized Mr Sugden was not liable, action against the two drivers was statute barred. The plaintiff, therefore, sued the solicitors for professional negligence in the conduct of his claim; they attempted to join the barrister in the action. He resisted on the grounds that he did not owe a duty of care when giving the advice. The House of Lords indicated two public policy reasons existed to explain why a barrister did not owe a duty to take care when conducting court work. These were:

(i) A barrister owes a duty to the court as well as to his client and sometimes these might conflict. Counsel could not deliberately mislead the court on the facts of the law and certain questions which might help his client might remain unasked because of legal etiquette. A barrister conscious of a possible negligence action might be unable to adequately perform his duty to the court.

(ii) If barristers could be sued by clients for negligence this would enable the re-litigation of issues between the client and his original opponent. A convicted criminal could obtain a retrial in a civil court by suing his barrister for negligence. This could involve a re-examination of witnesses, probably several years after the original

[2] Although this case does not refer to physical damage it effectively illustrates the 'public policy' arguments outlined in the preceding passages.

trial, and would necessitate one court commenting on the decision of another.

Having stated the policy reasons for excluding the duty of care whilst conducting a court case, their Lordships considered whether these applied to the provision of pre-trial advice. Where an action was dismissed, or judgment entered without a contested hearing, the majority of their Lordships felt that immunity should not be granted. If the case has never reached the court the barrister is unlikely to find a conflict between his duty to the court and his client and the circumstances are such that re-litigation is impossible, there having been no original litigation.

Where the advice precedes litigation the majority said that immunity would only be granted to advice which was an integral part of the trial. An example was quoted where counsel decides not to call Y as a witness because he believes his client's motive in calling the witness is solely to embarrass his opponent. This decision receives immunity and his client cannot claim this action was negligent. In the current case their Lordships decided by a majority of three to two that the barrister's advice did not attract immunity and so he owed a duty to take care. If he was in breach of this (and the mere fact that his advice was wrong was not proof of carelessness) he would be liable to pay damages in negligence.

In Batty's case the defendants (see footnote[1]) denied owing the plaintiffs a duty of care. They admitted the neighbour test expounded in *Donoghue* v. *Stevenson* (1932) applied but sought its exclusion on policy grounds.

They claimed a builder's duty should not extend to examining land adjoining the building site, or even to considering its effects on their houses, but be restricted to observable defects and possible symptoms of instability on their building site. This was rejected by the court who saw no policy reasons for so limiting the builder's duty. As a secondary defence the builders argued the duty should, again for policy reasons, be limited to defects discoverable without sub-soil investigation. This was also rejected. Damages awarded.

a) *Where public policy reasons exist the duty of care is excluded.* As Winfield says, 'An adult who stands by and watches a child (to whom he stands in no special relationship) drown in a foot of water may have to answer before some higher tribunal somewhere, sometime, but he is not accountable for negligence'

b) *Where the defendant's ACT causes the plaintiff to suffer ECONOMIC loss only.*
In *Spartan Steel & Alloys Ltd* v. *Martin & Co Ltd* (1973), the defendants negligently damaged an electricity cable thereby cutting off power from the plaintiff's factory. The latter claimed £1767

being the profit lost during the shutdown. Their action failed. Where the defendant's action causes economic loss only the courts have held that although the neighbour test may apply, no duty of care should exist for public policy reasons.[3]

c) *Where the defendant's WORDS cause the plaintiff to suffer PHYSICAL damage*, with or without economic loss (ie negligent mis-statement).

Where physical damage is suffered the court follows the same procedure as explained in (a) to decide if a duty of care exists. In *Clay* v. *Crump & Sons* (1963) the defendant architect stated that a wall on a demolition site was safe and could be left standing. It collapsed and injured the plaintiff who recovered damages.

d) *Where the defendant's WORDS cause the plaintiff to suffer ECONOMIC loss* (ie negligent mis-statement).

Although the plaintiff may successfully sue in deceit or misrepresentation this section considers liability for negligent mis-statement. To succeed the plaintiff must prove the defendant owed him a duty to take care when making his statement. The neighbour test produces too wide an area of liability hence, for public policy reasons, the court evolved a different test. Since the Hedley Byrne decision in 1964 the defendant will owe a duty to take care when a '*special relationship*' exists between him and the plaintiff. Although the principle is still being formulated it appears such a relationship exists when the plaintiff seeks advice from the defendant who holds himself out as competent to give this advice (*Hedley Byrne* v. *Heller*)

or,

has a statutory duty to give such advice (*Sharp* v. *Ministry of Housing*)

or,

where a business relationship exists between the parties or the adviser has a financial interest in the matter (*Evatt* v. *Mutual Life Insurance Co*).

> *Arenson* v. *Arenson*, 1975
> The plaintiff owned shares in a company and it was agreed if he left their employment he would sell them to 'A' at a 'fair price' to be determined by the auditors. He left their employment and the auditors valued the shares at £5000. After the sale the plaintiff discovered their value to be nearer £30 000. He successfully sued the auditors for negligence.

Where there is a special relationship the plaintiff may recover damages for purely economic loss unlike the situation in (b).

An accountant negligently advises a client that a business is worth £150 000. After buying it the purchaser discovers its real value is

---

[3] These can be found in *Winfield* v. *Jolowicz* on Tort (11th edition) page 82.

£75 000. He can recover this sum from the accountant in a negligence action.

Ross v. Caunters (1979)

The defendant solicitors drew up a will for a testator and sent it to him for signing. They failed to warn him that a beneficiary or their spouse should not witness it. The testator asked a beneficiary's husband to witness the will. On his death the solicitors discovered the situation and informed the beneficiary that she was not entitled to the gift in the will. She sued them in negligence. In their defence they claimed that the plaintiff could not recover for pure financial loss. The judge considered the authorities since Hedley Byrne and held that damages were recoverable.

Students may find the distinction between economic loss arising from the defendant's negligent act and that arising from his negligent misstatement illogical. This view is shared by several members of the House of Lords!

Situation	Duty	Authority	Facts
Does a banker owe a duty of care when giving credit references?	Yes	*Hedley Byrne Co Ltd* v. *Heller & Partners* (1964)	The plaintiff enquired whether a potential customer was credit worthy. The bank negligently answered yes. Credit was given. The company became bankrupt. The bank would have been liable except that the breach was covered by an exclusion clause.
Does an accountant owe a duty of care when providing information to those contemplating transactions with their employers?	Yes	*Candler* v. *Crane Christmas & Co* (1951)	
Does an estate agent acting for a vendor owe a duty of care to a prospective purchaser?	Yes	*Dodds* v. *Millman* (1964)	
Does a barrister owe a duty to clients when making statements unconnected with litigation?	Yes	*Saif-Ali* v. *Sydney Mitchell* (1978)	

2 The defendant has broken his duty of care

The duty is broken when the defendant fails to act as a reasonable man. Relevant considerations include
a) the likelihood of injury,
b) the seriousness of the injury,
c) the ends to be achieved, and
d) the practicability of prevention.

☐   ⮡Whilst driving home in the early hours of the morning along an isolated country lane, Jackson takes a bend on the wrong side of the road. He has broken his duty of care to other road users because although the chances of an accident are remote the consequences of a collision are likely to be serious.

Paris v. *Stepney BC* (1951)
The plaintiff, a one-eyed garage mechanic, was removing rusty bolts from the underside of a car. There was a risk of rust causing eye injury. The possibility was slight but because of the seriousness of any injury (total blindness) the employers were liable for not ensuring he wore goggles.

Only by balancing these and other factors can the actions of a reasonable man be determined.

Standards expected of the professional person
A person offering their services as an accountant, whether professionally qualified or not, must show the competence associated with a fully qualified accountant and not the reasonable man. If an accountant specializes in one area, such as taxation, he must exhibit a higher level of competence than the average accountant.

The plaintiff must prove the defendant has broken his duty of care. If his evidence raises the inference of negligence then the defendant must prove otherwise or be liable. In some cases the facts themselves raise the inference of negligence; the plaintiff can plead *res ipsa loquitur* (the facts speak for themselves). The court can assume there is negligence and require the defendant to show how the accident could have arisen without his negligence. The court can assume negligence if a barrel falls from an upstairs window or a vehicle mounts the pavement.

Ward v. *Tesco Stores* (1976)
The plaintiff was suing Tesco for negligence after slipping and falling on some yoghurt that had been spilt onto the floor. The issue was whether the customer had to prove Tesco had been careless or whether Tesco had to prove that there had been no want of care on their part. The court quoted Erle CJ in *Scott* v. *London*

and St Katherine Docks Co. 'There must be reasonable evidence of negligence. But where the thing is shown to be under the management of the defendant or his servants, and the accident is such as in the ordinary course of things does not happen if those who have the management use proper care, it affords reasonable evidence, in the absence of explanation by the defendants, that the accident arose from want of care.' Applying it to the facts the court stated that the floor was under the control of the manager (for whom Tesco was vicariously liable.) The accident would not have happened if the floor had been clean and spillages cleared up immediately. The onus was therefore on the defendants to show the accident did not arise from a want of care on their part.

Where res ipsa loquitur applies the burden of proof is transferred. The plaintiff does not have to prove negligence, the defendant must disprove it.

3   Damage

The plaintiff must firstly prove that the damage he suffered was caused by the defendant's breach of duty, ie would not have otherwise occurred.

☐   Wit's secretary has varicose veins and a date has been fixed for an operation. Due to his negligence she is injured which necessitates the identical operation. The damage (ie the operation) would have arisen *without* his negligence. He cannot be successfully sued.

Secondly the damage must be a foreseeable consequence of the wrong-doing otherwise it is irrecoverable, being too remote.

Having proved the case the plaintiff will succeed unless the defendant can establish a defence such as **volenti non fit injuria ('consent')**. This means that 'one who has invited or assented to an act being done towards him cannot, when he suffers from it, complain of it as a wrong.' Although obvious it needs emphasizing that the defence is not required unless a tort has been committed.

☐   Williams accepts a lift from Rees knowing Rees has drunk seven pints of beer. They are stationary when involved in an accident caused solely by Davies' negligence. The reason Williams cannot sue Rees is not because of volenti (which may apply) but because Rees has not committed negligence.

A burglar breaks into Connor's offices and is injured, as stated on page 189. Connor need not plead volenti or any other defence because no tort is committed.

Assuming there is a tort, volenti applies if the defendant can prove:

1 The plaintiff *consented to the legal risk* (ie not to sue if injured). Consent may be **express** (eg one party may agree to an exclusion clause) but this is subject to the Unfair Contract Terms Act 1977. Consent may also be **implied** from the circumstances. This is easily proved in intentional torts (a rugby player consents to batteries committed during the course of a game) but in negligence the facts must indicate the plaintiff consents to a lack of reasonable care on the part of the defendant. It is not enough to show that the plaintiff knew of the risk. Knowledge does not equate with consent. Thus in *Paris* v. *Stepney BC* the mechanic appreciated the risk from rust particles but volenti was still inapplicable. The defence did however succeed in the following case.

ICI v. *Shatwell* (1965)
The plaintiff and his brother, James, were testing detonators and they agreed to disregard the defendant's safety instructions. As a consequence they were injured. He sued his employer as being vicariously liable for James' negligence, but failed: volenti applied because the parties clearly consented to run the risk of injury.

This case also illustrates the second ingredient for volenti.
2 The consent must be *freely given*. Consent is not freely given when the plaintiff feels compelled to act. In Shatwell's case no pressure was exerted on the men to disregard the regulations, the opposite being true. Where however the plaintiff does not possess freedom of choice the defence fails. In *Saif Ali* v. *Mitchell* if, following the crash, one party were trapped in a blazing car and a passer-by were injured attempting a rescue, then volenti would not protect the negligent driver (who owes the rescuer a duty of care because his actions were foreseeable). The rescuer was under a duty to effect the rescue (ie he did not have a choice).

Haynes v. *Harwood* (1935)
The defendant negligently left a horse and van unattended. They bolted in a crowded street. The plaintiff was injured attempting to stop them. Because of the danger to the public his act did not constitute volenti because he had no choice.

If however the public had not been endangered the rescuer would not have been 'compelled' to act. There would have been a choice; if he had intervened he would have consented to the risk.

Cutler v. *United Dairies Ltd* (1933)
The defendant's negligence had resulted in a horse becoming

unsettled in a field. There was no danger to the public but the plaintiff went to the defendant's assistance. As he chose to run the risk volenti applied.

In 'rescue' cases where the rescuer is suing the original wrongdoer, the defendant may also plead the defence of **contributory negligence**. Unlike volenti this is not a complete defence to a negligence action. If the plaintiff is guilty of contributory negligence he still receives damages but these will be reduced. Section 1 of the Law Reform (Contributory Negligence) Act 1945 states that if the *damage* suffered is partly the plaintiff's responsibility his damages will be reduced. Thus a driver who is thrown through his windscreen will have his damages reduced if he is not wearing a seat belt because he contributed to his injuries. (Note: he need not be responsible for the accident.) A similar result occurs if, although wearing a seat belt, he is partly responsible for the accident in which his injuries occur. A stationary motor cyclist who is hit by a car will be guilty of contributory negligence if he suffers head injuries and was not wearing a helmet. His damages will not be reduced if he breaks an arm because wearing a helmet could not have prevented the injury.

Past examination questions

1a)   State and explain the general principles applicable to the tort of negligence.
b)   Albert is walking down a street when, for some unknown reason, a parked car starts to roll down the street and injures him.
Discuss Albert's claim for damages against the owner of the car.

A C A June 1977

2a)   Define the tort of negligence. What must the plaintiff prove in order to succeed in an action for negligence?
b)   The audit of XYZ Ltd's annual accounts was carried out by Smith & Co and on the strength of these accounts Fred lent the company £20 000. It has now been discovered that the accounts contained a serious error and this may cause the company to go into liquidation. Fred believes that he may lose the money he has invested in the company and wonders whether he can sue the auditors. Advise him.

A C A June 1979

22

Occupiers liability

The occupier of premises has certain obligations regarding their condition. The nature of these obligations depends on whether the person on the premises is a trespasser or a visitor.

☐ William Connor is starting his own accountancy practice. He rents offices from the local council. He cannot afford full-time secretarial assistance but his wife works from 9.15 am – 12.15 pm whilst Terry, their four year old son, is at a playgroup. Their eighteen year old daughter, Simone, works for her father and is taking her first professional examinations in June.

1 Visitors

Under s. 2 of the Occupiers Liability Act 1957 (to which all references apply unless otherwise indicated) the occupier owes a **common duty of care** to all visitors. This means taking such care as *in all the circumstances* is reasonable to ensure the visitor is reasonably safe in using the premises for the purposes for which he is entitled to be there.

Who, under the act, is the occupier? The occupier is the person with 'control' over the premises and can be the owner, tenant, or both. In our example Connor is the occupier.

A visitor is usually someone invited onto the premises but the Act also applies to strangers entering as a result of a contract between the occupier and a third party and to parties permitted by the law to be there.

☐ The local authority permit the Certified Accountants to use Plymouth College as an examining centre. Simone is a stranger to this contract but when she arrives for her examination she is a 'visitor' to the college.

An occupier discharges his duty by ensuring the visitor is reasonably safe in all the circumstances. The relevant circumstances 'include the degree of care, and want of care, which would ordinarily be looked for in such a visitor, so that in proper cases an occupier must be prepared for children to be less careful than adults' (s. 2(3)). Making all property safe for unaccompanied child visitors would place an

187

intolerable burden on occupiers, transferring to them the parental obligation of looking after children's safety. To avoid this situation, where a 'reasonable parent' would accompany the child the occupier discharges his duty providing the property is reasonably safe for a child accompanied by an adult.

☐   There is some waste ground near William's practice on which children are permitted to play football. Terry is in the office being a nuisance and William allows him to play, unaccompanied, on the waste ground. He is injured by a danger which would have been apparent to an eight year old. As the site is reasonably safe for eight year olds the occupier is not liable. He can assume four year olds will be accompanied by a parent to whom the danger would be obvious.

Phipps v. *Rochester Corporation* (1955)
The plaintiff, aged five, was picking blackberries on a building site with his seven year old sister. He fell into a trench, breaking his leg. The danger would have been apparent to an adult and as a reasonable parent would have accompanied the child the defendants avoided liability.

☐   The playgroup premises which Terry attends has a large unfenced pond in the garden. Terry wanders unsupervised into the garden, falls into the pond and is badly injured. When his mother arrives at 12.15 she is thinking about the menu for a dinner party. She falls into the pond. She cannot sue − the property was reasonably safe for an adult. Terry can successfully sue because he is expected to be alone and four year old children do not appreciate the dangers of water. The property is not reasonably safe.

Another relevant circumstance specified is that 'an occupier may expect that a person, in the exercise of his calling, will appreciate and guard against any special risks ordinarily incident to it, so far as the occupier leaves him free to do so.'

☐   There is an electrical fault in Connor's office. He calls in the electricity board. Whilst investigating the problem an electrician electrocutes himself. The premises are not safe but there is no cause of action. As Lord Denning said in *Roles* v. *Nathan* (1963), 'when a householder calls in a specialist to deal with a defective installation on his premises, he can reasonably expect the specialist to appreciate and guard against the dangers arising from the defect.'

The occupier can discharge his duty although his premises are unsafe where:

(i) He warns the visitor of the dangers providing this enables the visitor to be reasonably safe. A notice at the top of some stairs stating 'these are dangerous' would only discharge his obligations if a safe exit existed.

☐ A notice at Terry's playgroup states, 'the bannisters are loose, do not use'. The occupier remains liable because four year olds cannot read. The notice does not enable them to be reasonably safe.

(ii) The danger was created by an independent contractor's negligence providing the occupier acted reasonably in entrusting the work to an independent contractor and acted reasonably to satisfy himself that the contractor was competent and had properly performed the work.

☐ William employs a local cleaning contractor for his offices. In January after a heavy snowfall he asks one of their staff to clear his office forecourt. She does this by throwing hot water over it. This freezes and a client slips over. Connor is liable because he failed to take reasonable steps (ie look at the forecourt) to ensure the task was properly performed.

Where skilled technical work is involved the occupier need only conduct superficial checks: if he chooses a competent independent contractor he can probably avoid liability.

Under the Unfair Contract Terms Act (1977) the occupier of *business* premises cannot exclude his liability for any breach of the Act causing death or personal injury. Where the exclusion relates to other damage or loss it is valid if reasonable.

2 Trespassers

The 1957 Act does not extend to trespassers but the occupier does owe them a duty. He must act as a conscientious and humane person in all the circumstances. These include:

could the trespass be foreseen?
the nature of the likely trespasser (adult, child, thief, etc);
the likelihood and gravity of injury;
the cost of making the property reasonably safe;
the occupier's resources.

☐ The playgroup leader knows young children climb through a hole in her hedge in order to play on swings near the dangerous lake. If a child trespasser is injured the occupier is liable because a conscientious person would have repaired the fence. Connor's offices include a room with rotten floorboards. It is kept locked. One night a thief breaks into his offices and enters this room. He falls through the floorboards. He is owed a duty (although a thief and a trespasser) but this has been, in the circumstances, discharged.

Herrington v. *British Railways Board* (1972)
The defendants knew that children played on their railway line, gaining access through a hole in the fence. They failed to repair it. Three months later Herrington was injured playing on the line. Because they possessed adequate resources to mend the fence their failure to act rendered them liable.

Past examination questions

1   (i) Discuss the responsibilities of an occupier of premises for the safety of persons on the premises:
   a) lawfully, and
   b) as trespassers.
   (ii) Plaschem Ltd owns and manages a chemical works which adjoins a housing estate. Although the company has improved the fencing around the plant and erected warning notices, the staff still find that children manage to get into the works. Recently, two children aged 7 and 15, who had managed to climb over the fence, fell into a waste pit and were badly injured. The parents of the children are now threatening to sue the company.
Advise Plaschem Ltd.   A C A December 1979

23

Defamation

Defamation has been defined as,

> 'the publication of a false statement which tends to lower a person in the estimation of right-thinking members of society generally; or which tends to make them shun or avoid that person.'

It can be permanent, eg in writing, when it is a libel or it can be published in a transient form, eg speech when it is a slander. The distinction can be important; a person libelled can sue automatically but if slandered he or she can, as a general rule, sue only if he or she has suffered *special damage*. This involves proving that the defamation caused him or her to suffer financial loss. This could be loss of employment or even the loss of a friend's hospitality. In four circumstances however (itemized below), the court assumes the plaintiff has suffered such damage; the slander becomes actionable per se. Damage is presumed when the slander is so obviously damaging to the plaintiff's financial position that pecuniary loss is almost certain, or so intrinsically outrageous that the slander ought to be actionable even if no pecuniary loss results. An example of the first would be 'words calculated to disparage the plaintiff in any office, profession, calling, trade or business held or carried on by him at the time of the publication.' (s. 2 Defamation Act 1952). An example of the second would be an imputation that the plaintiff is suffering from a socially unacceptable disease.[1]

☐ During a luncheon, a group of businessmen discuss their accountant (Gerald Rope) and their solicitor (Thomas Wist). Amongst the comments made are:
'Rope is a crushing bore.'
'Rope cannot add two and two together.'
'Rope had an affair with his ex-secretary.'
'Wist is a good advertiser.'

[1] The two other occasions a slander is actionable per se are
a) an imputation that the plaintiff has committed a criminal offence punishable by imprisonment, and
b) an imputation of unchastity or adultery to any female.

The second slanderous statement is actionable per se because it suggests Rope is an incompetent accountant but in the other situations special damage must be proved. In addition the plaintiff must prove:

1   The statement is untrue
If Rope committed adultery with his ex-secretary, albeit ten years ago, he cannot sue. The comment may be morally unfair and his wife may leave him. Rope possesses no legal remedy.

2   The statement must be defamatory
Rope cannot sue because he is called a 'crushing bore'. It is mere abuse and does not affect his reputation. If however he had not committed adultery he has been defamed. The words are defamatory 'in their ordinary meaning.'

Sometimes words may appear innocent but because of facts known to certain individuals they possess a secondary meaning, there is an 'innuendo', which is defamatory. Thus the comment 'Wist is a good advertiser' appears innocent but to those who know he is a solicitor it implies he is guilty of malpractice because he is advertising for clients. He has been defamed.

> *Tolley* v. *Fry* (1931)
> The plaintiff, a famous amateur golfer, appeared in a Fry's advert. He had not consented to this. He claimed the advert implied he had accepted money from Fry thereby prostituting his amateur status. He was successful.

3   The statement must refer to the plaintiff
This is satisfied if the plaintiff is described in sufficient detail to be identifiable. A defamatory comment about a female politician who 'sounds as if she ought to be in the business of restoring cottage roofs' would allow Mrs Thatcher to sue.

Where a class is defamed. All 'solicitors are dishonest,' no one member may sue unless the class is so small the statement may be regarded as defamatory of each member. All the partners in Dolittle, Plunder and Grabbit are dishonest would be considered defamatory of each partner.

4   Publication
Publication is a technical legal term. It consists of communicating the defamatory statement to one person other than the party defamed or the maker's spouse.

☐   Dolittle sends a letter to Grabbit which wrongly accuses him of incompetence and dishonesty. If Grabbit opens the letter and reads it no action lies because the statement remains unpublished.

Grabbit, like most businessmen, does not open his own mail. This is performed by his secretary. She therefore reads the defamatory statements.

Does this constitute publication? Dolittle will claim it does not as the letter was addressed to her employer. Grabbit would claim his secretary read the accusations which lowered him in her estimation. The damage is done.

The law sympathises with both arguments and steers a middle course. It adopts the following test: 'Was the secretary's conduct unusual, out of the ordinary and not reasonably to be anticipated or was her action foreseeable?' If it was foreseeable the defendant ought to have realized she would open the letter. The court therefore holds that he intended her to read it and the libel has been published. If, however, her action was unforeseeable no publication occurs and the plaintiff has no claim.

Theaker v. *Richardson* (1962)
A letter was addressed to the plaintiff but her husband opened it; normally such an action is unforeseeable. On this occasion the envelope was not marked 'private', not stamped, it was brown and resembled election addresses currently being delivered. Under these circumstances the defendant should have anticipated that the husband might open the letter. The defamation was published.

The moral is clear. To avoid publication of a libellous statement to a secretary the sender must indicate, by using appropriate words, that the envelope is only to be opened by the addressee. If she opens it her action is unforeseeable and the sender will not be responsible. Defamatory statements should not be sent on a postcard because it is known that postmen read postcards!

In the above situation Dolittle will almost certainly have communicated the defamation to his secretary. Most businesspeople do not write letters themselves; they dictate them to secretaries to type. The secretary sees the libel. Does this constitute publication? As the defendant clearly intends to publish the statement to his secretary the answer must be yes.

He has defamed the plaintiff and the three ingredients, defamatory statement, reference to the plaintiff and publication, are all present. The defendant can only escape liability by successfully pleading one of the defences.

Defences

The only one applicable to Dolittle would be:

a) Qualified privilege
If a communication between A and B falls under the umbrella of

qualified privilege the law ignores it when deciding if the statement was published. If I dictate a defamatory letter to my secretary which is sent to the plaintiff the only relevant person regarding publication is my secretary. If that communication is covered by qualified privilege the plaintiff's action will fail for lack of publication.

In *Adam* v. *Ward* (1917) it was stated that qualified privilege arises on an occasion where 'the person who makes the communication has an interest (to protect) or a duty, legal, social or moral, to make it to the person to whom it is made *and* the person to whom it is so made has a corresponding interest (to protect) or duty to receive it. This reciprocity is essential.'

In what circumstances are communications between an employer and his secretary privileged? A secretary is under a duty to take the letter down and type it, but this fact alone is insufficient to raise the defence of qualified privilege.

Communications between employer and secretary only attract qualified privilege on the following occasions. Firstly, where the employer has a duty to send the letter. If I am asked for a reference regarding an employee I have a duty to provide it. The occasion is covered by qualified privilege; getting the letter written prior to despatch is also covered 'if under current business practice the reasonable and ordinary way of getting it written is to dictate it to a typist.'

Secondly, the defence exists where the defendant has an 'interest to protect' and the letter is dictated as part of the process of protecting that interest. The word 'interest' has a technical meaning; it must be the type of interest the law recognizes as meriting protection. A shareholder has a legitimate interest to protect if he or she believes company funds are being misappropriated by the managing director. A letter setting forth this belief is protected if sent to the appropriate body (which must have an interest or duty to receive that communication). A client who believes the solicitor is negligently dealing with his or her affairs has an interest to protect and a letter of complaint despatched to the Law Society is protected by qualified privilege. If getting the letter typed is reasonable (see above), the communication to the secretary is covered by the qualified privilege attaching to the letter.

In both cases the dictation is not directly covered by qualified privilege. That protects the letter written by the employer to another employer (if a reference), or the Council of the Stock Exchange (if a complaint about a managing director), or the Law Society (if about a solicitor). As the typing of the letter was necessary the original privilege attaches to the communication between employer and secretary.

☐   A client discovers Reedy, a partner in Dolittle, Plunder and Grabbit, is dishonest. Qualified privilege attaches to letters sent to the police, the professional body, the partners, but not to Reedy's wife or friends. The client has no 'interest' or 'duty' to communicate it to them.

Watt v. *Longsdon* (1930)
The defendant received a letter accusing the plaintiff of dishonesty and immoral conduct. The former showed it to their
employer and the plaintiff's wife. It was held he was under a duty
to communicate the information to his employer but not to the
wife. Only the former communication was covered by qualified
privilege.

Qualified privilege is lost if the maker is motivated by malice. This
occurs unless he or she honestly believes his or her statement to be true.
Other occasions attracting qualified privilege are:

a) communications between a solicitor and client (subject to the exception below);
b) fair and accurate reports of Parliamentary proceedings;
c) reports of judicial proceedings;
d) reports of public meetings.

b) Absolute privilege
In certain situations it is essential an individual can express opinions
without fear of legal action. Where the defence of absolute privilege
applies it is *impossible* to sue the maker of the statement no matter
how irresponsible or malicious the comments may be. Absolute
privilege covers:

a) statements made in Parliament;
b) communications between high ranking officers of state;
c) statements made during the course of judicial proceedings;
d) communications between solicitor and client relating to litigation.

c) Justification
As a defamatory statement must be untrue, if the maker can justify
his comments he escapes liability. He need not prove it was true in
every detail, it is sufficient if the 'gist' of the statement was accurate.

☐ If a newspaper reports that Wist was struck off by the Law
Society for misconduct on 5 January the defence applies if he was
struck off on the 12.

d) Fair comment
Individuals will wish to comment on matters of public interest and
because comments involve personal opinions which are often incapable of being proved right or wrong, this defence evolved. It applies
when there is a fact which is of public interest (thereby justifying
public comment) providing the maker believes his or her comments

are true (ie he or she is not motivated by malice).

☐   A well-known Labour politician who supports comprehensive schools sends his son and daughter to exclusive public schools. A newspaper article reported this and commented that it proved the politician was unfit for high office because he lacked integrity. Providing the fact (sending the children to public school) is correct the defence is applicable.

e) *Unintentional defamation*
Under s. 4 of the Defamation Act 1952 a printer or publisher of a defamatory article can escape liability if he publishes an apology and proves the statement was not
(i) intended to refer to the plaintiff, *or* obviously defamatory and he was unaware of any circumstances that rendered it so,
and
(ii) he took reasonable care in publishing the statement

☐   In an article defamatory comments are made about a fictitious accountant, Gerald Rope. Unknown to the publisher there is a Gerald Rope who is an accounts' clerk living in West Hartlepool. One of his friends reads the article and believes Rope is being referred to. The article is defamatory but providing the journal publishes an apology in its next issue it avoids liability.

Past examination questions

1a) What is defamation?
b) When is slander actionable without proof of loss?
c) What defences are available in an action for defamation?

C A May 1980

24

Trespass

This can be to the person, their land or their goods.

1 Trespass to the person

The three forms of trespass to the person are:

a) Battery

To successfully sue, the plaintiff must prove the defendant intentionally (or possibly negligently) performs an act which directly and physically affects him or her.

☐ TAS Ltd (Tax Avoidance Specialists) are being investigated by the Inland Revenue. Several incriminating documents, including diaries, are in a competitor's office. TAS wish to recover these but, afraid their competitor will realize their importance and hand them over to the authorities, arrange for them to be stolen. Because the office block has a sophisticated burglar alarm the theft must be during office hours. The 'recovery' team enter the offices just before lunch time. To avoid conflict they order the staff to sit and a hand is placed on the shoulders of one of the secretaries. She sits immediately. Nethercott, the office manager, protests and is struck by an intruder.

Nethercott and the secretary can sue in battery. They were the victims of intentional and direct application of force (touching someone constitutes 'force' in battery) and although the secretary did not suffer damage, battery is actionable 'per se'.

The usual tortious defences apply such as self defence, necessity and volenti non fit injuria (consent). Volenti non fit injuria (consent) is the most important; many batteries can be negatived by the express or implied consent of the other party. A commuter on London Transport impliedly consents to being jostled on the escalators or when entering a tube train during the rush hour.

b) Assault

This is an act which causes the plaintiff to believe he is about to suffer a battery.

☐   In the above situation, to frighten the staff one intruder carries an unloaded gun which he points at them.

As they believe the gun is loaded it is reasonable for the staff to fear the commission of a battery (ie one of them being shot), hence there is an assault. It is immaterial that there is no battery (ie nobody is shot) as the two torts stand alone. It therefore follows that assault is actionable 'per se'. If, when pointing the gun, the intruder said, 'I will fire the gun if anyone moves' it might be argued that this removes the fear of battery and negatives the assault. In the above it is unlikely but such a situation arose in *Turbervell* v. *Savage* (1669) where the defendant reached for his sword and said, 'If it were not assize time I would not take such language from you.' Since it was assize time the words clearly indicated he would not commit the battery, therefore there could be no assault. Words can negative an assault but, whilst the authorities conflict, words on their own probably cannot constitute an assault.

As with battery, the usual tortious defences apply.

c) *False imprisonment*
This arises when the defendant intentionally (or possibly negligently) imposes a total restraint on the plaintiff's liberty without lawful justification.

☐   Whilst in the office one of the intruders stands by the door. When they leave, to avoid the alarm being given, they disconnect the telephones and lock the door. Although there is a fire escape this is considered dangerous, quotes already having been obtained for its repair. When leaving the building in which the office is situated the front door is padlocked. The police open this before the other office workers realize they have been locked in.

The intruders have committed three acts of false imprisonment. When one of them stands by the door there is an implied threat that anybody attempting to leave will be stopped. This effectively 'imprisons' the staff within their office as does the locking of the door. The restraint on liberty must however be total hence if a reasonable means of escape exists there can be no false imprisonment.

Bird v. *Jones* (1845)
The defendants wrongfully fenced off part of a footpath. The plaintiff who was on the footpath was not allowed to continue along it although he was free to leave in the opposite direction. The restraint was not total, there was no false imprisonment.

The alternative route must be reasonable. As using the fire escape involves a risk of injury there was a total restraint of the office staff, there being no reasonable alternative exit. The staff in the remainder of the building were also falsely imprisoned when the front door was padlocked; knowledge is not an essential ingredient in false imprisonment.

> *Meering* v. *Grahame-White Aviation Co Ltd* (1919)
> The plaintiff was in a room being questioned about certain thefts. Unknown to him two works policemen were outside the room with instructions to restrain him if he attempted to leave. He successfully sued for false imprisonment.

As with other forms of trespass to the person, false imprisonment is actionable per se.

2 Trespass to land

This involves a direct and forcible interference with another's possession of land without lawful justification. The tort must be committed intentionally. This is satisfied if the defendant intends to enter onto the land. He need not intend to trespass; he may believe his entry is justified. Ignorance is no defence in trespass. The plaintiff is the person in possession of land such as the owner/occupier or a lessee. In the above scenario assuming the office is leased the lessee can sue and not the absentee owner. No physical damage need be caused as trespass is actionable per se.

Trespass to land can be committed in several ways. If the intruders forced an entry into the offices they are *entering without lawful justification* (such as the occupier's permission). They would also be trespassing if they obtained entry by deception and then *abused their right of entry*. This would arise if they obtained permission to enter the office by posing as potential clients but after obtaining entry disclosed their true intent. If a TAS director visited the office to discuss the return of the documents but became abusive when he discovered they had been handed over to the Inland Revenue and then refused to leave when asked, he commits a trespass. He has *remained on land* although his permission to stay has been withdrawn.

If the intruders left listening devices on the premises to monitor conversations between the police and the staff the trespass is committed by *placing an object on land*. Unlike the other types of trespass to land this is a continuing trespass which permits successive actions until the object is removed. Having been awarded damages the plaintiff can recommence proceedings until the object is removed.

3 Trespass to goods

A person interfering with another's goods may commit several torts, one being trespass to goods. This is a wrongful physical interference with the possession of the plaintiff's goods. As with all trespasses the interference must be direct and is actionable per se.

☐   Sid Lick, anxious to impress his new girl-friend, 'borrows' Johnson's new Mercedes without informing him. He intends to return it later that evening. He takes his girl-friend to a 'sleazy club', parking the car outside. X and Y, two young vandals, scratch the car and steal the tyres. All three have committed the tort of trespass. They have, in the case of Lick and Y, taken the goods out of Johnson's possession and X has damaged the car.

Johnson's action is for damages and although the usual tortious defences are available to the defendants none apply here.

Past examination questions

1 Explain the different forms that the tort of trespass may take.
A C A December 1976
2 What do you understand by the tort of 'Trespass to the Person'? Explain the various forms it may take.   A C A December 1978

25

Nuisance

Private nuisance

Private nuisance is an unlawful, indirect interference with a person's use or enjoyment of land or of some right over or in connection with it (ie a servitude). An example of the latter would be an interference with the use of a private right of way, a right to light or a right to support.

The most common type of private nuisance is, however, the interference with a person's enjoyment of land by smells, smoke, gas, heat, vibrations, noise etc. Where the interference affects *enjoyment* of land the court has a dilemma. D's use of his land restricts P's use of his land, but to enable P to 'enjoy' his land involves restricting D. Both parties cannot therefore 'enjoy' their land. To achieve a balance between a landowner's right to use his property without restriction with his neighbour's right to be free from interference, the court utilizes the concept of reasonableness. The court asks itself the question, 'is it reasonable for the plaintiff to have to put up with this interference?'

Whether D's use of land is reasonable depends on all the circumstances but relevant considerations include:

The locality: a noisy factory in an industrial area may constitute a reasonable use of land whereas the same noise level would be unreasonable in a country village.

The duration: a person may be expected to tolerate an interference of short duration although this depends on the seriousness of the interference.

The cost of eliminating the nuisance: a minor interference of short duration might be unreasonable if the cost of prevention is minimal. The failure to keep the interference to a minimum being unreasonable.

The defendant's motive: a reasonable act may become unreasonable if the defendant is motivated by malice[1].

[1]*Christie* v. *Davey* (1893). The parties lived in semi-detached houses in Brixton. The plaintiff taught music and the noise of pupils practising annoyed the defendant who retaliated by beating trays and rapping walls. He was liable in private nuisance but as the judge said, 'if what had taken place had occurred between two sets of persons both perfectly innocent, I should have taken an entirely different view of the case.'

The plaintiff's use of land: the court ignores any especially 'sensitive' use for which he uses his land in assessing the seriousness of the interference[2].

☐   A consortium of London businessmen purchase a large estate in Cornwall. Most of the estate is farmed by a tenant farmer but part contains a development of holiday chalets which they sell. The consortium obtains planning permission and sells 50 acres to a developer to construct 150 'executive' houses.

Where the gas, smoke, vibrations etc interfere with the plaintiff's use of his land by causing *physical* damage to his property the court, in assessing liability, ignores the locality. (See chart opposite.)

☐   The farmer sprays his crops with an insecticide. This drifts onto a neighbour's property seriously damaging his rosebushes. Although spraying is reasonable in that locality because there is physical damage to the rose bushes (which is not a sensitive use of land) the farmer is liable.

St Helen's Smelting Co v. *Tipping* (1865)
The plaintiff purchased a large estate near the defendant's smelting works. Vapours from the works caused physical damage to the shrubs and trees. The defendants were liable although the area was an industrial one.

Who is liable?
1   *The creator*   He is always liable.
2   *The landlord*   He is liable if he authorizes the commission of the nuisance. This includes letting the property for a purpose which he knows will be a nuisance.

☐   The consortium lease part of the estate near the holiday chalets to an organisation for the sole purpose of erecting a permanent funfair. Because of the locality this must be a nuisance. They are liable.

3   *The person in possession of the land*   He is liable for nuisances created by
a)   his servants,
b)   a trespasser, providing he knew, or ought to have known of the nuisance and failed to take *reasonable* steps to eliminate it.

Page Motors Ltd v. *Epsom and Ewell BC* (1980)
The defendants granted the plaintiffs a business lease on part of

---

[2]*Robinson* v. *Kilvert* (1889). The plaintiff's brown paper, which was especially sensitive to heat, was damaged when stored above a heated cellar. This was at a temperature that would have been harmless to most goods, hence his action failed.

	Facts	Complainant	Complaint	Reasonable use of defendant's land	Reason	Authority
1	The pig sheds are sited near the housing development	Owners of the houses	smell	√	locality	
2	Combine harvesters work for two weeks in September from 6.30 am to 9.00 pm	Owners of the houses	noise level	√	locality and short duration	
3	A pig herd is moved across the estate to a site adjacent to the housing development following a dispute between the farmer and the builder	Owners of the houses	smell	X	although locality reasonable the farmer is motivated by malice	*Christie* v. *Davey*[1]
4	The farmer refuses to instal a filter costing £500 to reduce the smell emanating from the battery hen house	Owners of the houses	smell	X	cost of prevention minimal	
5	Owners of holiday chalets cannot let them because of the smell from the pigs	Owners of chalets	smell	?	the reasonableness of the locality must be balanced against the seriousness of the injury	
6	Farm equipment is being repaired during the day	House owner who is on nightwork and cannot sleep during the day	noise	√	sensitive nature of user of land	*Robinson* v. *Kilvert*[2]

an estate in 1974. Gipsies occupied another part of the estate and their numbers escalated to 74 by 1977. Their behaviour, burning of tyres etc and their failure to control their dogs resulted in the plaintiffs losing business. Although the gipsies' occupation was unauthorized (ie they were trespassers) the council were sued because they failed to take *reasonable steps* to eliminate the nuisance ie set up another site for gipsies. The judge held that the council should have found an alternative site within two years (ie by 1975) and awarded the plaintiffs damages for losses incurred between 1975 and 1978.

c) process of nature if he fails to take *reasonable* steps to eliminate the nuisance. In *Leakey* v. *National Trust* (1980) soil and tree stumps had, as a result of an extremely dry summer, fallen from the defendant's land onto the plaintiff's land. The latter sued in nuisance. The court stated that an owner of land must take reasonable steps to prevent anything on his land causing damage to his neighbour's land. Given the resources of the Trust and the nature of the work involved their failure to act was unreasonable. They were liable in nuisance.

Who can sue?

Only the person in possession of land can sue. This includes a tenant or owner/occupier but not their spouse, children or lodger. A reversioner (ie a person entitled to possession at a future date) may sue where the nuisance affects his interest in the land, perhaps by creating permanent damage.

Defences

☐   The owners of some newly built houses object to the smells from a nearby riding stables. Because the area is designated for housing it is held that the keeping of horses is an unreasonable use of land. It is no defence to prove

a) the *plaintiff moved* to the nuisance,
or
b) that all *reasonable care* had been taken to reduce the smell,
or
c) that the *public benefited*, this being the only riding school in the neighbourhood.

The defences to an action in private nuisance include:

a) *Twenty years prescription*
If *this* plaintiff has accepted the nuisance for 20 years he cannot successfully sue.

☐ The riding stables have existed for over 20 years and nobody has previously complained. Until the houses were built there was no nuisance. The house owners could not have accepted the nuisance for 20 years. They can sue.

The period runs from the day the act became a nuisance for *this* plaintiff.

b) *Statutory authority*
Where a statute imposes a duty on the defendant to act and his actions must *inevitably* produce a nuisance the defence applies. If however the act can be performed without committing a nuisance the defence is inapplicable.

☐ The local authority are authorized by statute to build an incinerator adjoining the consortium's chalet complex. The incinerator is badly designed and belches forth smoke. There is an actionable nuisance and the defence of statutory authority is inapplicable

c) *Volenti non fit injuria* (see page 184)

Remedies

The remedy sought is usually an injunction to stop the nuisance although damages may be claimed for the losses incurred.

Public nuisance

Although bearing little resemblance to private nuisance they are considered together in view of examination requirements. Public nuisance is 'an act or omission which materially affects the reasonable comfort and convenience of life of a *class* of Her Majesty's subjects.' The offending act or omission must affect several people and not merely one individual as in private nuisance. Examples include obstruction of a public highway and selling impure food. Unlike private nuisance it is a crime and the Attorney-General may prosecute the wrongdoer or seek an injunction.

An individual may however sue in tort where he suffers a special loss above that suffered by the general public. This could involve personal injury, damage to property or loss of business profits. A blocked highway obstructs the public's right of way but if the obstruction blocks a shop entrance the retailer suffers a special loss (fewer customers) and can commence an action in public nuisance.

In *Halsey* v. *Esso Petroleum Co Ltd* (1961) dirt from the defendant's chimney damaged the clothes on the plaintiff's washing line and his car which was parked in the street.

Complaint	Tort	Explanation
damaged clothes on washing line	private nuisance	unreasonable interference with plaintiff's use of his land: locality irrelevant because there was physical damage.
car damaged	public nuisance	1 there can be no private nuisance because the damage occurred outside the plaintiff's property. 2 the plaintiff suffers a special loss (ie damage to his car) above the inconvenience suffered by the other road users.

Past examination questions

1 a) Distinguish between the torts of trespass and nuisance.
   b) Give one example each of a public nuisance and a private nuisance.
   c) Bill's garden is overrun with weeds, with the result that they spread into his neighbour Dorothy's garden. After Dorothy complains, Bill, in a fit of temper, throws his weeds over the fence into Dorothy's garden. Discuss Bill's liability for his action and Dorothy's remedies.   C A October 1979

26

Vicarious liability

Vicarious liability involves one party being responsible for the torts of another. The most common illustration today is insurance, the insurer being financially responsible for certain acts of the insured. Whilst there are numerous examples of vicarious liability, the most important for students is that which renders an employer liable for an employee's wrongful acts committed during the course of employment. A plaintiff wishing to sue the employer for a tort committed by an employee must therefore prove:

1   The wrongful act was committed by his *employee*.
    The law distinguishes employees from independent contractors. In most situations the status of the staff is obvious but the courts have found it impossible to formulate one working definition. For our purposes an employee is part of the employer's organization, operating under a contract of service as distinct from a contract for services. An employee can be told how to do the job whereas an independent contractor can only be told what to do (but not how to do it).

☐   Barl Enterprises engage Dolittle, Plunder and Grabbit as their accountants. They instruct one of their staff, George Reedy, to service the account. George's sister-in-law, Celia Rafty, is the financial director of Contours Ltd. She is responsible for the accounting procedures in the individual travel agents. Because of the travel involved she possesses a company car.
    Whilst discussing the accounts with the partners at Barl Enterprises Reedy carelessly knocks over a cup of coffee. It scalds one of Barl's staff. She can sue Reedy or Dolittle's (he is their employee) but not Barl Enterprises because Reedy is an independent contractor.

2   The wrongful act must be committed in the *course of employment*. Providing the employee is doing what he or she is employed to do, albeit mistakenly or carelessly, the employer is liable. Because the latter is insured the courts, in borderline cases, are likely to decide the act was within the course of employment.

□⁴ Rafty is visiting one of Contour's travel agents and due to her carelessness, is involved in a road accident. Contours are vicariously liable because although Rafty is employed as an accountant she is authorized to drive a car during her employment.

Century Insurance Co v. *Northern Ireland Road Transport Board* (1942)
The defendant's employee, a petrol tank driver, delivered petrol to a garage. Whilst watching it being pumped from his tanker he lit a cigarette. He threw away the lighted match. There was an explosion. His job involved supervising the transfer of the petrol. He was performing this task negligently. The employer was liable.

A criminal act may also be within the course of employment although performed purely for the wrongdoer's benefit.

□ Barl Enterprises' accounts are incomplete when Dolittles are appointed. To avoid further problems they suggest incoming cheques are made payable to them so detailed records can be kept. Reedy receives the cheques but endorses them to himself and vanishes with the proceeds. Dolittle are liable to make good Barl's losses.

Lloyd v. *Grace Smith & Co* (1912)
The defendant solicitor's managing clerk was allowed to work unsupervised when conveyancing. He advised the plaintiff to sell certain property and persuaded her to sign it over to him. He sold it, retaining the proceeds. The solicitors were liable because the clerk was performing his job, conveyancing, although in an illegal manner.

Where however the act is outside the course of employment — the employee is on a 'frolic of his own' — the employer is not liable.

□ Rafty drives her company car to a nightclub one Saturday. She has too much to drink and causes an accident driving home. Although using her company car she is not engaged in company business. They are not liable.

A prohibited act may fall either within or outside the employee's course of employment depending on the type of prohibition. If it *limits* the *scope* of employment by defining a person's job then prohibited acts fall outside the course of employment. If Rafty is prohibited from visiting branches this limits the scope of her employment. Contours are not liable for accidents caused whilst Rafty is driving to the branches. The second type of prohibition attempts to specify *how* a person performs a job. If Rafty was allowed to drive a company car but was prohibited from using it unless adequately insured this does not limit the scope of her employment (using a car) but merely determines how she should use the car. If such prohibitions were effective the concept of vicarious liability could be destroyed. If an employer prohibited an employee from committing tortious acts then all wrongful acts would be outside the course of employment! Only the former type of prohibition is therefore effective.

☐ Reedy is only allowed to collect cheques from Barl that have been crossed 'A/c payee only'. He collects cheques without this crossing, fraudulently endorses them and absconds with the proceeds. His actions are within his course of employment, the prohibition tells him 'how' to collect cheques. If he were told not to collect any cheques this might limit the scope of his employment thereby rendering his fraudulent activity outside the course of employment.

Independent contractors

Although an employer is not vicariously liable for an independent contractor's torts some of the employer's duties are non-delegable. If he employs an independent contractor who is negligent the employer is liable, not because he is responsible for the contractor's negligence but because he has broken *his* duty to ensure the task was carried out efficiently. Examples of non-delegable duties are:

(i) Where the task is inherently dangerous or extra hazardous. If a 200 foot chimney which needs demolishing is surrounded by other properties the task is inherently dangerous. The owner must ensure the task is performed safely and this duty cannot be delegated to an independent contractor. The task may be delegated but not the duty to see it is performed safely.
(ii) Where work is being carried out on the highway.
(iii) Torts of strict liability, including *Rylands* v. *Fletcher*.

Where vicarious liability exists the plaintiff can sue *either* the wrongdoer or his employer. As the latter is the 'man of substance' he is usually sued but he can claim an indemnity from the employee to the extent of his losses.

Past examination papers

1a) Explain the doctrine of 'vicarious liability'. In what circumstances may a person be liable in tort for the acts or omissions of his independent contractor?

b) Fast-Repair Garages employed a garage hand, part of whose duty was to remove cars parked in the garage. He was expressly forbidden to drive the cars. In breach of this prohibition and in order to make room for other vehicles, the garage hand negligently drove a van onto the highway causing a collision with Peter's van.

Peter wishes to know his rights against Fast-Repair Garages and their employee. Advise him.   A C A June 1976

2a) When may an employer be liable for the wrongful acts of his workers?

b) Roy, a lorry driver, leaves his normal route to call at home and, in the course of the deviation, damages another lorry through careless driving. After resuming his authorized journey he damages a car, again through carelessness. To what extent is his employer liable for the two accidents?   A C A June 1978

Section 4

The English legal system

27

Legal personality

A legal person is somebody recognized by the law as capable of having legal rights and duties. Legal persons can be either natural persons (human beings) or juristic persons (corporations created by the law).

Natural persons

Some of an individual's rights and duties have already been explained and many of these are determined by their **domicile**. This indicates a person's permanent residence and everybody must possess one domicile. A child's domicile is that of his or her father or, if illegitimate, his or her mother but anybody over sixteen may alter his or her domicile by taking up *permanent* residence in another country; a business trip to France does not involve the businessperson changing domicile because residence in France is temporary.

Domicile must be distinguished from **nationality**. This indicates a person's relationship with a state. Whilst a person must have a domicile it is possible not to possess a nationality (be stateless) or to possess dual or even triple nationality. A person's nationality follows that of their parents, hence a child with French and English parents possesses dual nationality.

The most common method of acquiring UK nationality is to be born in the UK, or its colonies, or to possess a British father (if the birth occurs overseas it must be registered with the British Consulate within one year). In the above circumstances nationality is acquired as of right.

An alien who has been resident in the UK for five years, is eighteen and possesses a good command of the English language may apply for naturalization but its award is discretionary. If granted the naturalized citizen's wife may acquire citizenship by registration with the Home Secretary; this right is open to anybody married to a UK citizen.

Note: It is possible to possess one country's domicile and another country's nationality.

In business, natural persons can be classified into:

(i) An individual businessperson – **sole trader**

This consists of a single individual working on their own account, with or without paid assistance. There are no formalities to be complied with in forming such a business, although if the sole trader is involved in credit or moneylending, he or she must also obtain a licence from the Director General of Fair Trading under the Consumer Credit Act (1974).

Probably the most important legal characteristic of a sole trader is that he possesses unlimited liability. In the event of bankruptcy his creditors can, if his business assets are insufficient, claim his personal belongings such as house, car and furniture.

☐ A R Leal is commencing business selling cassette tapes to professional students. He can commence business without complying with any formalities.

(ii) A group of individuals

Where several individuals combine together for a common purpose they become an **unincorporated association**. This association does not possess a separate legal identity (see below) and its property belongs not to the association but to the individual members. The individual member is liable for contracts he makes (even though acting on behalf of the association) and if they are not honoured he is the one sued. As he may have insufficient assets to pay the damages awarded it is possible to obtain judgment against the association's assets through a representation order.

The unincorporated association most relevant to the accountant is the partnership.

a) Partnership

This is primarily governed by the Partnership Act (1890). Section 1 defines a partnership as 'the relationship which subsists between persons carrying on a business with the common purpose of profit.'

Partnerships are most commonly found in the professions (solicitors, accountants etc) where professional ethics forbid the creation of companies which would permit their members to shelter behind the shield of limited liability. No formal requirements exist for the creation of a partnership. The partnership agreement may be oral, arise through implication (the fact of profit sharing gives rise to a presumption that a partnership exists) or by deed. The latter is the most common and normally contains details of the partners' rights and duties, the proportion in which they will contribute capital and share the profits and losses.

Like the sole trader, partners possess unlimited liability although the Limited Partnership Act (1907) enables a partner to possess limited liability providing at least one partner possesses unlimited liability.

A partner is an agent of the partnership, hence his contracts bind the partnership where he possesses actual or ostensible authority to make them (see Chapter 18). All partners are jointly and severally liable on the contracts and can be sued individually or collectively. The creditor may however only bring one action and if he sues one partner he cannot commence a second action against another.

☐   A R Leal decides to expand ARL Enterprises and take on two partners:
a) his wife, Barbara (for tax purposes) and
b) a friend, Bob, who will contribute additional capital for the purchase of more sophisticated dubbing equipment. He is to be a sleeping partner.
The name is to become Barl Enterprises.

By forming a partnership the sole trader would normally consult his partners before making decisions but with sleeping partners this is unnecessary as they play no active role in the running of the business.
b) *Trade unions* are another example of an unincorporated association.

Juristic persons

Corporations are artificial legal persons which possess a separate legal identity from the individual members. This was illustrated in *Salomon* v. *Salomon* (1897) in which the plaintiff was able to sue his own company because it possessed a legal identity separate from that of its shareholders (ie Salomon). As a corporation has its own identity it continues in existence despite changes in, or the death of, its members. In legal terminology it possesses 'perpetual succession.'
Corporations are of two types:

(i) *Sole*
A corporation sole is a recognised official position filled by one human being who is periodically replaced (bishops, treasury solicitor, public trustee etc). The corporation (juristic person) is distinct from the human being (natural person) occupying the position. It possesses a separate identity and perpetual succession: it remains constant although the individual holding the position varies. Today a corporation sole can only be created by statute.
The Monarch in her official capacity (the crown) is a juristic person. Because of the crown's unique status its position in law differs from other corporations and is governed by the Crown Proceedings Act (1947). Since that act the crown can be liable in contract and tort and for breach of duties arising out of the occupation of land. Although not liable for breaking a contract of service an employee who is wrongfully dismissed may possess a remedy under the common law.

(ii) *Aggregate*

A corporation aggregate is a legal person usually formed by a group of natural persons. There are three types:

a) Chartered

These are created by royal charter and are uncommon today. Examples include the Law Society, Chartered Institute of Secretaries and the Chartered Accountants. They possess full contractual capacity but their charters may be revoked if they act outside of their spirit.

b) Statutory

Parliament may create a corporation by passing a statute. Examples include the British Coal Board and British Railways Board. Their powers are laid down by the creating act and any contract outside these powers in void.

c) Registered

These are formed by complying with the requirements of the Companies' Acts and they comprise the majority of corporations. One of their main features is that the owners possess limited liability.[1] Their liability is limited to the extent of their shareholding[2] (investment in the business) and creditors cannot claim their private assets.

Registered companies can be private or public. Under the Companies' Act a **private** company may not invite the public to take shares in the company.

☐   Barl Enterprises is thriving and the partners are anxious to expand. They require more capital to produce video cassettes but because of the increased risks they want limited liability. The formation of a private company enables them to fulfil these objectives.

Any company not a private company must be a **public** company. Any such company possessing limited liability must include 'Public Ltd Company' as part of its name.

To form any registered company it is necessary to submit numerous documents to the Registrar of Companies. The two most important are the *memorandum of association* and the *articles of association*. The former relates to the external workings of the company, providing information to the outside world; contents include the company name

---

[1] There are unlimited companies but these are extremely rare.
[2] This is the most common type of liability and the company is said to be 'limited by shares.' Some companies are 'limited by guarantee' and do not possess shareholders. They possess members who guarantee to pay a fixed sum should the need arise. Their liability is limited to the extent of their guarantee.

(followed by the words 'public limited company') and the nature and objects of the company. The articles of association define the internal workings of the company, dealing with rights and duties of shareholders, directors, transfer of shares and the procedure at meetings. Under s. 8 of the 1948 Act a model set of articles (which is included in the Act) applies unless excluded. It is customary to accept these articles with minor modifications.

Other documents which must be submitted include:
a declaration that the Companies Act has been complied with;
a list of the first directors and secretary;
the address of the registered office;
details of the first shareholders.

After receiving the relevant documents the registrar will issue a certificate of incorporation bringing the corporation into existence unless he believes it is being formed for an illegal purpose or has an undesireable name.

Registered corporations obtain their powers through the memorandum of association. Any contract outside of these powers is ultra vires and, until 1972 was unenforceable. S. 9(1) of the European Communities Act 1972 states that, '*in favour of a person dealing with a company* in good faith, any transaction decided on by the directors shall be deemed to be one which is within the capacity 'of the company to enter into.' A company still cannot sue on a ultra vires contract but the clause enables the other party to sue on such a contract.

Comparison of partnerships and companies

	Partnership	*Public Company*	*Private Company*
1	Easy to form	More difficult to form: necessary to comply with requirements of Companies' Act	
2	Minimum of two partners maximum of 20[3] partners	Minimum of two shareholders No maximum	Minimum of two shareholders
3	Has no corporate existence	Possesses a legal identity separate from its shareholders	
4	Partners do not possess limited liability (subject to limited partners)	The owners possess limited liability	
5	Accounts less publicised	Generally accounts attract more publicity than with partnerships	
6	Difficult to raise finance because number of partners limited	Easier to raise finance because can issue shares to general public	Difficult to raise finance because limited number of shareholders and cannot issue shares to public

[3] Exceptions exist where there can be more than twenty partners.

| 7 | Owners participate in running of company | Owners delegate day to day running to board of directors | Owners more likely to be involved in day to day running |
| 8 | Difficult for partners to realize their assets by sale to new partner because other partners must approve any incoming partner | Easy to realize assets: sell shares on stock exchange | More difficult for owner to realize his assets than with a public company: restrictions on the sale of shares |

Past examination questions

1 Explain the difference in law between a partnership and a limited liability company.   A C A June 1977

2 Explain the difference between Nationality and Domicile and describe the various ways in which a person may acquire British Nationality.   A C A December 1977

3 'Once a corporation has come into being, it forms an entirely separate entity from the individuals who compose it.' Discuss. In what ways may corporations be created?   A C A December 1978

4 Compare and contrast partnerships and private limited companies.
                                       A C A June 1979

5 What is meant by a corporation in English Law? Explain the rules relating to the contractual capacity of corporations.   IAS June 1979

6 What is a partnership? What characteristics distinguish a partnership from a registered company?   I A S December 1980

7 a) Define what is meant by a limited liability company and state what are its characteristic features.

b) Smith and Jones are directors of a limited company which manufactures light bulbs. The company patented an indestructible light bulb, and after initially selling well, sales slumped because the bulbs never wore out. Consequently the company did badly and the creditors issued winding-up proceedings. The company owes £100 000. Smith retires to his £40 000 house and Jones takes over the running of his own stables, worth £60 000. Creditors demand that they sell their assets to pay the company's debts. Discuss the extent of the liability of Smith and Jones.

c) State three ways by which a corporation may be created, and give an example of each such creation.   C A May 1980

THE COMPANIES ACTS, 1948 to 1967

COMPANY LIMITED BY SHARES

𝔐emorandum of 𝔄ssociation

OF

THE BOOTS COMPANY LIMITED

1st. The name of the Company is " THE BOOTS COMPANY LIMITED."

2nd. The Registered Office of the Company will be situated in England.

3rd. The objects for which the Company is established are all or any of the following, the Company having power to do any part of the matters mentioned in one section apart from any other of the said matters, and none of the general or other descriptions given in this Clause being subject to be limited or restrained to matters of the same or some similar kind to those elsewhere in this Clause mentioned or referred to, or to be otherwise limited or restrained by any other part of this Clause not containing an express limitation or restriction, nor by any inference to be drawn from such other part.

(A) To purchase or acquire the business of patent medicine vendors, dispensers, drug merchants, herbalists, manufacturers of proprietary articles, and general store-keepers, carried on by " THE MIDLAND DRUG COMPANY, LIMITED," at Goose Gate, Island Street, and Arkwright Street, in the Town of Nottingham; at High Street, in the City of Lincoln; at Snig Hill, and at High Street, Attercliffe, both in the Borough of Sheffield; and elsewhere; and the lands, shops, warehouses, buildings, machinery, plant, material, stock-in-trade, book debts, goodwill and assets of the said business; and to issue fully paid-up shares in the Company to all or any of the shareholders of the before-mentioned selling Company as the whole or part consideration for the purchase.

(B) To carry on and extend the said business, and generally to carry on the business of wholesale, retail, manufacturing and dispensing chemists and druggists, herbalists and patent medicine vendors.

(C) To carry on the businesses of artists' colourmen, and of manufacturers of and merchants in oils, paints, colours and brushes, and artists' and painters' requisites of all descriptions.

(D) To manufacture and deal in mineral and aerated waters, syrups, and other beverages of all descriptions.

(E) To manufacture and deal in surgical, electrical, photographic, and other scientific apparatus, instruments, and requisites of all descriptions.

(F) To establish and carry on stores in any place or places, and to buy, sell, manufacture and deal in goods, stores, consumable articles, chattels and effects of all kinds, both wholesale and retail, to transact every kind of agency business, and to carry on the business in all its branches of a store-keeper.

(G) To carry on any trade, business or mercantile operation which in the opinion of the Directors of the Company may be incident, auxiliary or conducive to the objects aforesaid, or any of them, and whether on account of the Company alone, or with or for any other company or person.

(H) To acquire by purchase or grant, or otherwise, or take out and to work and sell any inventions, patent rights or privileges in connection with the said business, or any other business for the time being carried on by the Company, and to procure foreign patents in respect of any such inventions, and to grant or sell all or any estate or interest of and in the inventions, patent rights, or privileges of or to which the Company may from time to time be possessed or entitled, and to grant licences to use, work, or vend the same.

(I) To purchase or rent, or otherwise acquire and hold any freehold, copyhold or leasehold land, houses, factories, wharves, buildings, and hereditaments in the United Kingdom or elsewhere, and to sell, lease, let, and dispose of the same, and to make, construct, and build any buildings or works for the purposes of the Company.

(J) To sell the undertaking, assets, and property of the Company, or any rights or interests therein, or any portion of the same, to any other company, association, or person, for such price in money or shares, and on such terms, as the Company shall sanction, and to take over and acquire by purchase or otherwise the whole or any part of the undertaking, assets, and property of any other company or person, or to amalgamate with any other company established for objects similar in general character to the objects of this Company, and to take and hold any shares, stock, or debentures respectively in any company whatsoever in which the liability of the Members shall be limited to the amount of their shares or stock, and whether such company shall be established in the United Kingdom or elsewhere.

(K) To establish agencies in connection with the business for the time being of the said Company in this country, or in such foreign places as the Directors of the Company may from time to time determine.

(L) To draw, accept, endorse, and make bills of exchange, promissory notes, and other negotiable instruments.

(M) To borrow or receive deposits or loans of money at interest or otherwise, and to make and issue as security for the same, or for any moneys owing by the Company, debenture bonds or stock, or mortgage debentures, or mortgages, or charges, with or without powers of sale, of the whole or any part or parts of the undertaking and property of the Company (including its unpaid Capital, whether called or not), and to lend money upon such security as shall be thought fit, or without security, and to guarantee the payment of any money or the performance of any contract or work by any other company or person.

(N) To maintain, establish, and aid institutions for the benefit of persons whether employed by or having dealings with the Company or not, including schools, libraries, dispensaries, infirmaries, provident societies, clubs, mechanics' and other institutions, and friendly societies.

(o) To pay all or any servants and workmen employed by the Company such bonus, percentage, or share of the profits of the Company as the Directors of the Company may from time to time think desirable.

(P) To do all such things as are incidental or conducive to the attainment of the above objects.

4th.   The liability of the Members is Limited.

See Notes below.

5th.   The Capital of the Company is £80,000 divided into 800 shares of £100 each ; which shares, and all other shares of which the present or any future Capital shall consist may be issued at a premium, and may be divided into different classes, and may have such preference, guarantee, or privilege, as between themselves, as shall be in conformity with the regulations of the Company from time to time, and may, when fully paid up, be converted into Stock.

NOTES:—

1. The Capital of the Company at the date of this reprint (1st January, 1973) is £50,000,000 divided into 200,000,000 Ordinary Shares of 25p each, the original Capital having been increased from time to time and reduced, as follows:—

(A) On 21st December, 1900, increased to £180,000 by the creation of 100,000 new shares of £1 each.

(B) On 6th June, 1902, increased to £355,000 by the creation of 120,000 new shares of £1 each and 550 new shares of £100 each.

(C) On 11th September, 1905, increased to £600,000 by the creation of 245,000 new shares of £1 each.

(D) On 6th February, 1911, increased to £1,000,000 by the creation of 400,000 new shares of £1 each.

(E) On 23rd July, 1914, increased to £1,250,000 by the creation of 250,000 new shares of £1 each.

(F) On 3rd December, 1917, increased to £1,500,000 by the creation of 250,000 new shares of £1 each.

(G) On 5th January, 1920, increased to £1,750,000 by the creation of 2,500 new shares of £100 each.

(H) On 28th March, 1923, increased to £2,400,000 by the creation of 650,000 new shares of £1 each (on this date each of 3,600 shares of £100 each were divided into 100 shares of £1 each).

(I) On 12th January, 1926, increased to £2,900,000 by the creation of 500,000 new shares of £1 each.

(J) On 10th October, 1933, each of the 1,500,000 issued and fully paid Ordinary Shares of £1 each was divided into 4 Ordinary Shares of 5s. each.

(K) On 7th June, 1934, increased to £3,000,000 by the creation of 400,000 new Ordinary Shares of 5s. each.

(L) On 10th July, 1947, increased to £4,000,000 by the creation of 4,000,000 new Ordinary Shares of 5s. each.

(M) On 12th July, 1951, increased to £8,000,000 by the creation of 16,000,000 new Ordinary Shares of 5s. each.

(N) On 14th July, 1955, increased to £15,000,000 by the creation of 28,000,000 new Ordinary Shares of 5s. each.

(O) On 22nd November, 1960, increased to £40,000,000 by the creation of 100,000,000 new Ordinary Shares of 5s. each

(P) On 16th July, 1964, increased to £50,000,000 by the creation of 40,000,000 new Ordinary Shares of 5s. each.

(Q) On 31st March, 1965, reduced to £48,600,000 and immediately increased to £50,000,000 by the creation of 5,600,000 new Ordinary Shares of 5s. each (see Note 2 below).

2. On 31st March, 1965, pursuant to an Order of the High Court of Justice dated 22nd March, 1965, the Capital of the Company was reduced and subsequently increased. A copy of the Minute approved by the Court and set out in the schedule to such Order and which, by virtue of Section 69 of the Companies Act 1948, is deemed to be substituted for the corresponding part of the Company's Memorandum of Association, is annexed.

3. Authorised Share Capital increased from £50,000,000 to £100,000,000 by Ordinary Resolution dated 17th July 1975.

We, the several persons whose names, addresses and descriptions, are subscribed, are desirous of being formed into a Company in pursuance of this Memorandum of Association, and we respectively agree to take the number of shares in the capital of the Company set opposite our respective names.

NAMES, ADDRESSES AND DESCRIPTIONS OF SUBSCRIBERS.	Number of Shares taken by each Subscriber.
JESSE BOOT, Mapperley, Nottingham, Drug Merchant	One
THOMAS CUTLER, 15 College Street, Nottingham, Drug Merchant	One
HY. G. JALLAND, Heathcote Buildings, Nottingham, Wine Merchant	One
WILLIAM NEVILLE, SENIOR, Sherwood Rise, Lace Agent, Nottingham	One
WILLIAM NEVILLE, JUNIOR, Chilwell, Notts., Lace Manufacturer	One
FRANCIS WILLIAM VICTOR MITCHELL, 204 Hagley Road, Edgbaston, Penmaker	One
GEORGE COLLISON TUTING PARSONS, 120 Colmore Row, Birmingham, Chartered Accountant	One

DATED the 5th day of November, 1888.

WITNESS to the signatures of JESSE BOOT, THOMAS CUTLER, HENRY GIBSON JALLAND, WILLIAM NEVILLE, Senior, and WILLIAM NEVILLE, Junior—

ALFRED ROBINSON, Solicitor,
Clerk to Messrs. WELLS & HIND, Solicitors,
Nottingham.

WITNESS to the Signatures of FRANCIS WILLIAM VICTOR MITCHELL and GEORGE COLLISON TUTING PARSONS—

JOSEPH NICHOLLS,
54 St. Mary Street, Birmingham,
Clerk.

Figure 12 Memorandum of Association

Certificate of the Incorporation of a Company

I hereby Certify that

BOOTS PURE DRUG COMPANY, LIMITED

was INCORPORATED under the Companies Acts, 1862 to 1886, as a

LIMITED Company, on the Seventh day of November One thousand

eight hundred and eighty-eight.

GIVEN under my hand at London, this Eleventh day of January

One thousand nine hundred and eleven

GEO. J. SARGENT,
Assistant Registrar of Joint Stock Companies.

Figure 13 Certificate of the incorporation of a company

28

Nature and sources of English law *(Part I)*

Nature

Law can be defined and classified in various ways. The former is only relevant to a law student and the distinctions that are relevant to the professional student are those between:

1 **Civil and criminal law**
   The branch of law involved in a dispute depends not upon the act but upon the legal consequences following it.

☐   Trevor Wit leaves his car with a garage to have it serviced. The garage sells it. The same act is both a crime (theft) and a civil wrong (breach of contract).

   The same act produces both civil and criminal actions. It is however possible to generalize and state that where an act against an individual is also regarded as a wrong against the state it will be regarded as a crime and the state therefore institutes proceedings. In contrast in civil law there is simply a wrong against an individual who must decide whether to commence an action against the wrong-doer.

2 **Real and personal property**
   Property (something that can be owned) is either
  (i) real property   This consists of any freehold interest in land, or
  (ii) personal property   This consists of chattels real (any leasehold interest in land) and chattels personal (all other interests).
   The distinction between freehold and leasehold interests in land is purely arbitrary and exists for historical reasons. Chattels personal (personalty) are either

choses-in-possession − items possessing a physical existence

or

choses-in-action. Things capable of ownership but possessing no physical existence like the right to a legacy (see page 69).

Sources

Historical introduction
Prior to 1066, the law was administered by royal officials who presided over local assemblies and by landowners who exercised jurisdiction over their own tenants in their private courts. Both 'Courts' applied local customs and there was no uniform law throughout the country.

Development of common law
The catalyst for the development of common law was the Norman Conquest in 1066. The Normans created a strong centralized monarchy which was assisted by a council of powerful landowners (Curia Regis) which possessed administrative, legislative and judicial functions. Itinerant (or travelling) justices were sent out from the Curia Regis to exercise judicial functions and in 1179 circuits were organized around which they travelled. In the formative years each justice administered local customs but gradually, following discussions amongst the justices, good local customs were adopted and became common throughout the country. They formed the basis of the Common law.

Common law
Although most general customs (those nationally applied) were incorporated into the common law during this period, the customs of the Law Merchant (such as negotiable instruments) were incorporated from the seventeenth century onwards. Apart from those involving negotiable instruments general customs cannot be considered a current source of law. Local customs (those binding in a particular area) may however still be proved and are a current, although minor source of law.

> *Egerton* v. *Harding* (1974)
> The plaintiff's cottage and the defendant's farm adjoined common land on which the defendant's cattle grazed. Some of the cattle wandered into the plaintiff's garden causing damage. One of the questions the court had to decide was: was there a custom compelling the plaintiff to fence his land to protect his property from the grazing cattle? In the course of his judgment Lord Justice Scarman said 'Was there a custom? If one enlarges the horizon of investigation so as to bring into view all the lands surrounding and adjoining Binswood Common, the possibility of a local custom emerges. The judge (at first instance) did this: he examined with care all the evidence of usage and, applying the well-known criteria, came to the conclusion that a custom was proved. He posed the correct question − is there a custom requiring the occupier of the cottage to provide a fence against the

Common? He recognized that a custom, to be upheld as Local Law, has to be shown to be of immemorial origin, reasonable, continued without interruption, and certain'.

The four tests mentioned are:

1 *Immemorial origin* The person alleging the custom must prove it has existed since time immemorial ie 1189. The court presumes this providing the custom has existed as long as anyone can remember. The person contesting the custom must then prove it could not have existed since 1189 by perhaps showing the land involved was not reclaimed from the sea until the fourteenth century.
2 *Reasonableness*
3 *Continued without interruption* It is not necessary to prove that the custom has been continuously exercised merely that the right has always existed, even if not always enforced. It is enough that the cottage owner could have been required to erect a fence. In addition the custom must have been exercised *peaceably*, *openly*, *and of right* to show that the local population have consented to the custom, their agreement being essential.
4 *Certain* Everyone must know what the right is if there is to be genuine consent.
   In addition the locality within which the custom operates must be definite.

Growth of equity

By the fourteenth century certain defects had become apparent in the common law:

a) There was a restricted right of appeal from the common law courts. Appeals were through a procedure called 'writ of error' and only certain types of error could be considered and even then the appellate court could only set aside the decision, not reverse it.
b) The common law might not provide a remedy. Legal proceedings were initiated by issuing a writ; in the early years new writs were framed for new situations but by the end of the thirteenth century there was a reluctance to issue new writs. The changing patterns within society meant many potential plaintiffs were remediless, unable to obtain a writ. Even where a writ existed the plaintiff lost if he issued the wrong one, the common law being concerned more with technicalities than justice.
c) The only common law remedy, damages, was often unsuitable. As explained on page 82 a modern plaintiff can apply for specific performance or an injunction, both equitable remedies.
d) Their procedures meant an influential party could ignore the court.

It was common practice during this period for aggrieved citizens to petition the monarch, hence when somebody was dissatisfied with their treatment in the common law courts it was natural to petition the king for relief.

The early petitions, addressed to the monarch, were referred to a committee of the Curia Regis. As the *Chancellor* issued letters after a favourable decision it was logical for him to head this and during the fourteenth century petitions came to be addressed directly to him. The Court of Chancery evolved during the fifteenth century.

This Court differed from the common law courts in that, because early Chancellors were ecclesiastics, it attempted to dispense justice ('equity'). The Chancellor was concerned to do what was just and fair in order to save the defendant's soul. The court's procedure reflected these objectives. On receiving a petition (bill) the Chancellor issued a subpoena instructing the parties to appear before him to be questioned (at common law the parties could not give evidence). After questioning them the Chancellor exercised his discretion to make the 'just' decision. Equitable remedies were therefore discretionary. A defendant would be instructed to do whatever was necessary to clear his conscience. The order was made against him, not his property, and a failure to comply meant imprisonment. Hence equity was said to act 'in personam' (against the person).

Later development of equity

Initially Chancellors decided cases on their merits with no reference to earlier decisions. This created uncertainty and equity was said to vary with the 'length of the Chancellor's foot' (Selden). As Chancellors became lawyers rather than ecclesiastics they began following their own decisions and by the eighteenth century equity had become more certain with the establishment of settled equitable principles.

When equity developed there was no friction with the common law, indeed Chancellors often sought advice from common law judges. By the sixteenth century however, the latter were viewing the increased influence and power of Chancery courts with distrust. Dispute arose over Chancellors' determination to issue injunctions preventing a man from enforcing his legal rights if this was unconscionable. If a writ were issued but the Chancellor considered that its enforcement would be against the plaintiff's conscience, he would issue an injunction which forbade the plaintiff continuing with the action. If he ignored this he would be imprisoned. The conflict was heightened by the personal animosity between Coke (the common lawyer) and Ellesmere (The Chancellor) and in 1616 the king was asked to ajudicate. His decision was that in the event of conflict between the two systems equity was to prevail.

Characteristics of equity
Equity presupposes the existence of common law which it seeks to make fairer and more equitable. Therefore:

(i) it will not intervene where the common law is adequate. When considering specific performance on page 82 the reader will recall it is not available where damages are adequate. This is because it is an equitable remedy.

(ii) Equity is a 'gloss' on the common law acting in areas in which it is deficient. The most commonly quoted example is the law of trusts but readers will already be familiar with other examples. Thus duress, a common law concept, failed to cover non-violent forms of persuasion hence equity developed the doctrine of undue influence (see page 55). Under Section 40 of The Law of Property Act (1925) a contract for the sale of land must be evidenced in writing; to avoid a party using this to 'defraud' another party equity devised the doctrine of part-performance (see page 25).

(iii) Equitable remedies are discretionary and will be withheld if the party has acted unfairly. In *D & C Builders* v. *Rees* (see page 21) the defendant sought to rely on the equitable defence of promissory estoppel. She lost because of her unprincipled conduct.

Judicature acts (1873–5)

The procedure in the court of Chancery eventually become slow and cumbersome and this deficiency applied to most other courts. In addition the existence of separate common law and chancery courts was untenable and there was still no logical system of appeals. The nineteenth century saw numerous improvements, the most sweeping of which were the above Acts. These reorganized the court structure and simplified procedures to improve the efficiency and reduce the cost of the judicial process. The main reforms were:

1 *Creation of the Supreme Court* consisting of the Court of Appeal and High Court. All appeals from the latter being heard by the newly created Court of Appeal and then the House of Lords, the other appeal courts being abolished.

2 *Simplified procedure* The old forms of action were abolished and procedures simplified so that a plaintiff would not lose his action on a purely technical error.

3 *The fusion of law and equity* Prior to 1875 they were administered by separate courts but post 1875 each court administers both systems although if a clash occurs equity prevails.

Judicial precedent

Judicial precedent exists when decisions of certain courts are binding on other courts. Judges even as early as the thirteenth century, attempted to be consistent in their judgments but a prerequisite of judicial precedent is a recognized hierarchy of courts and a system of law reporting. In the early nineteenth century these were lacking hence, although a principle from a previous decision of a superior court bound an inferior court, the establishment of the current system had to wait until the Acts of 1873–75. These produced the hierarchy of courts and in 1866 the Incorporated Council of Law Reporting had been established. Their Law Reports have a semi-official status and, because their reporters are barristers, counsel can cite them in court. Their accuracy is ensured because judges can revise the wording of their judgments before publication.

Precedents can either be binding or persuasive.

Binding

This is a precedent a lower court must follow in a case with the same material facts. Thus the *ratio decidendi* (defined as the reason for the decision, or the legal principle on which it was based or the material facts of the case plus the decision) of:

(i)   The House of Lords binds all other English courts in similar cases although it is not binding on itself.

(ii) The Court of Appeal (civil division) is binding on itself (even where the earlier decision was obviously wrong), except:

a) Where two previous inconsistent Court of Appeal decisions exist it must choose which to follow.

b) The court must ignore an earlier decision explicitly or impliedly overruled by the House of Lords.

c) It can ignore a decision given 'per incuriam' (by oversight) eg where a relevant authority or statute was not quoted.

Where an appellant cannot succeed in the Court of Appeal because a binding precedent exists he can utilize the leap-frogging procedure and appeal direct to the Lords.

Lord Denning has however claimed that the civil division of the Court of Appeal is not bound by its previous decisions. In *Davis* v. *Johnson* (1978) *five* Court of Appeal judges agreed by a majority to ignore two earlier decisions on statutory interpretation. Lord Denning claimed the decisions were not binding on the Court but the other two majority judges overruled the earlier cases on narrow technical grounds. The House of Lords on appeal reiterated that the Court of Appeal was bound by its previous decisions but indicated that this ruling might, at some future date, be changed.

The criminal division can overrule its previous decisions because an individual's freedom is considered more important than achieving certainty in the law.

Decisions of the Court of Appeal bind all lower courts.

(iii) Divisional court binds itself.

A single High Court judge does not bind other High Court judges and decisions of inferior courts do not bind anybody, even themselves.

Note: Only a case's ratio decidendi is binding.

A lawyer discovers a case's ratio decidendi by ascertaining the *material* (ie relevant) facts. In *Holwell Securities* v. *Hughes* the fact that the plaintiff was exercising an option to purchase property was immaterial (the acceptance could have related to anything) but the words 'notice in writing' were material. Thus in

Holwell Securities v. *Hughes* (Court of Appeal) the ratio decidendi was that the words 'notice in writing' expressly exclude the operation of the postal rule.

Saif Ali v. *Sidney Mitchell* (House of Lords) the ratio decidendi was that barristers owe a duty of care when advising clients whether to commence litigation. Any lower court called upon to decide this point must follow the Lords' decision.

Persuasive

This is a precedent which does not bind a judge, only influences him. Persuasive precedent includes obiter dicta ('other words', ie the judgment other than the ratio decidendi), Privy Council decisions and the ratio decidendi of inferior courts. The persuasiveness of the precedent depends on various factors including the rank of the court, prestige of the judge and date of the decision. Thus in

Saif Ali v. *Sidney Mitchell* the House indicated, by way of illustration, that a barrister did not owe a duty when giving pre-trial advice which was closely connected with the conduct of the case (eg not to call a witness). This obiter dictum is only persuasive but, being a carefully argued Lords' case, would carry great weight. In *Holwell Securities* v. *Hughes* the judges commented that if the postal rule's application would lead to absurdity it would be impliedly excluded by the offeror. This was obiter dictum and is only persuasive. Even the ratio decidendi of this case would only be persuasive on the House of Lords.

Advantages of judicial precedent

Its main *advantages* are:

1 *Certainty* Because judges must follow previous decisions a barrister can usually advise his client on the outcome of a case. A customer wishing to sue a publican who refused to sell him beer offered in an off-licence window can be advised against litigation

because goods in a shop window constitute an invitation to treat.

2   *Flexibility*   It is claimed that case law can be extended to meet new situations thereby allowing the law to adjust to new social conditions. The growth of duty of care situations has been cited as proof (see pages 117ff).

Its main disadvantages are:

1   *Uncertainty*   As indicated below various techniques have evolved which enable judges to avoid following a ratio decidendi they disapprove of. It is claimed that as whether a case is followed or not is a matter of judicial discretion, this produces uncertainty. In most cases the amount of discretion is limited but in 'grey' areas judges do possess considerable discretion.

2   *Rigidity*   Because old decisions must be followed bad case law is perpetuated and it is difficult to alter, as opposed to modifying law. Thus exclusion clauses were acceptable but with growing inequality of bargaining power it became necessary to protect the weaker party. The courts were unable to do this and Parliament was forced to legislate (see pages 30–34).

Because judges sometimes wished to avoid following a previous case avoidance techniques evolved. One such, 'distinguishing', occurs when the judge finds a material distinction between the current case and that cited as an authority. By distinguishing the cited case he can ignore it. Thus the judge in *Hartly* v. *Ponsonby* distinguished *Stilk* v. *Myrick* because the crew desertions were greater in the former (see pages 18–19).

The rigidity and inflexibility of judicial precedent (stare decisis) has been mitigated by two developments. The first was the practice statement made in July 1966,

> 'Their Lordships regard the use of precedent as an indispensable foundation upon which to decide what is the law and its application to individual cases. It provides at least some degree of certainty upon which individuals can rely in the conduct of their affairs, as well as a basis for orderly development of legal rules. Their Lordships nevertheless recognize that too rigid adherence to precedent may lead to injustice in a particular case and also unduly restrict the proper development of the law. They propose therefore, to modify their present practice and, while treating formal decisions of this House as normally binding, to depart from a previous decision when it appears right to do so. In this connection they will bear in mind the danger of disturbing retrospectively the basis on which contracts, settlement of property and fiscal arrangements have been entered into and also the special need for certainty as to the criminal law. This announcement is not intended to affect the use of precedent elsewhere than in this House.'

The House is still extremely reluctant to overrule earlier cases and may restrict these powers to areas where changed social conditions make the earlier decision unrealistic. As Lord Reid said in *Jones* v. *Secretary of State for Social Services* (1972),

> 'My understanding of the position when this resolution was adopted was and is that there were a comparatively small number of reported decisions of this House which were generally thought to be impeding the proper development of the law or to have led to results which were unjust or contrary to public policy and that such decisions should be reconsidered as opportunities arose. But this practice was not to be used to weaken existing certainty in the law. The old view was that any departure from rigid adherence to precedent would weaken that certainty. I did not and do not accept that view. It is notorious that where an existing decision is disapproved but cannot be overruled courts tend to distinguish it on inadequate grounds. I do not think that they act wrongly in so doing: they are adopting the less bad of the only alternatives open to them. But this is bound to lead to uncertainty for no one can say in advance whether in a particular case the court will or will not feel bound to follow the old unsatisfactory decision. On balance it seems to me that overruling such a decision will promote and not impair the certainty of the law.
>
> But that certainty will be impaired unless this practice is used sparingly. The typical case for reconsidering an old decision is where some broad issue is involved, and that it should only be in rare cases that we should reconsider questions of construction of statutes or other documents.' In that case the majority of their Lordships disagreed with the earlier decision but were unwilling to overrule it.

The importance of certainty was again stressed by Lord Reid in *Knuller* v. *DPP* (1972) where the appellants were charged with a conspiracy to corrupt public morals following the earlier House of Lords decision in *Shaw* v. *DPP*. As he said, 'It was decided by this House in *Shaw* v. *Director of Public Prosecutions* (1962) that conspiracy to corrupt public morals is a crime known to the law of England. So if the appellants are to succeed this House must reverse that decision. I dissented in Shaw's case. On reconsideration I still think that the decision was wrong and I see no reason to alter anything which I said in my speech. But it does not follow that I should now support a motion to reconsider the decision. I have said more than once in recent cases that our change of practice in no longer regarding previous decisions of this House as absolutely binding does not mean that whenever we think that a previous decision was wrong we should reverse it.'

Was however the 1966 statement necessary as a full-time body now exists (the Law Commission) to review the Law and propose amending legislation where necessary? Until the 1930's the development of the law was mainly the responsibility of judges but they were unable to keep the law abreast of the times. Therefore in the 1930's and 1950's two part-time unpaid committees of judges, lawyers and civil servants were constituted to consider proposed law reforms submitted by the Lord Chancellor. Although useful the members' time was limited. This eventually led to the Law Commissions Act (1965) which set up two full-time Law Commissions, one for England and Wales and one for Scotland.

The Commissions are required to 'take and keep under review the whole of the law ... with a view to its systematic development and reform, including in particular ... codification ... the elimination of anomolies, the repeal of obsolete and unnecessary enactments, the reduction of the number of separate enactments and generally the simplification and modernization of the law'.

The Commissions must receive and consider proposals for law reform which are referred to them, prepare and submit programmes of law reform and of consolidation and statute law revision, undertake the examination of particular branches of the law and formulate proposals for reform by means of draft bills or otherwise. They produce two kinds of publication, working papers and reports. Following research the commission publishes a working paper outlining the defects of a certain law, the alternatives for reform and a provisional proposal. The paper is sent to interested parties for consideration. Following comments a report is presented to the Lord Chancellor. This differs from the working paper because it includes recommendations for reform and perhaps a draft bill. The report is laid before Parliament for possible enactment onto the statute book.

Two types of report deal with simplification of statute law. Revision bills repeal obsolete enactments and consolidation bills combine statutes dealing with the same topics. These bills are reviewed by a Joint Standing Committee of both Houses and are then enacted without further debate.

By 1980, 74 working papers and 98 reports had been published including fourteen annual reports which must be submitted to the Lord Chancellor (which he submits to Parliament). 70% of its proposals had been implemented with over 2700 obsolete acts repealed and over 100 Consolidated Acts passed. Its deliberations have also led to legislation such as the Theft Act (1968) and the Matrimonial legislation (1969–1973).

29

Nature and sources of English law *(Part II)*

Statute (Act of Parliament)

An Act of Parliament is a bill that has passed through both Houses of Parliament and received the Royal Assent. If statute and common law clashes the former prevails and the courts cannot question the validity of any Act.

> *Pickin* v. *British Railways Board* (1974)
> Per Lord Morris 'In my view, it is beyond question that the substance of the plea advanced is that the court is entitled to and should disregard what Parliament has enacted. The question of fundamental importance which arises is whether the court should entertain the proposition that an Act of Parliament can be so assailed in the courts that matters should proceed as though the Act or some part of it had never been passed. I consider that such a doctrine would be dangerous and impermissable. It is the function of the courts to administer the laws which Parliament has enacted. In the processes of Parliament there will be much consideration whether a bill should or should not in one form or another become an enactment. When an enactment is passed there is finality unless and until it is amended or repealed by Parliament. In the courts there may be argument as to the correct interpretation of the enactment: there must be none as to whether it should be on the Statute Book at all.'

The purpose of statutes are to change or modify the existing law and they can be classified under three broad headings:

1 Statutes involving isolated areas of law eg, Unfair Contract (Terms) Act.
2 Consolidating statutes which re-enact in one statute the existing law as continued in numerous Acts. Thus the Sale of Goods Act 1979 consolidated the Sale of Goods Act 1893 and the Sale of Goods (Implied Terms) Act 1973.
3 Codifying statutes such as the Bills of Exchange Act (1882) which enact in one statute the whole of one area of law (including the case

law). In most European countries statutory codes form the main source of law and one of the Law Commission's functions is the possible codification of English Law.

Statute has always been a source of English Law and by the nineteenth century it rivalled decided cases as a source. Today it is the most important new source of law. This is because:

a) The complex nature of commercial and industrial life has necessitated legislation to create the appropriate organizations and legal framework.
b) Modern developments, such as drugs and the car, necessitated legislation to prevent their abuse.
c) There are frequent changes in the attitudes of modern society (such as that relating to the role of females) and law must change to keep in step. Thus it is now accepted that limits must be imposed on groups with excessive economic power (see pages 32–36 for the law on exclusion clauses).

Delegated legislation

This is legislation made by a body other than Parliament and includes regulations made by a government minister or bye-laws passed by a local authority. It has increased considerably since the last war (in any one year its volume exceeds statute) because a rapidly changing society necessitates increased legislative activity but parliamentary time is limited. Parliament possesses neither the time to initiate every detailed item of legislation nor the technical knowledge to deal with the complexities often involved. It can only legislate on broad principles leaving the relevant minister to fill in the details following consultation with experts. Where an act is introduced in stages, as was the 1980 Companies Act, this can be achieved by Regulations made under statutory instruments.

Whilst essential to the smooth running of the nation, the growth of delegated legislation can be criticized because law making is transferred from the elected representatives to the minister (in effect his civil servants). Thus the Consumer Credit Act gives the minister considerable delegated powers but, because of pressures of work, these will be delegated to his civil servants with the minister merely signing the orders to give them legislative force. It is therefore essential that controls exist over the executive's law-making powers.

The validity of delegated legislation can be challenged in the courts as being ultra vires (ie beyond the powers of the party making it) and therefore void. This judicial safeguard depends on the parent legislation (ie the act giving the powers). If this confers extremely wide powers this restraint may become almost ineffectual. The courts, when interpreting the parent (enabling) statute will therefore, unless it contains clear words to the contrary, presume the Act does not confer a power to make:

(i) restrospective rules;
(ii) unreasonable or uncertain rules, or
(iii) rules that cannot be challenged in a court.

As the astute reader will realize from the last presumption, it is possible to exclude judicial review by using the appropriate words.

The second check on the executive is that all delegated legislation must be laid before the House of Commons. Some becomes effective on being presented to Parliament; some must be approved within forty days or else it lapses whilst some becomes effective unless rejected within forty days. Parliamentary control is strengthened by the existence of the Select Committee on Statutory instruments, which reviews delegated legislation and occasionally refers it to the House. The volume of delegated legislation means however only a small part is examined and only one per cent of that examined is in fact laid before the House.

All legislation (delegated or otherwise) requires **interpreting**. The object of interpretation is to ascertain Parliament's will as expressed in the Act; the court is thus in theory concerned with what is stated and not with what it believes Parliament intended. Seventy five per cent of reported cases in the House of Lords and fifty per cent in the High Court involve questions of statutory interpretation and in many of these the legislature's intention is impossible to ascertain because it never considered the question before the court. In such circumstances the intention of the legislature is a fiction. The judge must do what he thinks Parliament would have done had they considered the question. He is acting as a legislator. A statute refers to a 'vehicle'. Does this include a pram? Assuming the judge has no guidance he must use his common sense and act accordingly. His decision will therefore either extend or curtail that statute.

When faced with interpretation of a statute (or legislating in the sense outlined above) judges can apply numerous rules. The one adopted often reflects the judge's conception of the role of judge as legislator. At one extreme, judges believe they should implement the literal words of Parliament and if these cause absurdity or hardship Parliament must enact new legislation. The opposite view is that judges possess a creative role in ensuring that statutes are sensibly interpreted (even if this involves a 'liberal interpretation). The former judges would utilize the *literal* rule. This states that words are given their literal meaning even though this causes hardship. The more liberal judges will adopt the *golden* rule which states that if a literal interpretation results in an absurd situation the courts, presuming this was not Parliament's intention, interpret the Act accordingly. These judges can also utilize the *mischief* rule, the court considering the mischief the Act was designed to prevent and interpreting it accordingly.

The rules regarding interpretation are complicated, extremely numerous and are often said to 'hunt in pairs' because they often contradict each other. This, it is suggested, gives judges a choice and their decision depends on which of the opposing rules they apply.

> *Bushell* v. *Faith* (1972)
> Lord Upjohn said, 'My Lords, when construing an Act of Parliament it is a canon of construction that its provisions must be construed in the light of the mischief the Act was designed to meet. In this case the mischief was well known.'
> In contrast, Lord Donovan said, 'My Lords, the issue here is the true construction of s. 184 of the Companies Act, 1948: and I approach it with no conception of what the Legislature wanted to achieve by the section other than such as can reasonably be deduced from its language.'

If the judge is seeking assistance in questions of interpretation to what may he refer? He can consider the Act's title and preamble but he cannot usually seek guidance from the reports of committees, Royal Commissions or Parliamentary speeches.

> *Assam Railways* v. *CIR* (1935)
> Per Lord Wright, 'The question, which is by no means free from difficulty, depends on the true construction of the section. (Counsel) sought to introduce into his argument certain recommendations from a report of a Royal Commission on Income Tax in 1920: he argued that, as the Act of 1920 followed these recommendations, it should be presumed that the words of the section were intended to give effect to them and hence they could be used to show what was the intention of the Legislature in enacting the section ... It is clear that the language of a Minister of the Crown in proposing in Parliament a measure which eventually becomes law is inadmissable and a Report of Commissioners is even more removed from value as evidence of intention because it does not follow that the recommendations are accepted.'

Today however there is an increasing amount of legislation and this development has led the Law Commission to recommend that judges should consider non legislative material to ascertain an Act's purpose and that they should be instructed to interpret Acts in a liberal manner to ensure the 'attainment of the object of the Act ... according to its true intent, meaning and spirit'. This indeed appears to be the practice of at least one senior judge.

Watchel v. *Watchel* (1973)

Following a divorce the court had to decide how to divide the family assets especially the matrimonial home. This involved interpreting the Matrimonial Proceedings and Property Act 1970.

Per Lord Denning MR 'How is the court to exercise its discretion under the Act of 1970 in regard to the matrimonial home?' We will lead up to the answer by tracing the way in which the law has developed. Twenty-five years ago, if the matrimonial home stood in the husband's name, it was taken to belong to him entirely.

In 1965 Sir Jocelyn Simon said:

'In the generality of marriages the wife bears and rears children and minds the home. She thereby frees her husband for his economic activities. Since it is her performance of her functions which enables the husband to perform his, she is in justice entitled to a share in its fruits.' But the courts have never been able to do justice to her. In *Pettit* v. *Pettit* (1970) AC 777, 811, Lord Hodson said: 'I do not myself see how one can correct the imbalance which may be found to exist in property rights as between husband and wife without legislation.' Now we have legislation. In order to remedy the injustice Parliament has intervened. (s. 5(1)(f) of the Act) … In their Report on financial provision in matrimonial proceedings the Law Commission emphasised the importance of s. 5(1)(f) and the change which it would make. It has sometimes been suggested that we should not have regard to the reports of the Law Commission which lead to legislation. But we think we should. *They are most helpful in showing the mischief which Parliament intended to remedy.*'

Reports of Royal Commissions *are* admissable under the mischief rule to discover the mischief an Act was designed to remedy but inadmissable under the other rules. It is however possible that such documents may soon become admissable in all cases involving statutory interpretation.

In addition to the rules there are various presumptions to assist judges. These include:

  (i)   the statute is not retrospective;
 (ii)   it applies to all the United Kingdom;
(iii)   it does not bind the crown;
 (iv)   that mens rea is required for criminal liability.

Textbooks as a source

Textbooks, although important in the development of the common law, are not *original* sources of law as are statutes. Their importance as a source diminishes as law reports grew in reliability. Thus in the formative years, when there were inadequate reports, textbooks were regarded as a main source of authority. Ancient textbooks (those before 1765) are therefore in practice, considered to be books of authority and quoted as a source of the common law.

Modern textbooks would not be quoted as a source of law but textbooks by academics such as Cheshire and Winfield (whether alive or dead) are however highly persuasive. Although judges can and do decline to follow principles enunciated in such works this is extremely rare and in many cases judges have adopted as law the views expressed by such authors.

European law

Since Britain's entry into the European Economic Community on 1 January 1973 it has been bound by Community Law. Under s. 2(1) of the European Community Act (1972) all existing and future community law which is self-executing is immediately incorporated into English Law. A self-executing law therefore takes immediate effect: it does not require action by the United Kingdom Legislature.

European law is mainly concerned with agriculture, customs duties, free movement of labour, services, capital, transport and restrictive trade practices hence most United Kingdom domestic law (eg contract and tort) is unaffected, but where a clash exists community law is paramount.

European law consists of Primary Law and Secondary Law. The former is found in the articles of the three Community Treaties whilst secondary law is that enacted by the European Commission or the Council of Ministers under Section 189 of the Treaty of Rome. It takes the form of a:

Regulation
This is of general application and becomes law immediately it is passed by the Council or Commission. It does not need parliamentary approval, being self-executing.

Directive
This states the objects to be achieved but each member state decides the best method of implementing these. It binds member states but requires domestic legislation to bring it into effect. Thus the Companies Act (1980) implemented the European Economic Community's second directive on Company Law.

Decision
This is a formal method of enunciating policies or initiating action. It is addressed to the person or state involved and is only binding on the recipient. It could be used for example, to impose a fine on a company for non-compliance with community law.

The Commission may also issue *recommendations* and *opinions* but these are not binding although they may be implemented by further legislation.

The European Court interprets European treaties under s. 177 of the Treaty of Rome and its decisions bind the House of Lords and all inferior courts. Thus article 119 of the European Economic Community Treaty states that 'men and women should receive equal pay for equal work' and in *McCarthy's Ltd* v. *Smith* (1979) the Court of Appeal, uncertain as to its meaning, referred the matter to the European Court under s. 177. Their decision was that 'the principle that men and women should receive equal pay for equal work ... is not confined to situations in which men and women are contemporaneously doing equal work for the same employer.' This ruling was implemented by the Court of Appeal.

Past examination questions

1 What do you understand by 'delegated legislation'? Explain the reasons for the increased delegation of legislative powers by Parliament in modern times. Outline some of its advantages and disadvantages. To what extent, if at all, is it subject to control by the Courts and Parliament? A C A June 1976

2 Outline the more important changes brought about by the Judicature Acts 1873–75 and explain why they were thought to be necessary. A C A December 1976

3 'In spite of the enormous bulk of Statute Law, the most fundamental part of English Law is still the Common Law.'
Comment on this statement and explain the position where there is a conflict between the provisions of a Statute and the rules of the Common Law. A C A June 1977

4 Outline the development and growth of Equity. A C A December 1977

5 Explain the rules which govern the interpretation of Statutes. A C A June 1978

6 'The doctrine of precedent is the corner-stone of English Law.' Discuss this statement and explain what is meant by the doctrine of precedent. Describe the advantages and disadvantages of the English system of case law. A C A December 1978

7   Explain the reasons for the growth of Equity and consider its contribution to English Law.   A C A June 1979

8   Explain the nature and legal effect of Regulations, Directives and Decisions made by the Council of Ministers and the Commission of the European Economic Community.   I A S June 1979

9   'Equity is a gloss on the common law.' Discuss this statement with reference to equity as a source of law today.   I A S December 1980

10 a)   Briefly compare and contrast civil and criminal law.

    b)   Give an example of an act which can be both a crime and a tort.

    c)   Pat and Harry are neighbours, but they are always quarrelling. One day Harry breaks into Pat's home and brutally assaults her. She is badly injured. What legal action can be taken against Harry, and by whom?   C A May 1980

11 a)   Explain the differences between a consolidating statute and a codifying statute.

    b)   What are the principles of interpretation used by the judiciary?
                                        C A October 1979

12   Write a short essay on the development of Equity and its importance in the English legal system.   C A 1980

Note: In Chapters 30 and 31 the amounts of money quoted are correct at time of going to press. We suggest that students should check the most recent figures.

30

English courts

Historical introduction

The previous chapter briefly mentioned the Common Law courts but their growth and development requires examination in more detail as many current courts trace their origins back to Norman times. The Norman kings ruled with advice from a council of noblemen (Curia Regis). This body possessed legislative, administrative and limited judicial functions, hearing disputes involving the king's tenants-in-chief. Initially the council met three times a year. Later the Curia Regis split into two separate assemblies and the smaller met more frequently with its members undertaking specialized work, each with their own staff. From these the main Common Law courts developed.

The first court to emerge from the Curia Regis was the **Court of Exchequer** which evolved during the twelfth century. Originally an administrative body concerned with the collection of royal revenue, it possessed jurisdiction to hear cases concerning royal revenue, ie involving the king's debtors. It extended its jurisdiction to other debtors by developing the fiction that P sued D and because of D's non-payment P was unable to pay his debts to the king. In theory the action concerned the king's revenue. As it was cheaper to sue in this court than the Court of Common Pleas this fiction was widely used.

The **Court of Common Pleas** developed from the thirteenth century. Magna Carta had stipulated a court should exist at a 'certain place' to hear disputes between subjects. The place chosen was Westminster and the first Chief Justice was appointed in 1272. The court possessed a wide jurisdiction but as only senior members of the legal profession could appear before it, actions were expensive and subjects chose to commence actions regarding debts in the Court of Exchequer and actions involving land in the Court of Kings Bench. In addition applicants could seek redress in the local courts because actions only commenced at Westminster providing they had not already been heard locally ('nisi prius').

The final court evolving from the Curia Regis was the **Court of Kings Bench**. The monarch originally attended this court personally, hence it possessed wide powers, hearing any action concerning the king, and was the only one of the three to possess criminal jurisdiction. As junior counsel had the right of audience it was cheaper than the Court of Common Pleas hence fictions developed to extend its jurisdiction.

As explained earlier, a limited right of appeal existed from the Common Law courts. This led to the development of the Court of Exchequer Chamber. Its composition changed four times between 1358 and 1830 but by the latter date it heard appeals from the three Common Law Courts.

A final appeal from the Court of Exchequer Chamber lay to the House of Lords.

Appeals from the Court of Chancery (see page 228) lay to the Chancellor until 1851 when the Court of Appeal in Chancery was established. Miscellaneous courts also existed prior to 1873. These included the *Court of Admiralty* which possessed jurisdiction over maritime matters, the *Court of Probate* whose jurisdiction included wills and the *Court for Divorce and Matrimonial Causes* which considered family matters.

Modern court structure

The modern system was primarily created by the Judicature Acts (1873–75) as modified by the Administration of Justice Act (1970) and the Courts Act (1971), (see page 245).

The most important court is the European Court.

European Court
When there are purely internal disputes between United Kingdom citizens, the House of Lords remains the final appellate court and in implementing European legislation it is the final arbitrator. If however doubt exists over the interpretation of such legislation the House of Lords must refer to the European court for a decision. It consists of eleven judges (who must be senior judges or 'recognized jurists') assisted by three advocate generals who present the cases to the court. The president is appointed for three years from amongst the judges. In addition to its interpretive function the court hears complaints brought by one member state (or community body) against another member state. It also reviews the legality of the actions of the Commission and the Council.

House of Lords
This is the highest civil and criminal appellate court. It comprises the Lord Chancellor, nine Lords of Appeal (Law Lords) who are barristers of fifteen years standing or Supreme Court judges of two years standing. In addition any member of the House of Lords holding high judicial office may attend. Five Lords usually hear appeals although a

COURTS POSSESSING MAINLY CIVIL JURISDICTION

	Structure before 1875	1875	1880	1970	Present Structure
11 C	Curia Regis				
12 C	—Court of Exchequer	Exchequer Division			
13 C	—Court of Common Pleas	Common Pleas Division	Queen's Bench Division	Queen's Bench Division	Queen's Bench Division (with Admiralty and Commercial courts)
13 C	—Court of King's Bench	Queen's Bench Division			
15 C	Court of Chancery	Chancery Division		Chancery Division	Chancery Division
14 C	Court of Admiralty	Probate, Divorce and Admiralty Division		Family Division	Family Division
1857	Court of Divorce				
1857	Court of Probate				
1858	Courts of Exchequer Chamber	Court of Appeal		Court of Appeal (Civil Division)	Court of Appeal (Civil Division)
1851	Court of Appeal in Chancery				

quorum is three.

It hears criminal appeals from the Court of Appeal and the Divisional Court of the Queens Bench Division. (The Administration of Justice Act 1969 allowed appeals to go direct from the High Court to the Lords.) Appeals must be on a point of law of general public importance and leave to appeal must be given by either the lower court or the Lords.

Its civil appeals stem from the Court of Appeal and 'leave' of one of the courts is required. Although the appeal need not involve a point of law it must involve a question of public importance. The 1969 Act also applies allowing the Lords to hear appeals direct from the trial judge providing the parties agree, a point of law of public importance is involved (eg construction of a statute) and the Lords give leave.

The House of Lords gives opinions, not decisions, and the trial judge must translate these into action.

Court of Appeal

Together with the High Court and Crown Court it forms the *Supreme Court*. Since 1966 it has consisted of

a) *Civil division*

This comprises the Master of the Rolls and up to fourteen Lord Justices of Appeal drawn from High Court judges or barristers of fifteen years standing. In addition the Lord Chancellor can co-opt High Court judges if the pressure of work necessitates this. Usually three judges hear appeals, which can be on law or fact, from the High Court, the County Court or the Employment Appeals Tribunal. It usually rehears the case, using the original transcript, and can

  (i) reverse the original decision,

 (ii) amend the decision,

(iii) order a retrial,

(iv) enforce the decision.

b) *Criminal division*

This comprises the Lord Chief Justice plus judges of the Queens Bench Division. Usually three judges hear appeals from the Crown Court. The accused has an appeal of right on points of law but appeals against sentence or on the facts require the leave of one of the courts. The Attorney-General may refer a point of law to the court for an opinion but this only affects future cases, not the current one. No appeal exists against an innocent verdict. The court can

  (i) increase or reduce a sentence,

 (ii) quash a conviction,

(iii) order a new trial if there is new evidence available *and* its effect on a jury is unclear. If its effect is obvious a new trial will be unnecessary, or

(iv) enforce the conviction.

High Court
There are three specialist divisions (although theoretically each can hear any case) and there is no upper financial limit on their jurisdiction.

a) *Queens Bench division*

This comprises the Lord Chief Justice and puisne judges (barristers of not less than ten years standing). The busiest division it deals with contract, tort, commercial matters (in its two specialist courts) plus matters falling outside the jurisdiction of the other two divisions. Its appellate function is exercised by its Divisional Court, usually consisting of three Queens Bench Division judges.

The Queens Bench Divisional Court hears appeals by way of case stated from the Crown and Magistrates courts and from certain tribunals. It also exercises supervisory jurisdiction through the issue of applications for judicial review (superseding the former prerogative orders of mandamus, prohibition and certiorari). This ensures inferior courts exercise their powers properly and remain within their jurisdiction.

b) *Chancery division*

This comprises the Vice Chancellor and puisne judges. It deals with the administration of estates, trusts, mortgages, bankruptcies and contentious probate issues. Its divisional court exercises its appellate function hearing appeals from bankruptcies arising outside of London.

c) *Family division*

This comprises the President and puisne judges. Its jurisdiction is now restricted to family matters such as contested divorce, its old admiralty jurisdiction transferring to the Queens Bench Division and probate to Chancery. Its divisional court exercises its appellate jurisdiction hearing appeals from the magistrates and the crown court on family matters.

County Court
There are over four hundred and fifty County Courts. They hear actions (providing they arise within their own district) in contract and tort where the amount claimed is less than £5,000; actions for the recovery of land where the net annual value for rating does not exceed £1,000; equity proceedings where the sum involved does not exceed £30,000; admiralty proceedings (although the jurisdiction is restricted to certain courts) and, outside of London, bankruptcy claims. Additional powers have been vested in the County Court by numerous statutes (such as Rent, Hire Purchase and Matrimonial Causes Acts).

Note: In contract and tort the parties can agree to waive the financial limits.

The court comprises a circuit judge assisted by a registrar who is a solicitor of seven years standing. The latter mainly performs administrative tasks but, with the leave of the judge, he may hear actions in which the defendant does not appear, admits liability or (unless the parties object) where the claim does not exceed £2,000. Where the registrar hears the case appeals lie to the County Court judge, otherwise appeals are to the Court of Appeal except in bankruptcy cases where they go to the divisional court of the Chancery Division.

Crown Court

This comprises either a High Court judge (Queens Bench Division), or a circuit judge (who may also sit in the county court) or a part-time paid recorder (who is a barrister or solicitor of at least ten years standing). In addition two to four magistrates attend to hear appeals from the magistrates court against sentence or conviction.

Its jurisdiction extends to all indictable offences. These are categorized into four classes:

Class one   The most serious (eg murder), these must be heard by a High Court judge.
Class two   These are less serious but are tried by a High Court judge except in exceptional circumstances.
Class three   These can be heard by a judge or recorder.
Class four   These are indictable offences which may be tried summarily in the magistrates court. If the accused opts for trial in the crown court the case will probably be heard by the circuit judge or recorder.

Appeals are by way of the case stated to the divisional court of the Queens Bench Division or to the Court of Appeal.

Magistrates Court

This comprises a minimum of two unpaid part-time lay Justices of the Peace (although usually three sit) or one paid full-time stipendary magistrate. It possesses civil and criminal jurisdiction over local matters of minor importance.

a) *Civil*   It can recover certain debts (eg those imposed by affiliation and domestic orders) and can issue affiliation and matrimonial orders. Appeal lies to the divisional court of the Family Division.
b) *Criminal*   Summary (less serious) offences are dealt with by the magistrates, the maximum penalty they can impose being a fine of £1,000 or a prison sentence of up to 6 months. Most summary cases involve offences under the Road Traffic Acts to which the accused can plead guilty by post. Indictable (more serious) offences merit

jury trial but the less serious indictable offences may be heard by the magistrates if the accused agrees, although the magistrates may send him to the Crown Court for sentencing if their sentencing powers are inadequate.

The magistrates possess no jurisdiction over serious indictable offences. One magistrate will however hold committal (preliminary) hearings in such cases to determine if the prosecution's evidence establishes a sufficient case to justify a trial in the crown court.

If an accused wants a retrial an appeal lies to the Crown Court. If however either party appeals on a point of law, it goes to the Divisional Court of the Queens Bench Division by way of case stated.

Incorporated within the magistrates' criminal jurisdiction is the *Juvenile Court*. This hears matters involving children and young persons (under seventeen) and comprises three JP's, one being a woman, drawn from a panel of those suitably qualified. The proceedings are informal with restricted publicity.

Magistrates also perform administrative functions, including the issue of alcohol licences, summonses and warrants and the granting of bail.

Specialist Courts

a) *Coroners Court*

The coroner is a solicitor, barrister or medical practitioner of not less than five years standing. He holds enquiries (inquests) into deaths occuring in unusual circumstances, being assisted by a jury if there is reasonable suspicion of 'foul play'. Inquests are also held where there is hidden treasure to ascertain ownership.

b) *Judicial Committee of the Privy Council*

This comprises the Lord Chancellor, Law Lords, Privy Councillors who have held high judicial office and co-opted holders of high judicial office from Commonwealth countries. In practice its composition is similar to the House of Lords, hence although its decisions are not binding they are highly persuasive. It does not give judgments but offers an opinion which is enforced by an order-in-council.

It is not an English appellate court although it hears final appeals on ecclesiastical law and from disciplinary bodies such as the General Medical Council. It hears civil and criminal appeals from many overseas territories (eg the Channel Islands, Isle of Man and many commonwealth countries), although the independent commonwealth countries can pass legislation excluding appeals to the Privy Council.

c) *Tribunals*

These can be administrative or judicial. The latter comprise of judges, lawyers and laymen possessing specialist subject knowledge. Many 'domestic' tribunals are statutory creations empowered to regulate the professions (eg solicitors, doctors) and the empowering act provides a right of appeal. Even non-statutory domestic tribunals which offer no right of appeal can be compelled by the courts to abide by the rules of national justice.

'Industrial' tribunals enforce statutes such as the Contracts of Employment Act, Redundancy Payments Act and the Sex Discrimination Act considering questions of unfair dismissal, sex discrimination etc. Appeal lies from these tribunals to the

d) *Employment Appeals Tribunal*

Although titled a tribunal it is really a court (replacing the National Industrial Relations Court). It comprises judges from the High Court or Court of Appeal, one being President, plus laymen (representing employers and employees) specialized in industrial relations. Its jurisdiction is limited to hearing appeals, being the final adjudicator on questions of fact although on points of law there is an appeal to the Court of Appeal.

Note: The amounts involved change regularly. The student must check the text and complete with accurate figures.

31

Settlement of legal disputes
(Part I)

When faced with a legal problem the first step is to seek legal advice and assistance.

Legal advice and assistance

The Legal Advice and Assistance Act (1972) provides free legal advice, up to a maximum of £25. To obtain the free advice the applicant completes a 'green form', providing details of income and capital. If this is below the minimum the applicant receives £25 of advice free but this figure decreases if the applicant's income and capital rise and, above a certain figure, the applicant becomes ineligible for free advice.

Inflation causes the figures to be frequently reassessed.

Current figures:

minimum: disposable capital £ 1,200   disposable income £ 40 weekly.
maximum: disposable capital £ 2,500   disposable income £ 85 weekly.

Under the scheme solicitors provide general advice and assistance in negotiating a settlement. The scheme *does not* (with certain exceptions) extend to instituting proceedings or participating in a court action.

An applicant whose income exceeds the maximum must pay the full price for advice. He may however (under a scheme instigated by the Law Society) obtain a thirty minute interview for £5 from the 75% of solicitors who participate in the scheme.

Any party obtaining legal advice will usually meet a **solicitor**.

Solicitors can qualify through the routes shown on page 253. Once qualified they are controlled by the Law Society who possess wide ranging statutory powers although disciplinary proceedings are the responsibility of an independent statutory body, the Solicitors' Disciplinary Tribunal. Appeals lie to the Divisional Court of the Queens Bench Division.

Solicitors main functions are:

(i) *General administrative paperwork* Conveyancing is the most important, accounting for 40-60% of their gross income.
(ii) *Conducting the preparatory stages of litigation* This includes interviewing witnesses, preparation of documents, issuing of writs

and liaison with a barrister (the client's advocate in court).

(iii) *Appearing in 'inferior' courts*   (magistrates and county courts).

Solicitors, unlike barristers, may form partnerships and sue for their fees. Where the work is contentious (ie work prior to a case commencing) the court, if requested, will assess the fees and in non-contentious (all work where proceedings are not actually commenced) the fees are determined according to guidelines although the client may request they be assessed by the court or the Law Society.

Serious or complicated disputes will probably involve the solicitor engaging, on behalf of the client, the services of a **barrister**.

The examination structure is illustrated opposite. Although he has passed his examinations and spent one year as a 'pupil' of a senior barrister the student cannot practice unless he has been 'called to the bar' at one of the four Inns of Court. This involves keeping eight terms at the particular Inn (in practice this means having twelve dinners at the Inn over two years). The barristers governing body is the Senate of the Inns of Court and the Bar who regulate the admission of students, control legal education and administer discipline.

A barrister's main function is advocacy, having access to all UK courts, although he also drafts documents such as pleadings and writes 'opinions' on areas of law. The highest judicial offices are almost exclusively reserved for barristers.

A feature of the UK system is the division of the legal profession into solicitors and barristers as opposed to all-purpose lawyers found elsewhere. This division was one matter considered by the Royal Commission on Legal Services which reported in 1979. Having received over three thousand five hundred written submissions it recommended against fusion of the two professions. It was however, concerned over a young barrister's financial problems (during the first six months of pupillage he receives no income) and suggested grants be available during pupillage and whilst young barristers build up their practices. It also recommended solicitors he allowed to advertise, subject to Law Society control, to stimulate competition and allow the public to select 'specialist' solicitors.

Having consulted the legal profession the individual may, willingly or unwillingly, become involved in a court action. He will therefore wish to know the availability of legal aid.

Legal aid

This is concerned with representation in court. It is available in all **civil** cases except for undefended divorce and defamation, although it is not generally available in judicial or administrative tribunals or in arbitration, and will be granted if:

Solicitors' training

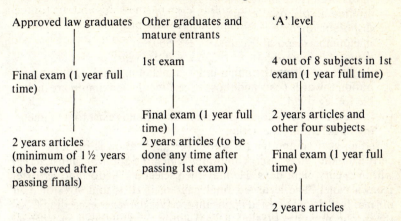

Approved law graduates	Other graduates and mature entrants	'A' level
	1st exam	4 out of 8 subjects in 1st exam (1 year full time)
Final exam (1 year full time)		
	Final exam (1 year full time)	2 years articles and other four subjects
2 years articles (minimum of 1½ years to be served after passing finals)	2 years articles (to be done any time after passing 1st exam)	Final exam (1 year full time)
		2 years articles

Barristers' training

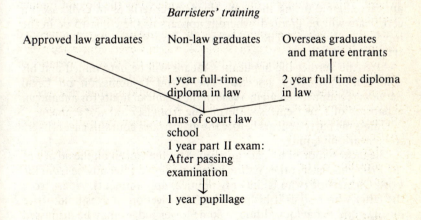

Approved law graduates	Non-law graduates	Overseas graduates and mature entrants
	1 year full-time diploma in law	2 year full time diploma in law

Inns of court law school
1 year part II exam:
After passing examination

↓

1 year pupillage

254 Essential law for accountancy students

a) the applicant and his spouse's disposable income (net income minus deductions for dependents, rent etc) and disposable capital are within the prescribed limits.

minimum: disposable capital   £ 1,200
disposable income   £ 1,700   year
maximum: disposable capital   £ 2,500
disposable income   £ 4,075   year

Applicants within the minimum − maximum band make a contribution towards costs and those exceeding the maximum are ineligible for legal aid.

b) in the Committee's opinion reasonable grounds exist for commencing or defending the action.

If the local committee (to whom the application is made) grant a certificate they may insert conditions which the applicant must accept within twenty eight days. He may then select a solicitor and barrister from a panel. The legal aid fund pays their costs and 90% of their normal fees. If the assisted applicant receives damages exceeding £ 000 the surplus must pay off the legal aid subsidy and any costs awarded go directly into the legal aid fund. An assisted applicant ordered to pay costs may be required to pay a 'reasonable sum' but the legal aid fund may pay the costs awarded to the unassisted party.

In **criminal** proceedings the application is made at the trial court and the need for speed means an investigation into resources prior to the grant of aid is impossible. The applicant provides details of his means to the court and if a contribution appears likely he is informed. If he appears eligible (using the same financial criteria as in civil cases) a certificate will be granted 'where it appears to the court to be in the interests of justice.' The certificate is always available for serious crimes.

After the verdict the applicant's means will be determined and his contribution, if any, assessed. The Royal Commission on Legal Services recommended an increase in the financial limits for aid and an expansion of Law Centres with funding from Central Government.

Unless the party appears before the magistrates court his case is likely to be heard by a **judge**.

The most senior judges are appointed by the Queen on the advice of the Prime Minister, other judges being appointed after advice from the Lord Chancellor (who is the only political appointment). Apart from the latter who resigns if his party loses an election, judges hold office during good behaviour although some lower judges may be dismissed by the Lord Chancellor for incompetence.

Their function is to decide cases by applying existing laws. In theory they cannot create law but in practice judges can and do create new law. An earlier chapter outlined their legislative role when interpreting legislation, and they can extend or modify the common law through

cases. In 1947 Lord Denning 'created' law with the High Trees decision
and the need to develop law through cases was implicit in the 1966
Practice Direction.

The extent to which a judge will 'make' law depends on his view of
the role of a judge. The different approaches are illustrated in the
following quotes:

Per Lord Simon in *Miliangos* v. *George Frank (Textiles) Ltd* (1975)

'I am sure that an expert committee, including or taking evidence
from departmental officials, would apprehend a great number of
not immediately apparent repercussions of the decision which my
noble and learned friends propose to take. Such a committee
might conclude that the repercussions make the decision
unacceptable. Or they might suggest some means of mitigating
any adverse effect. Or they might advise that the repercussions
were on balance acceptable. But at least the crucial decision
would be taken in the light of all the consequences involved.

By contrast, the training and qualification of a judge is to eluci-
date the problem immediately before him, so that its features
stand out in stereoscopic clarity. But the beam of light which so
illuminates the immediate scene seems to throw surrounding
areas into greater obscurity; the whole landscape is distorted to
the view. A penumbra can be apprehended, but not much
beyond; so that when the searchlight shifts a quite unexpected
scene may be disclosed. The very qualifications for the judicial
process thus impose limitations on its use. This is why judicial
advance should be gradual. 'I am not trained to see the distant
scene: one step enough for me' should be the motto on the wall
opposite the judge's desk. It is, I concede, a less spectacular
method of progression than somersaults and cartwheels; but it is
the one best suited to the capacity and resources of a judge. We
are likely to perform better the duties society imposes on us if we
recognise our limitations. Within the proper limits there is more
than enough to be done which is of value to society.'

Per Lord Diplock in *Manchester Corporation* v. *Connolly* (1970)

'This is an unfortunate case, because it deals with a group of
people who have hitherto at any rate found themselves unable to
adjust to modern social conditions ... The duty of the court when
its aid is sought is to administer the law. While I should be the last
to say that it is no part of the function of the courts to develop
the Common Law so as to adapt it to changing social conditions,
it is not within the court's power, and no part of its function,
to provide solutions to sociological problems which call for

administrative action by central or local government such as would be involved in the construction and supervision of suitable sites for gipsies.'

Per Lord Denning in *Dutton* v. *Bognor Regis UDC* (1972)

'In previous times, when faced with a new problem, the judges have not openly asked themselves the question: what is the best policy for the law to adopt? But the question has always been there in the background.

Nowadays we direct ourselves to considerations of policy. In *Rondel* v. *Worsley* (1969) we thought that if advocates were liable to be sued for negligence they would be hampered in carrying out their duties. In *Dorset Yacht Co Ltd* v. *Home Office* (1970) we thought that the Home Office ought to pay for damage done by escaping Borstal boys, if the staff was negligent, but we confined it to damage done in the immediate vicinity. In *SCM (United Kingdom Ltd)* v. *WJ Whittall & Son Ltd* (1971) some of us thought that economic loss ought not to be put on one pair of shoulders, but spread among all the sufferers. In *Launchbury* v. *Morgans* (1971) we thought that as the owner of the family car was insured she should bear the loss (reversed by the House of Lords). In short, we look at the relationship of the parties: and then say, as matter of policy, on whom the loss should fall'

and Viscount Simonds in *Shaw* v. *Director of Public Prosecutions* (1962)

'In the sphere of criminal law I entertain no doubt that there remains in the courts of law a residual power to enforce the supreme and fundamental purpose of the law, to conserve not only the safety and order but also the moral welfare of the State ... The law must be related to the changing standards of life, not yielding to every shifting impulse of the popular will but having regard to fundamental assessments of human values and the purpose of society.'

In Shaw's case the appellant published a 'ladies directory' containing names, addresses and photographs of prostitutes. Shaw had broken no existing law and was therefore charged with a 'conspiracy to corrupt public morals.' On appeal to the House of Lords it was held (despite a very strong dissenting judgment from Lord Reid) that such an offence was known to English Law. In reality the offence was created by the House of Lords.

Between 1972 and 1975 the House of Lords 'created' numerous

conspiracy offences (ie it changed the criminal law). In 1975 however, in *Regina* v. *Withers* it was asked to create a new conspiracy charge. It refused. During the course of his judgment Lord Diplock said,

> 'My Lords, on five occasions in the last three years, this House has had to consider the protean crime 'conspiracy' under one or other of the various shapes that it assumes. In each of these five cases what was proved against the defendant at the trial was that he had done something of which the judge and jury strongly disapproved. In each of them what the defendant did was not itself a criminal offence. In each of them the subject matter of the charge was the prior agreement with other persons to do that which they did.
>
> It would be disingenuous to try to conceal my personal conviction that this branch of the criminal law of England is irrational in treating as a criminal offence an agreement to do that which if done is not a crime; and that its irrationality becomes injustice if it takes days of legal argument and historical research on appeal to your Lordships' House to discover whether any crime has been committed even though the facts are undisputed.
>
> If what the defendants did ought to be made a crime, it is for Parliament to legislate accordingly.'

Note: The amounts involved change regularly. The student must check the text and complete with accurate figures.

32

Settlement of legal disputes
(Part II)

When a judge tries a case, regardless of the court, it is heard according to the rules of evidence.

Evidence

The rules of evidence are crucial in criminal trials but many also apply in civil actions. In any proceedings the party must know **two** things:
1   What facts *must* be proved if he is to succeed? Such facts are called *facts in issue*. In criminal cases the facts in issue to be proved by the prosecution are laid down in the criminal law and in civil cases they are found in the pleadings.

☐   Trevor Wit alleges the hot water bottle he purchased was of unmerchantable quality because it burst when filled with hot water. Facts in issue include whether the bottle was filled with hot water and whether it burst.

Facts in issue are **relevant** facts and can be proved *providing* they are **admissable**.
2   What facts *may* be proved? Facts in issue may be proved plus facts not in issue providing they are **relevant** (such as circumstantial evidence ie facts from which facts in issue can be inferred) *and* **admissable**.

☐   If Wit produces a burst hot water bottle this is circumstantial evidence inferring that it burst when filled with hot water.

Whether a fact is admissable under this heading is a matter of logic and depends on the special facts of each case.
Irrelevant evidence
Facts not falling into these categories are **irrelevant** and may not be proved. Unfortunately many facts a layman would consider relevant are legally irrelevant and some of these must be considered.
Thus:

1   Similar facts are legally irrelevant and incapable of proof. These are facts indicating the party had behaved in a similar way on previous occasions.

☐ Wit cannot bring evidence to show the retailer has been successfully sued for breach of contract.

In criminal cases an accused's previous convictions are irrelevant. Merely because somebody acted in a certain way in the past is not proof that he is still acting the same way
but
where a stronger link other than mere similarity exists between previous conduct and the present situation the similar fact evidence is admissible (eg where it proves the existence of a 'system') but the dividing line between admissible and inadmissible similar fact evidence is too complicated for this work.

2 A party's character (reputation and disposition) is legally irrelevant
but
in **civil** cases *witnesses* may be cross-examined regarding their reputation to cast doubts on their credibility but their answers must usually be accepted as final. A party's reputation/criminal record can only be proved where it is relevant in the action (eg defamation) or admissible under the Civil Evidence Act, 1968.

In **criminal** cases witnesses may be cross-examined as above. The accused, if he chooses to give evidence, cannot be questioned about his character (including previous convictions) and evidence on this matter is irrelevant. Evidence of previous criminal convictions may however be given under the Criminal Evidence Act (1898) where:

(i) it is relevant similar fact evidence (eg part of a system) or
(ii) if the accused seeks to establish his good character, or
(iii) where his defence involves imputations on the character of the prosecutor or prosecution witnesses (this involves more than claiming the witness is not telling the truth) or
(iv) where the accused gives evidence against a co-accused.

The judge has a discretion however to exclude any evidence he feels is unfair.

Summary
A party can only prove **relevant** facts that are **admissible**. Certain relevant facts are however *inadmissible*: thus

(i) if estoppel operates a party cannot prove a relevant fact. In the example on page 139 P is estopped from denying that his wife was acting as his agent and on page 129 Greenwood was estopped from proving his wife had forged his signature.
(ii) if disclosure of a fact would be prejudicial to the public interest it is inadmissible on grounds of public policy.

Burden of proof
Having ascertained the facts that must or may be proved, on whom does the burden of proof lie and what is the extent of that burden? The

legal burden of proof is usually on the plaintiff/prosecution and never shifts. During a case however the other party will have to rebut their evidence, hence the *evidential burden* shifts throughout a trial.

Civil cases must be proved on a balance of probabilities whereas in a criminal case it is 'beyond all reasonable doubt.' Per Lord Denning

> 'Proof beyond a reasonable doubt does not mean proof beyond the shadow of a doubt ... If the evidence is so strong against a man as to leave only a remote possibility in his favour, which can be dismissed with the sentence 'of course it is possible but not in the least probable' the case is proved beyond reasonable doubt, but nothing short of that will suffice.'

Proving relevant and admissable facts
Counsel, when deciding his court strategy, must determine the best method of proving the facts in issue although they will not need proving if they are:

(i) *Formally admitted* If the retailer formally admits he sold the hot water bottle to Wit, this need not be proved.
(ii) *A fact of which the court takes judicial notice* These are facts so obvious they need not be proved, for example that a week has seven days.
(iii) *Covered by a presumption* Unless this is irrebutable, it shifts the burden of proof once certain facts have been established (see page 183 for res ipsa loquitur).

The most common methods of proving facts are the use of:

a) *Witnesses*
Most people are both *competent* (ie they can give evidence) and *compellable* (ie they can be compelled to give evidence) but;
(i) Children too young to appreciate the need to tell the truth are incompetent.
(ii) The accused cannot give evidence for the prosecution. Thus if there are co-defendants one cannot give evidence against the other.
(iii) Spouses of accused persons cannot be compelled to give evidence for the defence and they are, subject to statutory exceptions, incompetent witnesses re the prosecution.

Most witnesses give oral evidence (although written evidence in lieu of oral is permitted in certain cases). The party calling the witness will question to elicit the relevant facts during the *examination-in-chief*. Because the witness is favourable leading questions (eg Did you see the accused commit the offence?) are forbidden and counsel cannot cross-examine his own witness if his evidence proves less favourable than anticipated. If however the witness proves 'hostile' (ie he shows hostility towards the party calling him) a limited right of cross-examination exists. When opposing counsel *cross-examines* the witness he is allowed greater freedom and leading questions are permissable. Opening counsel may then *re-examine* his witness to clarify matters already raised but new evidence cannot be introduced at this stage.

Whilst giving evidence a witness can refuse to answer questions that may incriminate himself and a spouse may refuse to disclose information given by their spouse during their marriage. Legal advisers receive similar protection regarding disclosures made whilst giving legal advice but this protection does not extend to accountants and their clients.

In most cases a single witness may be sufficient (although having more obviously improves your chances of success)
but
some evidence must be *corroborated*. This means producing supporting evidence of the witness's testimony.
Corroboration is required in:

(i) perjury cases,
(ii) affiliation proceedings, the mother's evidence requires corroboration. Showing the couple spent a night in a hotel during the appropriate period would be sufficient.
(iii) cases involving procuration of women, or
(iv) cases involving unsworn evidence of a child (ie the child does not give evidence on oath).

In the above a jury *cannot* convict without corroboration. Where the evidence of a child is given on oath or the evidence comes from an accomplice corroboration is not essential although juries must be warned at the dangers of convicting without corroborative evidence.

If in *Godley* v. *Perry* the retailer denied selling the plaintiff the catapult this would be a fact in issue. If counsel called a witness who stated, 'I was told by my friend that she saw the retailer sell the plaintiff a catapult' this would be **hearsay** evidence and inadmissable to prove the fact in issue. Counsel must call as a witness the friend who saw the transaction.[1] Where another's words are repeated to prove the truth of what was said the evidence is hearsay. To the general rule – hearsay is inadmissable – there are over seventy exceptions including:

(i) Under the Civil Evidence Act (1968) a written document by a first-hand witness is admissable as proof of the facts stated in the document.
(ii) Statements forming part of the 'res gestae' are admissable ie any

---

[1] In a defamation action for example, a witness could give evidence as to what the defendant said because this is to prove what words were spoken and not to prove the truth of what was said – it is therefore not hearsay.

statement 'made in circumstances of spontanaeity or involvement' with the facts in issue. The statements made at the time of an incident may be repeated by a third party as evidence that what was said was true eg if 'X' shouts 'Jenkins is stabbing me' this can be repeated by a third party to prove that Jenkins did stab X.

(iii) Informal statements against the interests of the maker. In criminal cases these are called 'confessions' and may be repeated by a third party as evidence that what was said was true.

(iv) Statements of dead persons (in certain circumstances).

(v) Statements in public documents (such as bankers books) or documents forming part of business records (Criminal Evidence Act (1965)).

b) *Documentary evidence*

In theory, contents of a document must be proved by the production of the original but as this is frequently impossible, exceptions have arisen. The contents of most documents may now be proved by secondary evidence.

c) *Real evidence*

This includes material objects (exhibits) such as weapons, a person's appearance where perhaps assessment of damages is relevant, or a view where the judge or jury visit the site perhaps to 'view' evidence relevant in an action involving Occupier's Liability.

In establishing his case counsel cannot use certain methods of proving facts. Thus *opinions* of non-expert witnesses are inadmissible. In *Godley* v. *Perry* testimony that when the child pulled the elastic back the catapult snapped is admissable. It is evidence of a fact that has been seen. A comment by a non-expert that the catapult snapped because the plastic was faulty would be inadmissable being an opinion and not a perceived fact. Experts' opinions are however admissable. The opinion of a plastic's expert that the plastic had an inherent defect would be admissable.

Having described the general law applicable to disputes, specific types of action are now considered.

Civil courts

a) A civil dispute involving damages of £50.

The plaintiff would probably utilize the County Court small claims procedure. He provides the court with written details of his claim and the relevant facts eg, broken arm causing pain and £20 lost wages following an accident caused by the defendant's negligence. This document is a *particulars of claim* and a plaintiff wishing to go to arbitration rather than to a formal court indicates accordingly. Accompanying this is a *request* which provides the court with the information (identity of parties etc) necessary to prepare a *summons.* The plaintiff then pays the appropriate court fee plus a sum for serving the summons. The court registrar prepares the summons (the document sent to the defendant informing him of the claim and his rights) and the plaintiff receives a *plaint note* containing the title of his action and a reference number.

A summons can be:

(i) An **ordinary summons**   This fixes the date for the pre-trial review (preliminary hearing),

or

(ii) A **default summons**   This generally involves a claim for a debt or specific sum of money. This summons does not set the date for a pre-trial hearing but gives the defendant fourteen days to accept liability or make a counter-claim. The court, in the latter case, fixes a pre-trial review.

If the defendant fails to attend a pre-trial review the registrar can find for the plaintiff. Following this review, unless the parties settle, the case goes before the registrar who listens to the evidence and reaches a verdict. Solicitors are discouraged and if a successful plaintiff is awarded costs his legal costs are excluded.

b)   A civil dispute involving £700.

This case falls within the county court jurisdiction where there is a similar procedure up to the pre-trial review. The case is however heard by a judge not registrar. In a defended action the plaintiff's solicitor makes an opening address, examines his witnesses who are cross-examined by the defendant's solicitor. The latter follows the same procedure and makes his final comments. The plaintiff's solicitor will then make his final address before the judge decides the issue.

c)   A breach of contract case involving damages of £50 000.

This falls within the jurisdiction of the High Court. A *writ of summons* is obtained from the Central Office or District Registry of the High Court. This contains details of the claim, specifies the division hearing the case and orders the defendant to enter an appearance within fourteen days. If this is not done, judgment is given in default and any unliquidated damages are assessed by a **master**. If the action is contested the master deals with preliminary matters. The parties submit documents including a statement of claim, a statement of defence (perhaps accompanied by a counter-claim) and a traverse (a repudiation of the defence). The plaintiff then takes out a Summons for Directions and the Master may order discovery of documents, etc. A notice of trial follows. Trial procedure is as in the county court except barristers replace solicitors.

Not all civil disputes are heard in the county or high court; many are dealt with by arbitration.

10.— *Request for Default Summons against Defendant in District.*

Two copies of the Plaintiff's particulars of Claim are required before a plaint can be entered, and if there are two or more Defendants to be served, an additional copy for each additional Defendant.

In the

County Court

Order 6, Rule 3 (1) (a).

To be served by

Entered .... 19 . .

No. of Plaint

Statement of Parties

1. PLAINTIFF'S names in full, and residence or place of business.
2. If a female, state whether married, single, or a widow.
3. If suing in a representative capacity, state in what capacity.
4. If an infant required to sue by a next friend, state that fact, and names in full, residence or place of business, and occupation of next friend.
5. If an assignee, state that fact, and name, address and occupation of assignor.
6. If co-partners suing in the name of their firm, add "(Suing as a Firm)".
7. If a company registered under the Companies Act, 1948, state the address of the registered office and describe it as such.

8. DEFENDANT'S surname, and (where known) his or her initials or names in full: defendant's residence or place of business (if a proprietor of the business).
9. Whether male or female, and if female, whether Mrs. or Miss.
10. Occupation (where known).
11. If sued in a representative capacity, state in what capacity.
12. If co-partners are sued in the name of their firm, or a person carrying on business in a name other than his own name is sued in such name, add "(Sued as a Firm)".
13. If a company registered under the Companies Act, 1948 is sued the address given must be the registered office of the company, and must be so described.

The Defendant is not a person under disability

SIGN HERE:

WHAT THE CLAIM IS FOR

AMOUNT CLAIMED	
FEE ON ENTERING PLAINT	
SOLICITOR'S COSTS	
TOTAL...............	

Plaintiff.

Solicitor's Name and Address for service

[Strike out if inappropriate:- I apply for this action, if defended to be referred to arbitration].

The certificate overleaf should be completed if service by post is required.

Figure 14   A summons

In the High Court of Justice

QUEEN'S BENCH DIVISION

19 .— .—No.

District Registry

A.4

Writ indorsed with
statement of claim
(Liquidated demand)
District Registry.

Oyez Publishing
Limited,
Oyez House,
237 Long Lane,
London SE1 4PU
a subsidiary of
The Solicitors' Law
Stationery Society
Limited.

F4418 16-9-75 BW18839

★★★★

Between..

....

....

....

PLAINTIFF

AND

....

....

....

DEFENDANT

Elizabeth the Second, by the Grace of God, of the United Kingdom of Great Britain and Northern Ireland and of Our other realms and territories, Queen, Head of the Commonwealth, Defender of the Faith: To

.

.

.

of

in the   of

WE COMMAND YOU that within 14 days after the service of this Writ on you, inclusive of the day of service, you do cause an appearance to be entered for you in an action at the suit of

.

.

.   ;

and take notice that in default of your so doing the Plaintiff may proceed therein, and judgment may be given in your absence.

Witness,   Lord High Chancellor of Great Britain, the   day of   , 19 .

NOTE.—This Writ may not be served later than 12 calendar months beginning with the above date unless renewed by order of the Court.

DIRECTIONS FOR ENTERING APPEARANCE.

If the Defendant resides or carries on business, or (in the case of a limited company) has a registered office, within the district of the above-named District Registry or the Writ is indorsed with a statement that any cause of action in respect of which the Plaintiff claims relief wholly or in part arose in that district, the Defendant must enter an appearance in person or by a Solicitor in the District Registry and may do so either (1) by handing in the appropriate forms, duly completed, at the office of the District Registrar,*

*Insert address of office

or (2) by sending them to that office by post.

If the Defendant neither resides nor carries on business, nor (in the case of a limited company) has a registered office, within the district of the above-named District Registry and the Writ is not indorsed with a statement that any cause of action in respect of which the Plaintiff claims relief wholly or in part arose in that district, the Defendant may enter an appearance in person or by a Solicitor either (1) by handing in the appropriate forms, duly completed, at the office of the District Registrar, or by sending them to that office by post, or (2) by handing in the said forms, duly completed, at the Central Office, Royal Courts of Justice, Strand, London WC2A 2LL or by sending them to that office by post.

The appropriate forms may be obtained by sending a postal order for 9½p with an addressed envelope, foolscap size, to (1) The District Registrar, High Court of Justice,†

†Insert address of District Registry.

if the appearance is to be entered in the District Registry, or (2) The Clerk of Accounts, Vote Office, Royal Courts of Justice, Strand, London WC2A 2LL, if the appearance is to be entered in London.

NOTE.—If the Defendant enters an appearance, then, unless a summons for judgment is served on him in the meantime, he must also serve a defence on the Solicitor for the Plaintiff within 14 days after the last day of the time limited for entering an appearance, otherwise judgment may be entered against him without notice.

[OVER

Figure 15 A writ

Arbitration

This involves referring a dispute to a third party for decision and many commercial contracts contain an arbitration clause. Procedure is basically governed by the Arbitration Acts 1950–1979. There is usually a single arbitrator who deals with all matters. A simple case may be decided on written evidence but in complicated cases the arbitrator deals with pleadings, counter-claims, discovery of documents etc. At the hearing all outstanding issues are dealt with including damages and costs. Decisions are not normally given at the end of hearings but the arbitrator prepares his award which he despatches to the parties on payment of his fee. His award is final and binding and a losing party can be compelled to pay the award through a High Court order. An award is immediately enforceable *unless* the High Court orders a stay of execution pending appeal on a point of law (not fact). Appeals are only allowed if the point of law involved seriously affects one party's rights and the court may impose restrictions on the appellant.

The parties can agree to exclude the review of the High Court providing the agreement is made after the arbitration has begun. (The High Court can always remove an arbitrator guilty of misconduct during the proceeding and may revoke the award.)

Advantages:

 (i) Privacy. There is no right of public admittance.
 (ii) The proceedings are often quicker than court proceedings.
(iii) The arbitrator possesses technical expertise. The Chartered Institute of Arbitrators has a panel of three hundred and fifty arbitrators covering thirty eight different areas (lawyers, engineers, accountants, surveyors etc).
(iv) Costs are often lower than in judicial hearings.

Disadvantages:

 (i) Costs can escalate, arbitrators' fees being higher than anticipated.
 (ii) Arbitrators may not be legally qualified.
(iii) Precedent does not apply. Each case is decided separately and full reasons are not always given. Thus practitioners are denied one reliable source of law.

The other non-judicial method of solving disputes is through administrative tribunals.

Administrative tribunals

To adjudicate in disputes in areas covered by social legislation (eg consumer protection, housing, health and safety, employment, rent control) administrative tribunals have emerged. They have been chosen instead of the traditional courts because:

a) the disputes often require policy decisions and involve discretion.
b) the ordinary courts are overburdened.
c) tribunal procedure is more informal, quicker and therefore cheaper.
d) their adjudicators possess specialist knowledge. Thus rent tribunals comprise one third lawyers, one third surveyors and valuers and one third laymen.

Disadvantages

(i) As tribunals often sit in private, justice may not be seen to be done.
(ii) Chairmen are not always legally qualified and their decisions are often unpredictable.
(iii) Legal aid is not always available.
(iv) There may not be a right of appeal on a point of law.

To meet some of the criticisms, The Tribunals and Enquiries Act (1971) set up a Council on Tribunals, consisting of ten to fifteen members, which presents an annual report to Parliament on the constitution and working of certain tribunals. The Lord Chancellor also chooses Chairmen of specified tribunals from a panel. Judicial control can also be exercized as seen in chapter 30.

Criminal

Criminal prosecutions are usually initiated by the Crown acting through the Attorney-General or the Director of Public Prosecutions. In serious cases the latter prosecutes but often this role is delegated to the police. Crimes are either summary (less serious) or indictable and the nature of the offence determines which court hears it.

Summary offences are tried in the Magistrates' Court. The magistrate's clerk prepares a *summons*, which the magistrate signs, from *information* provided by the police. It is served on the defendant who may, if the offence is covered by the Magistrates' Courts Act 1952, plead guilty by post. If he attends personally he may plead guilty or not guilty. Following a guilty verdict or plea, the accused's solicitor may make a plea of mitigation before sentence is passed. Ninety eight per cent of crimes committed in the United Kingdom are tried summarily by the 23 000 lay magistrates and 50 stipendaries. The former need no legal qualifications and are appointed by the Lord Chancellor to serve within their particular locality. They receive legal advice from the clerk to the justices who is a barrister or solicitor of at least five years' standing. The only full-time paid magistrates are the stipendaries who mainly sit in London. They must be legally qualified.

With more serious crimes (indictable offences) the filing of information is followed by a *warrant for arrest*. Following his arrest, the accused appears before the local magistrates. With less serious offences he can opt for trial before the magistrates but where he chooses the crown court (or the case is a serious one), the magistrates *commit* him for trial. He is remanded on bail or in custody until his trial. The clerk of the court receives a *bill of indictment* and the judge (or recorder) instructs him to sign the bill which then becomes the indictment.

The clerk arraigns the accused (ie calls and requests his plea). A not guilty plea is followed by the empanelling of a jury and a trial. If he is found guilty or makes a guilty plea, then his previous offences are stated, a plea of mitigation is made and sentence passed.

Juries are found in crown court trials, deciding all questions of fact (the judge deciding questions of law) and whether the accused is guilty. They may return a majority verdict (10-2), and if they cannot agree the judge may order a re-trial. Anybody may be a juror providing;

  (i)   they are on the electoral register,
 (ii)   between 18–65, and
(iii)   have been resident in the United Kingdom for at least five years since reaching eighteen,

unless they are

  (i)   members of the judiciary, police officers, ministers of religion, or
 (ii)   have in the last ten years, served a prison sentence of more than three months.

Other groups, including MP's and members of the armed forces may be excused jury service. A jury is selected by ballot at a trial's commencement from a list prepared by the Lord Chancellor. Either side may challenge a juror; the defendant can remove up to three jurors without giving cause but valid reasons must be given to remove further jurors. The prosecution can 'stand down' any number of jurors without giving reasons.

The defence cannot question jurors before deciding whether to challenge them but both sides can inspect the list of potential jurors and conduct pre-trial enquiries into their backgrounds. Although juries are a fundamental part of our criminal law and regarded as a bulwark of liberty, criticisms like those listed below have been voiced.

  (i)   Jurors are not a cross-selection of the community.
 (ii)   Being laymen they are susceptible to barrister's rhetoric, may be confused by legal technicalities and be unable to weigh the evidence.
(iii)   Jury service is often unpopular, because it involves a loss of pay, and cases may be boring causing jurors to lose interest.
(iv)   Juries are biased, thus they adopt a lenient attitude towards

motoring offences.

Although juries are primarily found in crown courts they exist in coroner's courts and play an insignificant role in the civil courts.

Past examination questions

1 **a)** State two of the functions performed by laymen in the administration of justice in England.

    b) Distinguish between the roles of solicitors and barristers in the English legal system.

    c) State your views as to whether the professions of solicitors and barristers should be fused.   C A 1980

List of cases

Aluminium Industrie Noasen BV v. *Romalpa Aluminium Ltd* (1976), 108
Anns v. *Merton London Borough* (1977), 178
Arenson v. *Arenson* (1975), 181
Assam Railways v. *CIR* (1935), 238
Avery v. *Bowden* (1885), 75

Barton v. *Armstrong* (1976), 54
Bird v. *Jones* (1845), 198
Bolton v. *Mahadeva* (1972), 72
Bourhill v. *Young* (1945), 178
Bowmakers Ltd v. *Barnet Instruments Ltd* (1945), 61
Bushell v. *Faith* (1972), 238
Butler Machine Tool Co Ltd v. *Ex-Cell-O Corporation (England) Ltd* (1978), 6

Cahn v. *Pocketts Bristol Channel Steam Packet Co Ltd* (1899), 102
Carlill v. *Carbolic Smoke Ball Co* (1893), 8
Cellulose Acetate Silk Co Ltd v. *Widnes Foundry* (1925) *Ltd* (1933), 78
Century Insurance v. *NIRTB* (1942), 208
Chapelton v. *Barry UDC* (1940), 35
Christie v. *Davey* (1893), 201
Christoforides v. *Terry* (1924), 144
Commercial Plastics v. *Vincent* (1964), 63
Cooper v. *Phibbs* (1867), 51
Cottrill v. *Steyning and Littlehampton Building Society* (1961), 80
Cox v. *Phillips Industries Ltd* (1976), 81
Cundy v. *Lindsay* (1878), 50
Curtis v. *Chemical Cleaning Co Ltd* (1951), 33
Cutler v. *United Dairies* (1933), 185

D & C Builders v. *Rees* (1966), 21
Davis Contractors Ltd v. *Fareham UDC* (1950), 74
Decro-Wall International SA v. *Practitioners in Marketing Ltd* (1971), 31

Index

278 *Index*